Ian Young

Further science

GW00762358

000023

LONGMAN

General editors

David Rowlands and George Snape

Authors

Sue Creamer, Eric Deeson, Sheila Hands, Jackie Hardie, Penny Johnson, Gabrielle McSharry, Libby Mooney, Jude Park, Jen Scarsbrook, Maggie and Peter Williams, Chris Wilshaw, Paul Wright.

The publishers acknowledge with thanks all those who have contributed to the previous editions of *Science at work*. We are particularly grateful to John Taylor, the original project director, and Keith Johnson, the original project co-ordinator. The publishers would also like to thank Dr Peter Borrows for advice on safety matters.

Acknowledgements

We are grateful to IPC Magazines Ltd for permission to reproduce the article 'Heat camera helps pilots see through fog' by Jonathan Beard from *New Scientist* (26.9.92)
We are indebted to Guardian News Service Ltd for permission to reproduce the headline and an extract from the article 'Climate report confirms worst fears of experts' by Paul Brown from *The Guardian* newspaper (June, 1992), © *The Guardian*.

Longman Group UK Limited
Longman House, Burnt Mill, Harlow, Essex CM20 2JE, England and Associated Companies throughout the world.

© Longman Group Limited 1993

All rights reserved. No part of this publication may be reproduced, stored in a retrieval system, or transmitted in any form or by any means, electronic, mechanical, photocopying, recording, or otherwise without either the prior written permission of the Publishers or a licence permitting restricted copying issued by the Copyright Licensing Agency Ltd, 90 Tottenham Court Road, London, W1P 9HE

First published 1993
Set in 11/13 point Helvetica Light (Linotron)
Designed, typeset and illustrated by
Ken Vail Graphic Design, Cambridge
Printed by Scotprint Ltd, Musselburgh

Photo acknowledgements

We are grateful to the following for permission to reproduce photographs; Ace Photo Library, pages **120** left (photo Superstock), **122** TV detector van (Roger Howard), **122** travel agent (Vibert Stokes), **129** above right (Andre Csillag), **129** below left (Martin Bond), **129** below centre (A. Dobravska), **130** above right (K. Kirkwood), and **141** left (Vibert Stokes); Allsport UK, pages **13** (Bob Martin), **14** (Tony Duffy), **15** (Vandystadt/Loubat), **19** (David Cannon), and **147** above (Simon Bruty); BBC, pages **140** and **141** centre; Biophoto Associates, pages **20**, **25**, **27**, **35** above, **36** and **65** above right; British Geological Survey, page **125** below; British Petroleum, page **116**; English Electric Valve Company, page **136** centre and below left; Environmental Picture Library, page **39** below (Herbert Giradet); Vivien Fifield, page **106** above left; Leslie Garland Picture Library, page **89**; Geoscience Features, pages **34** above right, **61** left, **94**, **124**, and **139** below right; Robert Harding Picture Library, pages **131** above centre left (Paul van Riel), **131** centre right (Kozeny Gonter/Silvestris) and **131** below right (JAC Wilson); Hutchison Library, pages **45** (Sarah Garington), **48**, **64** above (Tony Souter), **131** above left (Mick Csaky), **131** above centre right (Michael MacIntyre) and **131** above right; ICCE Photo Library, pages **64** centre left (Mark Boulton), **65** below left (Chris Rose), **155** (Mark Boulton) and **158** centre (Mark Boulton); Image Bank, page **147** below (Bernard Roussel); Immitor, page **50** above left; International Stock Exchange Photo Library, page **122** fax and **123** CAD; Andrew Lambert, pages **81**, **109**, **112**, **114**, **127** above left and below, **135** below, **141** right, **144** and **148**; Landform Slides, pages **54** below left, **60** below left (Colin T. Scruton) and **61** right; Frank Lane Picture Agency, page **38** above right (L. Lee Rue); Life Science Pictures/Ron Boardman, pages **135** above left and above right and **136** right; NASA, page **73** above right; National Medical Slidebank, pages **17**, **133** below left and below right; Nature Photographers, pages **31** below left (E. A. Janes), below right (Paul Knight), **38** above left and above centre (Hugo van Lawick), below left (Roger Tidman) and **38** below right (Owen Newman); Novosti Picture Library, page **153** left; Oxford Scientific Films, page **38** below centre (David Thompson); Panos Pictures, pages **47** (Dylan Garcia), **63** above right (Susan Cunningham), **64** below left and **157** below left (Jeremy Hartley); Planet Earth Pictures, page **133** centre right (Doug Perrine); Popperfoto, pages **37** above left, **39** above and **146**; Quadrant Picture Library, pages **143** and **147** centre (Auto Express); Ann Ronan at Image Select, page **106** above right and below left; Science Photo Library, pages **35** below (Petit Format/CSI), **57** (NASA), **67** centre (National Centre for Atmospheric Research), **67** below right (Claude Nuridsany and Marie Perennou) **69** (Julian Baum), **70** (US Geological Survey), **71** left (John Sanford), **71** right (NASA), **72** (Roger Ressmeyer/Starlight), **73** left (Julian Baum), **75** below left (D. Jean Lorre), **73** below right (Lorenz Denney), **75** below right (NASA), **79** (Roger Ressmeyer/Starlight), **96** (Simon Fraser/Northumbria Circuits), **106** below right, **118** above left (Lawrence Livermore National Laboratory/University of California), **118** right, **118** below left (Alexander Tsiaras), **121** (Jerome Yeats), **122** virtual reality (James King-Holmes/W. Industries), **125** above (Peter Menzel), **126** (Orville Andrews), **127** above right (Martin Dohrn), **130** below left (Jonathan Watts), **134** above right (Pekka Parviainen), **134** below left (David Parker), **135** centre left (Adam Hart-Davis), **135** centre right (Barney Magrath), **136** above left (Los Alamos National Laboratory), **137** (Tony Craddock), **138** above right (Princess Margaret Rose Orthopaedic Hospital), **138** above right (Tony Craddock), **138** below right (NASA), **138** below centre (Kapteyn Laboratorium), **139** above right (David Ducros), and **139** above centre (Alex Bartel); Still Pictures, page **63** below left (Mark Edwards); TRH Pictures, page **37** below right; John Walmsley Photo Library, page **119**; Tony Waltham Geo Slides, pages **67** above right and **157** above right; Zefa Picture Library, pages **34** below left (Richard Nicholas), **50** below right, **54** above left, **60** above right, **64** centre right (T. Ives), **64** below right, **149**, **153** above right, **153** centre (Photri), **157** above centre (Boutin), **157** centre (Stock Market), **158** above right, **159** above (Stock Market), **159** below left (J. Pfaff) and **159** below right (N. Bahnsen).

Photographs on pages **30**, **31** above right, **120** right, **122** teletext, **133** above left and above right, **139** below left were taken by John Birdsall, Nottingham, and on pages **90**, **91**, **92**, **93**, **98**, **100**, **101**, **102**, **103** by Andrew Lambert, Ilkley.

Picture research by Marilyn Rawlings and Charlotte Deane.

Cover The cover photograph of a satellite map showing a severe depletion or 'hole' in the ozone layer over Antarctica on October 3rd, 1990, is reproduced by permission of Science Photo Library (NASA).

Safety notes

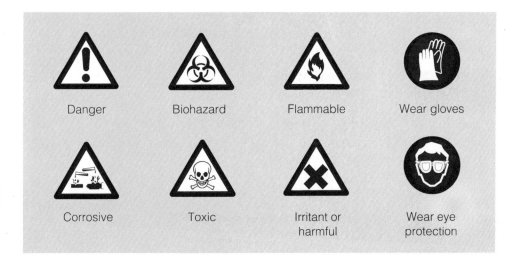

Danger   Biohazard   Flammable   Wear gloves

Corrosive   Toxic   Irritant or harmful   Wear eye protection

Good laboratory practice

These are the safety symbols used in Further science. You should get to know them so that you can recognise hazards (dangers) that you might come across during your science lessons.

To avoid accidents you should:

☐ take special care when you see one of these symbols

☐ always read through **all** the instructions given before you start doing your experiments

☐ check with your teacher if you are not sure about any of the instructions

☐ always check with your teacher before beginning any investigation that you have designed yourself

☐ always wear eye protection when your teacher tells you

☐ always stand when you are handling liquids so that you can move out of the way quickly if you spill anything

☐ if you do spill any cultures of microbes on the bench tell your teacher. Be careful not to get it on your hands

☐ if you spill anything on your skin wash it off immediately with plenty of water. If you spill anything on your clothes tell your teacher

☐ if you get anything in your eyes flush it out with plenty of water and tell your teacher immediately.

CONTENTS

CONTENTS

INTRODUCTION

Further Science is designed to introduce the student to some of the ideas covered by the higher levels of Science in the National Curriculum. These ideas take the student further towards understanding the world in which we live.

This book is intended to extend the work covered in the very successful *Science at Work* series of student books and copymaster extension sheets. Also linked to this book is a pack of activity sheets which extend and develop the concepts introduced here in a more practical way.

Examination syllabuses

The *Further Science* book is based on the requirements of the National Curriculum, and so is ideally suited for **any syllabus** which covers the Science topics specified by the orders for Science in the National Curriculum at Key Stage 4.

The book has been designed to link with the nine modules in the two GCSE examination syllabuses which have been specifically developed for this series of books. These syllabuses are:

Modular Science, Single and Double Award; Southern Examining Group (SEG) Science (Modular II), Single and Double Award; University of London Examinations and Assessment Council (ULEAC).

Students studying for the Double Award will need to cover all nine modules shown in the table. For a Single Award in science, students need to cover the five modules prefixed with **S**.

The table also shows which National Curriculum Attainment Targets each module is linked to. This will help if you are following a different syllabus.

Module	Attainment Targets and Strands
S1 Processes of Life	Sc2 strand i
S2 Reproduction and Inheritance	Sc2 strands i and ii
3 Ecosystems	Sc2 strands iii and iv
4 Earth and space	Sc3 strand iv, Sc4 strand v
S5 Materials	Sc3 strands i and ii
6 Chemical changes	Sc3 strand iii
S7 Electricity and Magnetism	Sc4 strand i
8 Light and Sound	Sc4 strand iv
S9 Forces and Energy	Sc4 strands ii and iii

The Science at Work series of books

The *Science at Work* series consists of eighteen practically based student books and a series of copymaster extension sheets. Together these give excellent cover for the Foundation and Intermediate tiers of the examinations. *Further Science* and the associated pack of activity sheets (*Further Science Copymasters*) have been written for the Higher tier of the examinations, and these concentrate on levels 8, 9 and 10.

The Further Science Book and Copymasters

Further Science has been designed to be interesting and helpful to you. Topics have been chosen to link to aspects of everyday life.

The book has been laid out to link with the examination modules. The pages are designed so that each topic starts on a new page. Each topic is cross referenced against work covered in the eighteen students' books and extension sheets. This will enable you to check up on or revise earlier work, or perhaps work covered at a lower tier.

Reading a book, however, will not always ensure that you pass the examination. You will need to

practise your answers and test your understanding of the topics. Each double page topic has a set of questions designed to do just this. The questions have been graded so that the easier ones come early on. You will obviously have to give much more thought to the harder ones. To help you eliminate simple mistakes there are answers to the numerical questions on page 172.

The final pages of this book (160–162) give help and advice on how to revise and pass examinations. The summary pages (163–171) contain a list of all the essential facts, laws, definitions and equations to help you with your last minute revision.

How to use this book

Each page is laid out like this:

Title of topic covered by double page

Cross references to Copymaster activity sheet

SEG/ULEAC syllabus module title

Page title

Cross references to Science at Work book and Extension sheet

Technical word in bold

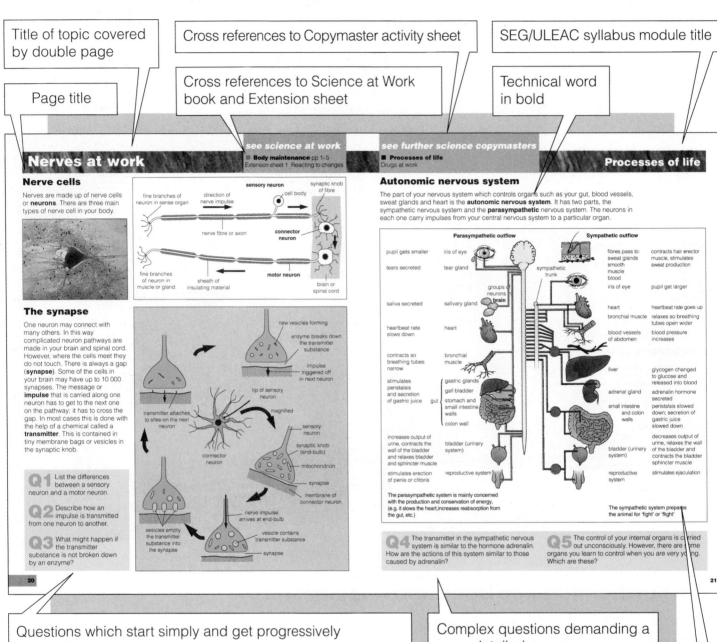

see science at work
■ Body maintenance pp 1–5
Extension sheet 1. Reacting to changes

see further science copymasters
■ Processes of life
Drugs at work

Nerves at work

Nerve cells

Nerves are made up of nerve cells or **neurons**. There are three main types of nerve cell in your body.

The synapse

One neuron may connect with many others. In this way complicated neuron pathways are made in your brain and spinal cord. However, where the cells meet they do not touch. There is always a gap (**synapse**). Some of the cells in your brain may have up to 10 000 synapses. The message or **impulse** that is carried along one neuron has to get to the next one on the pathway; it has to cross the gap. In most cases this is done with the help of a chemical called a **transmitter**. This is contained in tiny membrane bags or vesicles in the synaptic knob.

Q1 List the differences between a sensory neuron and a motor neuron.

Q2 Describe how an impulse is transmitted from one neuron to another.

Q3 What might happen if the transmitter substance is not broken down by an enzyme?

20

Autonomic nervous system

The part of your nervous system which controls organs such as your gut, blood vessels, sweat glands and heart is the **autonomic nervous system**. It has two parts, the sympathetic nervous system and the **parasympathetic** nervous system. The neurons in each one carry impulses from your central nervous system to a particular organ.

The parasympathetic system is mainly concerned with the production and conservation of energy, (e.g. it slows the heart, increases reabsorption from the gut, etc.)

The sympathetic system prepares the animal for 'fight' or 'flight'

Q4 The transmitter in the sympathetic nervous system is similar to the hormone adrenalin. How are the actions of this system similar to those caused by adrenalin?

Q5 The control of your internal organs is carried out unconsciously. However, there are some organs you learn to control when you are very young. Which are these?

Processes of life

21

Questions which start simply and get progressively more difficult.

For example 'List' means a simple list of differences. No explanation or expansion is required.

'Describe' demands a more detailed answer. You need to use several sentences and you could use a diagram to help with your description of what happens.

However, if the question states 'Explain what might ...' then your answer needs to be more detailed again. Go further than describing what happens. Try and explain why and how something happens.

Complex questions demanding a more detailed answer.

Artwork which summarises the necessary information clearly

This Copymaster activity sheet extends the information presented on the double page spread. It is suitable for classwork or homework.

Drugs at work

see science at work

■ Body maintenance
pp 23-26

Getting drugs into your body

There are three ways of getting drugs into your body. You can swallow them, sniff them or have them injected. The time it takes for a drug to have its effect depends on the amount you have taken and the way it has been put into your body. A large amount will produce a quicker and longer lasting effect than a small amount. A drug that is injected will show its effect quickly as it is put straight into the circulating blood. One you swallow may not show its effect for half an hour or more as it has to be absorbed before getting into the blood.

There is no such thing as a harmless drug; even an aspirin can damage your body. If you have ever had 'flu, you will have been given aspirin to bring down your body temperature.

The normal dose is two tablets every four hours until the temperature is back to normal. If larger doses are given over a long period of time, aspirin may cause the lining of the stomach to bleed.

Intravenous:
the drug is injected directly into a vein (1) and travels to the heart (2) where it is pumped into the arteries and carried to the brain (3) or the rest of the body (4)

Oral:
the drug is taken by mouth (1) and travels down the oesophagus (2) to the stomach (3) or intestines where it passes into the bloodstream and travels to the liver (4) and to the heart (5) where it is pumped to the brain (6) and the rest of the body (7)

Actions of drugs

Many drugs act on the nervous system, especially the synapses.

Drug	Site of action	Effect
Alcohol	Brain cells	Changes in mood, body co-ordination and judgement
Amphetamines ('pep' pills)	Cause the release of the transmitter in the sympathetic nervous system	Changes in the ways some of the body organs work
Atropine	Blocks the transmitter in the parasympathetic nervous system	Changes in the ways some of the body organs work
Curare	Blocks transmission between neurons and muscles	Movement of limbs impossible
Heroin	Pain centre in the brain	'Kills pain'
LSD	Works as a transmitter substance in the brain	Hallucinations
Morphine	Pain centre in the brain	'Kills pain'
Nicotine	Increases the activity of the sympathetic nervous system	Changes in the ways some of the body organs work
Strychnine	Stops the breakdown of the transmitter at many synapses	Effects of nerve impulse may be prolonged; increases the activity of the heart and breathing system

Q1 Why do injected drugs usually work quicker than ones you have swallowed?

Q2 Why is it wise to follow the dose advice on any drug container?

Q3 Why is morphine given to patients after an operation?

Q4 Curare was used on the tips of blow-pipe darts by South American Indians when they hunted animals. What effect would it have on an animal?

Q5 In what ways are the effects of amphetamines and atropine on the heart, lungs and gut different?

© Longman Group UK Ltd. 1993

7

Hormones, menstrual cycle and pregnancy

After puberty, a woman's body goes through a series of regular monthly cycles. The only visible sign of the changes is the shedding of blood at a period. When a woman is pregnant, the cycle is interrupted. The diagrams show the changes that take place in the uterus lining, the ovary, the neck of the womb, the blood and the body temperature during one menstrual cycle.

Non-pregnant woman

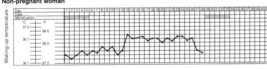

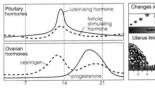

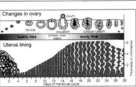

Pregnant woman

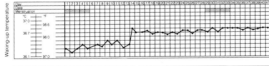

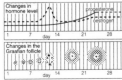

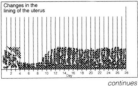

continues

© Longman Group UK Ltd. 1993

5

9

Homeostasis

Feedback mechanism

The cells in your body work best in a narrow range of conditions. Each of your body cells is bathed in tissue fluid so the substances in this must be kept steady or within a narrow range. The way the levels are regulated is called **homeostasis**. (This comes from two Greek words, *homos*, meaning the same and *stasis* meaning state). Homeostasis means keeping a constant or steady state inside your body.

This steady state is controlled by a **feedback** mechanism. Imagine you are heating a beaker of water with a Bunsen burner and you want to keep it at 37 °C. First of all you would heat the water with the Bunsen burner. If the water temperature rose above 37 °C, you would take the burner away and let the water cool slightly. If the temperature went below 37 °C, you would put back the burner under the beaker and the temperature of the water would rise. The change has been detected and actions have taken place to correct it. You can show this as a diagram. ▶

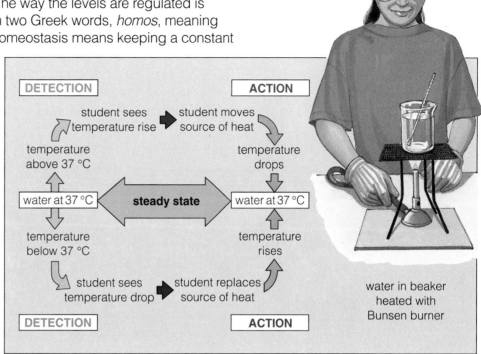

water in beaker heated with Bunsen burner

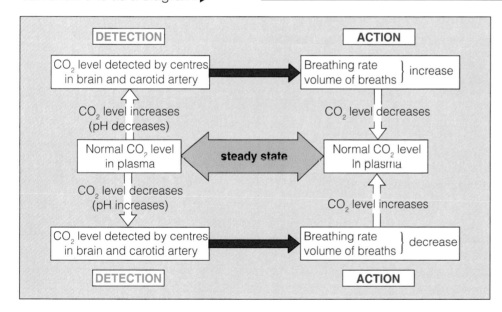

Control of breathing

Your cells release energy from food in respiration. Carbon dioxide is made. This gas will dissolve in the water of the tissue fluid and blood plasma to make carbonic acid. The pH of these fluids will change. However your cells will be affected if the pH changes, so the carbonic acid (carbon dioxide) must be got rid of. There are detectors in one of your arteries and your brain that are sensitive to pH. If the pH drops, these centres pass messages to your breathing system and you will breathe deeper and faster.

Q1 What other examples of feedback mechanisms can you find around your school or home?

Q2 If the amount of carbon dioxide in your blood increases, what will happen to the blood's pH?

Q3 Why will a change in pH affect the way your cells work?

Q4 Explain how your breathing will change if there is a decrease in the level of CO_2 in your blood.

Body Temperature

see science at work
■ Body maintenance
p 7 Energy in Foods
p 12 Body Temperature
p 13 Keeping warm and keeping cool

Heat gain and loss

Air temperature can change a lot during one day. Animals that live on land have to cope with these changes. The body temperature of most animals changes with the air around them. They rely on the heat from their surroundings to raise their temperature and so are known as **ectotherms**. Others rely on the production of heat by their body. These are called **endotherms** and can keep their temperature steady regardless of the weather.

You can keep your temperature steady between 37 °C and 38 °C even though your body produces enough heat to raise your temperature about 1 °C every hour.

So in warm weather your body must lose some of the heat it makes. In very cold weather your body will need to make more heat. You can make more heat by taking in more fuel (food) and keeping active, but you can also gain and lose heat by **radiation**, **convection** and **conduction**.

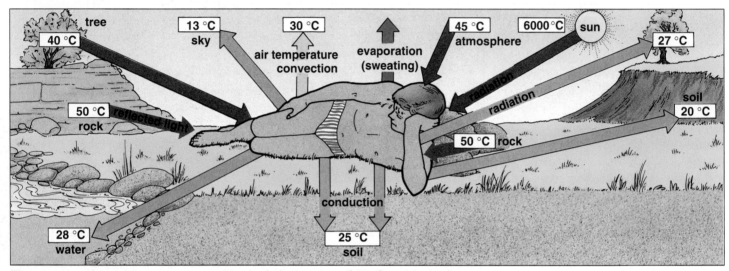

The energy exchanges between a man with a body temperature of 37 °C and the environment on a hot sunny day with an air temperature of 30 °C

Body size and temperature

The main source of heat is the breakdown of food in your body cells. The amount of heat made by a resting animal is known as the **basal metabolic rate** (BMR) and it gives us a way of comparing the activity of different animals or the same animal doing different things. In one day an average man will need 8000 kJ to match his BMR. The exact amount of energy you need depends on your age, size and sex.

A bulky person has lots of body cells producing heat but compared with this only a small surface area through which to lose heat to the surroundings. Animals like the elephant face overheating while small ones like the shrew lose heat quickly. Small animals with a large surface area compared to their bulk will lose heat quickly, and so to compensate, break down their food rapidly. Scientists believe that no mammal can be smaller than the smallest shrew because it could not get energy from its food quickly enough to make good the heat lost at its body surface.

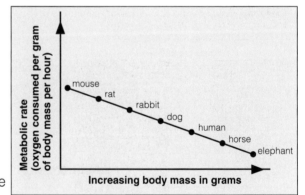

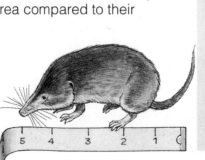

Q1 What are the body processes that work best at 37 ˚C?

Q2 Name two animals that are ectothermic. Name two animals – other than humans – that are endothermic.

Q3 Why could small babies die when put in a cold bedroom?

Processes of life

Skin

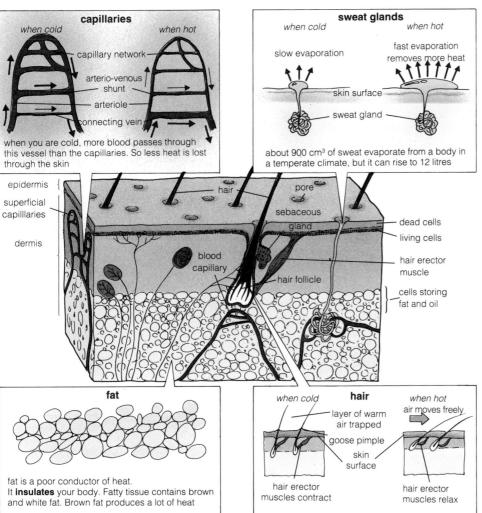

capillaries

when cold — *when hot*

- capillary network
- arterio-venous shunt
- arteriole
- connecting vein

when you are cold, more blood passes through this vessel than the capillaries. So less heat is lost through the skin

sweat glands

when cold — *when hot*

slow evaporation

fast evaporation removes more heat

- skin surface
- sweat gland

about 900 cm³ of sweat evaporate from a body in a temperate climate, but it can rise to 12 litres

- epidermis
- superficial capillaries
- dermis
- hair
- pore
- sebaceous gland
- blood capillary
- hair follicle
- dead cells
- living cells
- hair erector muscle
- cells storing fat and oil

fat

fat is a poor conductor of heat.
It **insulates** your body. Fatty tissue contains brown and white fat. Brown fat produces a lot of heat

hair

when cold — *when hot*

air moves freely

- layer of warm air trapped
- goose pimple
- skin surface
- hair erector muscles contract
- hair erector muscles relax

Your body is covered by a layer of skin 1 to 2 millimetres thick. If you could take off your skin it would be about the size of a single bed sheet. You can control the loss of heat through your skin. The blood capillaries, sweat, hair and fat all play a part in controlling your temperature.

Clothes

Some athletes wear kit made of two layers. The inside layer soaks up the sweat given off by the skin as the body gets hotter during exercise. The outer layer loses this water quickly by evaporation. So the athlete loses heat and keeps the temperature near normal.

Sea water can be very cold. Diving suits are made of neoprene which is a heat insulator. Wearing a diving suit means the diver cuts down heat loss.

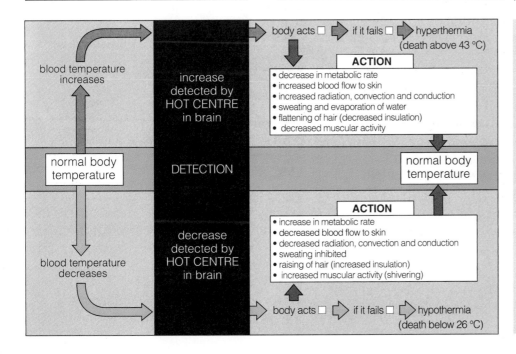

blood temperature increases

increase detected by HOT CENTRE in brain

body acts ☐ ➡ if it fails ☐ ➡ hyperthermia (death above 43 °C)

ACTION
- decrease in metabolic rate
- increased blood flow to skin
- increased radiation, convection and conduction
- sweating and evaporation of water
- flattening of hair (decreased insulation)
- decreased muscular activity

normal body temperature

DETECTION

normal body temperature

blood temperature decreases

decrease detected by HOT CENTRE in brain

ACTION
- increase in metabolic rate
- decreased blood flow to skin
- decreased radiation, convection and conduction
- sweating inhibited
- raising of hair (increased insulation)
- increased muscular activity (shivering)

body acts ☐ ➡ if it fails ☐ ➡ hypothermia (death below 26 °C)

Q4 Explain how sweating lowers your body temperature.

Q5 Explain why mammals can be no smaller than a shrew.

Q6 What are the advantages of being able to control your body temperature? What are the disadvantages?

Q7 Why do you shiver on a cold day? Explain how this action is brought about.

The working units of the kidney

Your kidneys are the organs which adjust the amount of water and substances like salt (sodium chloride) in your body. They also get rid of the waste products of working cells (urea), and the remains of drugs and food additives. These substances are passed out of your body in urine. If you have drunk a lot of liquid, you will make a lot of weak urine. If your body is short of water, you will get rid of a small amount of strong, dark yellow urine. This is evidence of the body maintaining the water and solute balance. You need to keep this balance so the concentration of your body fluids stays the same and the cells can work properly. If your body loses this balance, movement and co-ordination are difficult. You may see athletes suffering in this way at the end of a marathon race.

Each kidney contains about a million fine tubes. These are called **nephrons** and they remove waste from the blood and regulate water loss.

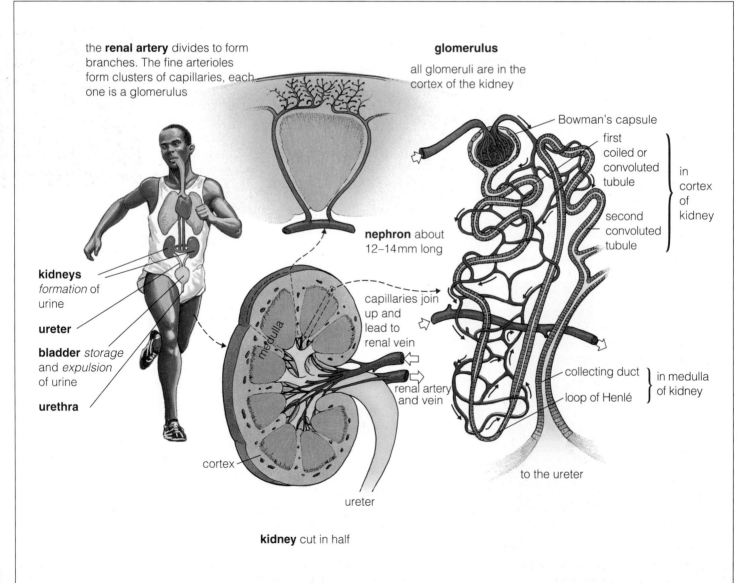

the **renal artery** divides to form branches. The fine arterioles form clusters of capillaries, each one is a glomerulus

glomerulus

all glomeruli are in the cortex of the kidney

Bowman's capsule

first coiled or convoluted tubule

second convoluted tubule

in cortex of kidney

nephron about 12–14 mm long

kidneys *formation* of urine

ureter

bladder *storage* and *expulsion* of urine

urethra

medulla

capillaries join up and lead to renal vein

renal artery and vein

collecting duct

loop of Henlé

in medulla of kidney

cortex

to the ureter

ureter

kidney cut in half

Controlling water

You have a group of cells in the brain that detects if the blood plasma is getting more or less concentrated than normal. These cells can turn on or off the release of **antidiuretic hormone (ADH)** from the posterior pituitary gland. ADH increases the movement of water from the collecting duct of the nephron into the blood and so the kidney will produce urine with less water. The urine will be very dark yellow. ADH is released when you need to cut down the loss of water.

Urine and health

Urine contains many substances. International athletes have to give urine samples for testing. Traces of drugs, such as anabolic steroids, can be identified in urine. Women who think they may be pregnant also give urine for testing. The urine of a pregnant woman will contain a hormone (human chorionic gonadotropin). This hormone can be detected using a reaction with antibodies. When you are ill, your doctor might ask you for a sample of urine. If you are ill, the urine may have substances in it that are not usually there. For example, anyone suffering from sugar diabetes will have glucose in their urine.

Ben Johnson (left) winning the final of the 100m race at Seoul, 1988. He was subsequently disqualified after urine tests.

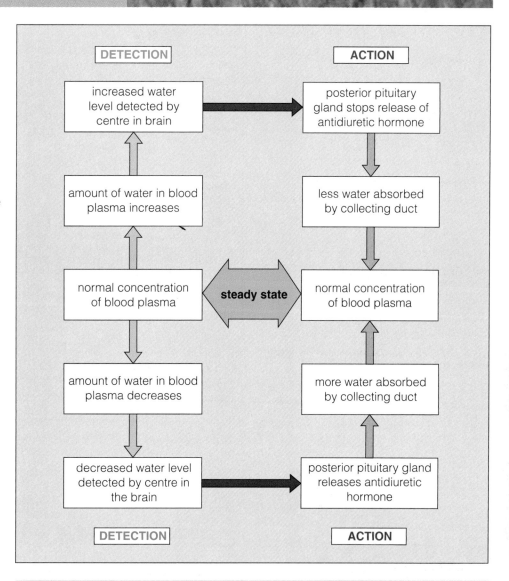

Q1 Explain as accurately as you can, the place where each of the following is found in your body:
a Bowman's capsule
b loop of Henlé
c bladder.

Q2 Why does your body need to stay in water and solute balance?

Q3 What do you predict would happen to each of the following if you were sitting in a hot, humid classroom;
a the production of sweat
b the production of antidiuretic hormone
c the permeability of the collecting ducts in your kidney.

Q4 Explain how your kidneys produce weak urine to keep your body in water balance.

Cell wars

Protecting your body

Your body is always under attack from microbes, so to stay healthy it either has to keep them out or deal with them if they get in. Everyone is born with *six* ways of defending themselves from invasion by microbes. They are the skin, breathing tubes, stomach acid, tears, blood clotting and microbe-eating cells (**phagocytes**).

The skin acts as a barrier to microbes. Mucus in the breathing tubes trap microbes. Cilia sweep mucus to the mouth where it is swallowed and goes to the stomach. Acid in the gastric juices of the stomach kills microbes. Tears contain an enzyme which damages microbes. Blood clotting proteins in blood plasma form sticky threads which trap red blood cells to form a scab. White blood cells attack and digest any microbe that enters the body.

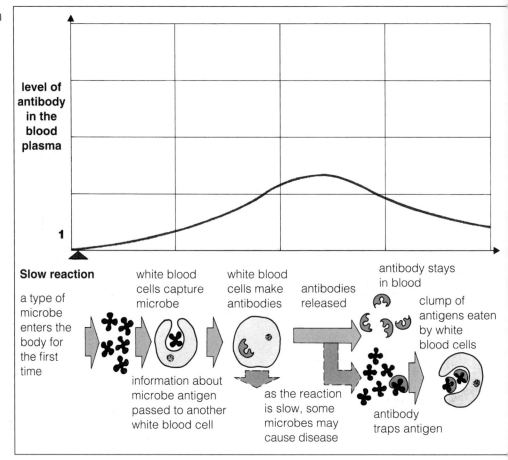

level of antibody in the blood plasma

1

Slow reaction

a type of microbe enters the body for the first time

white blood cells capture microbe

information about microbe antigen passed to another white blood cell

white blood cells make antibodies

antibodies released

as the reaction is slow, some microbes may cause disease

antibody stays in blood

clump of antigens eaten by white blood cells

antibody traps antigen

Q1 Why should mothers be encouraged to breast feed their babies?

Q2 Why do you need to have 'booster' vaccinations to protect you from diseases like polio?

Q3 Edward Jenner deliberately infected James Phipps with smallpox. Was Jenner right to risk James' life?

Q4 Vaccination campaigns like those organised by WHO could wipe out infectious diseases such as measles and whooping cough which kill many young children in developing countries. What do you predict could be the impact of this in such countries?

Antibodies and immunity

There are some microbes, like the foot and mouth virus, that cause disease in animals, but cannot live inside your body and infect you. You are **naturally immune** to such diseases.

However you can also develop or **acquire** immunity to certain diseases. If a microbe gets into your blood, the white blood cells will recognise it as an invader or **antigen** and they will make a defence chemical called an **antibody**. The antibody will either destroy the antigens or stick them together, making it easier for phagocytic cells to engulf them. Because your body is working to make antibodies, this type of defence is called **active acquired immunity**. A fetus or new-born baby gets antibodies from its mother, either across the placenta or in breast milk. As the antibodies are not made by the baby itself this is called **passive immunity**. This type of immunity only lasts for a short time because the antibodies will be destroyed by the liver. So, new-born babies are resistant to some diseases for about three months. After this, the baby must be given treated antigens to give it active immunity against infectious microbial diseases (**vaccination**).

If there is an outbreak of a dangerous disease – like meningitis or diphtheria – people need to be protected very quickly. They are treated with ready-made antibodies. This is another example of passive immunity.

see further science copymasters
■ **Processes of life**
The changing pattern of disease

Processes of life

The immune reaction

The type of antibody your body makes depends on the type of antigen that is invading. An invading measles virus (antigen) will make the body produce measles antibodies. These antibodies will stay in the blood for a short time and then almost disappear. However, if your body is invaded by the same antigen again, the antibody level rises further and will stay high for some time. Once your body has made an antibody, it can produce more of the same very quickly. It's like a boat builder. The builder will take some time to make the mould for a glass fibre boat, but once it is made, then many glass fibre boats can be made quickly. So, if the measles antigen attacks your body for a second time, some of the antibodies remaining after the first attack will destroy a few and your body will have the 'mould' for more of the antibodies, so more can be made quickly. You will not catch measles even if the virus enters your body.

2

Time

Fast reaction

the same type of microbe enters the body for a second time

white blood cells recognise the antigen. The cell makes antibodies quickly

clump of antigens eaten

antibody stays in blood

some antibodies already in blood

antibody traps a few antigens

as antibodies are either in the blood or made quickly, the microbes do not damage the cells – the person is immune

Edward Jenner

Edward Jenner was a country doctor. He noticed that dairy maids who had milked cows with the cowpox disease, were less likely than other people to catch the dangerous disease of smallpox. The dairy maids sometimes developed sores on their hands. He also knew that people with cowpox sores rubbed them into scratches on other people's bodies and they didn't catch smallpox. So, in 1797, Jenner took some of the liquid from a dairy maid's cowpox sore and scratched it into the skin of a boy called James Phipps. Later Jenner scratched James with liquid from a smallpox sore. James didn't catch the disease. We now know that James had become actively immune to smallpox.

World Health Organisation (WHO)

The WHO tries to improve the health of all people in all countries. It was established in 1948 and its headquarters are in Geneva, Switzerland. Their medical experts and advisers work in many ways. They keep detailed records of any outbreak of a dangerous disease. They organise campaigns to vaccinate people against infectious diseases like measles, polio and smallpox. In fact they have completely wiped out smallpox, except for the occasional accident with the virus in laboratories. The last known case was in Somalia in 1977. They also provide advice about sanitation, housing and medical services.

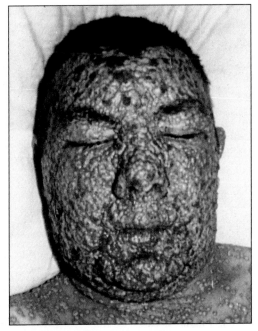
A case of smallpox.

Glands, hormones and targets

Your glands are groups of cells that make substances needed by your body. The substances are called **secretions**. There are two kinds of glands, **exocrine** and **endocrine**.

Exocrine glands like your sweat glands and salivary glands pour their secretions into tubes or ducts. These secretions go to the outside of your body or into a space inside one of your organs.

The endocrine glands pour their secretions, which are called **hormones**, into the blood. These hormones affect many processes but some may affect just one part of the body. This is called the target. Endocrine glands help to co-ordinate the way your body works.

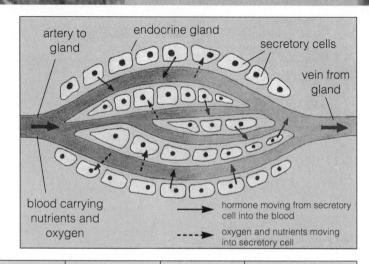

artery to gland — endocrine gland — secretory cells — vein from gland — blood carrying nutrients and oxygen

→ hormone moving from secretory cell into the blood

‑‑‑> oxygen and nutrients moving into secretory cell

hypothalamus (a control centre in the brain)

parathyroid gland

thyroid gland

thymus gland

Endocrine gland	Controlled by	Hormone(s) secreted	Target(s)	Effect
Anterior pituitary gland	Growth factor from hypothalamus	Growth hormone	Body cells	Growth of body cells
	Sex hormone levels in the blood	Gonadotropic hormones (ICSH, FSH, LH)	Sex organs	Development of sex cells and control of reproduction
Posterior pituitary gland	Water level in plasma	Antidiuretic hormone (ADH)	Nephrons in the kidney	Urine becomes concentrated
Adrenal gland	Nerves	Adrenalin	Many body processes	'Fight or flight' reaction
Pancreatic islets of Langerhans	Glucose level in the blood	Insulin and glucagon	Liver	Homeostatic control of blood glucose level
Ovaries *or*	Gonadotropic hormones (FSH, LH)	Oestrogen and Progesterone	Uterus and ovaries	Regulating the menstrual cycle
Testes	Gonadotropic hormones (ICSH, FSH)	Testosterone	Male sex organs	Production of sperm, libido

Q1 Name three exocrine glands and describe how their release of secretions differs from endocrine glands.

Q2 How does the way adrenalin works differ from other hormones?

Q3 Male and female athletes used to take testosterone as a drug. Now this is banned. Suggest reasons why it has been banned.

Q4 Why is the body's failure to produce insulin a greater hazard to health than failure

Hormones at work

The release of hormones from your endocrine glands is controlled in three ways:
● by the action of nerves (e.g. the release of adrenalin from the adrenal gland)
● by the presence of a substance in the blood (e.g. the presence of a lot of glucose causes the release of insulin from the islets in the pancreas)
● by the presence of a stimulating hormone (e.g. the presence of a pituitary hormone in the blood causes the testes to release testosterone).

Most endocrine glands work by the second two ways. The timing of the release of hormones is controlled by a feedback mechanism (see *Homeostasis*).

Your endocrine and nervous systems work together to control the activities of your body.

Nervous control	Hormonal control
Message is an electrical – chemical impulse	Message is a chemical
Message travels along nerve cells	Message is carried in the blood
Response usually quick and in one part of the body	Response is usually slow and over many parts of the body
Effect lasts for a short time	Effect usually lasts a long time
Controlled by brain or spinal cord	Most controlled by pituitary gland

Sex hormones

In teenage boys and men, two hormones from the anterior pituitary gland stimulate the testes. One (FSH) is produced all the time and causes the testes to make sperm.

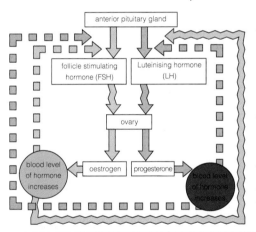

The other (ICSH) causes the testes to make another hormone, testosterone. This hormone causes the growth of the male reproductive parts and affects the sex drive (**libido**). The level of testosterone in the blood is regulated by feedback.

In girls and women, there are also two hormones released by the anterior pituitary gland. FSH stimulates the maturing of eggs, but in women this does not take place continuously. It is in a cycle of events that takes place once a month and so it called the **menstrual cycle** (*mensis* is the Latin word for month). This hormone, FSH, also causes the ovary to make oestrogen. This helps the egg to develop, makes the lining of the womb thicken and stops the

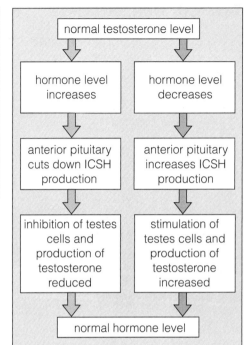

release of more FSH. Oestrogen stimulates the anterior pituitary gland to release its second hormone (LH). This hormone makes sure the egg completes its development and is released. The cells left in the ovary develop into the yellow body which releases the hormones oestrogen and progesterone. The hormones that regulate the menstrual cycle also affect the breasts, abdomen and brain.

Insulin

In your pancreas are the islets of Langerhans, which have two kinds of cell. They are alpha and beta cells and they are both sensitive to the level of glucose in your blood. Alpha cells secrete glucagon and beta cells secrete insulin and these act in opposite ways.

In some people, the beta cells do not make insulin. These people suffer from sugar diabetes. Since 1921, these people could be treated with insulin from other animals, but the immune response (see Cell Wars) caused problems when they got older. Human insulin can be made by genetic engineering, and this should free diabetics from the harmful side-effects of using animal insulin.

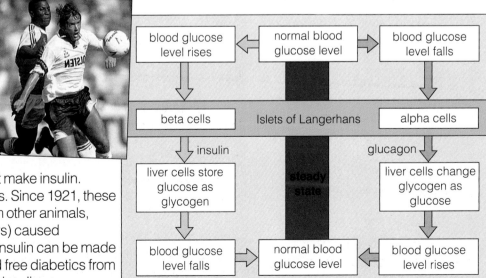

Nerves at work

see science at work
Body maintenance pp 1–5
Extension sheet 1 Reacting to changes

Nerve cells

Nerves are made up of nerve cells or **neurons**. There are three main types of nerve cell in your body.

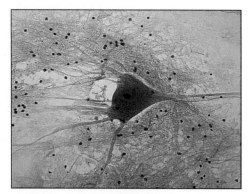

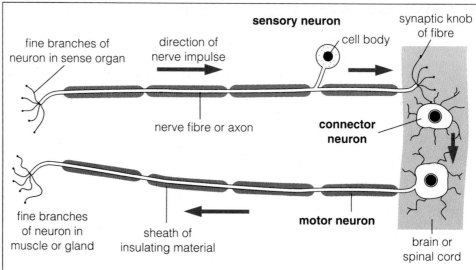

The synapse

One neuron may connect with many others. In this way complicated neuron pathways are made in your brain and spinal cord. However, where the cells meet they do not touch. There is always a gap (**synapse**). Some of the cells in your brain may have up to 10 000 synapses. The message or **impulse** that is carried along one neuron has to get to the next one on the pathway; it has to cross the gap. In most cases this is done with the help of a chemical called a **transmitter**. This is contained in tiny membrane bags or vesicles in the synaptic knob.

Q1 List the differences between a sensory neuron and a motor neuron.

Q2 Describe how an impulse is transmitted from one neuron to another.

Q3 What might happen if the transmitter substance is not broken down by an enzyme?

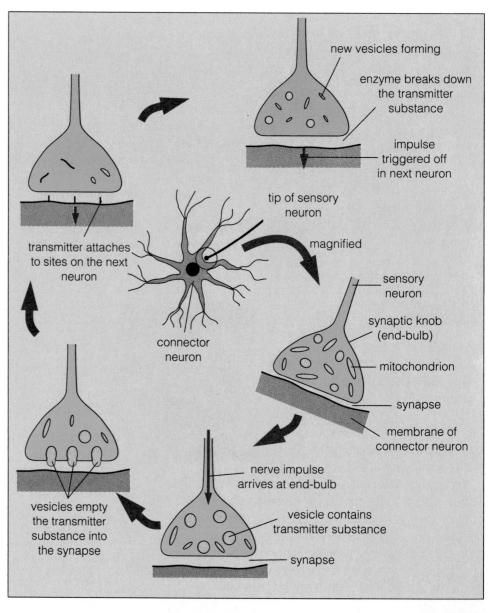

Autonomic nervous system

The part of your nervous system which controls organs such as your gut, blood vessels, sweat glands and heart is the **autonomic nervous system**. It has two parts, the sympathetic nervous system and the **parasympathetic** nervous system. The neurons in each one carry impulses from your central nervous system to a particular organ.

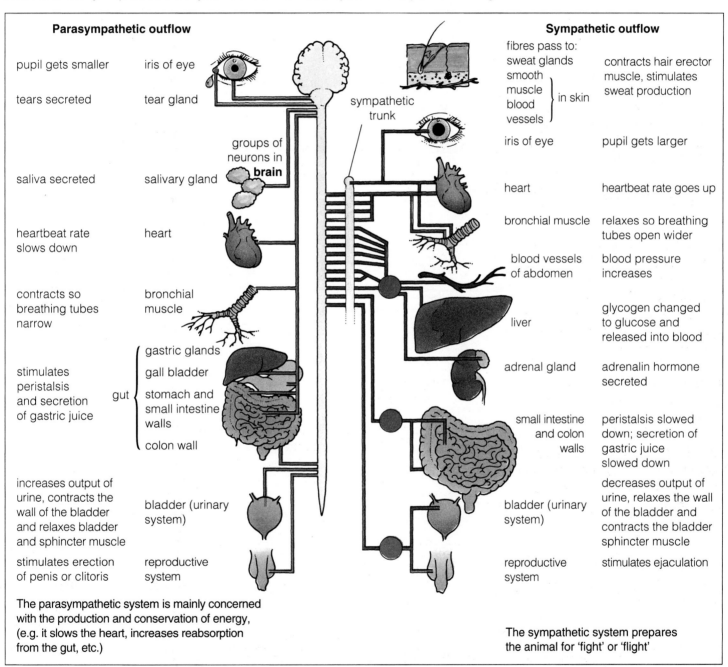

Parasympathetic outflow

pupil gets smaller	iris of eye
tears secreted	tear gland
saliva secreted	salivary gland
heartbeat rate slows down	heart
contracts so breathing tubes narrow	bronchial muscle
stimulates peristalsis and secretion of gastric juice	gut { gastric glands, gall bladder, stomach and small intestine walls, colon wall }
increases output of urine, contracts the wall of the bladder and relaxes bladder and sphincter muscle	bladder (urinary system)
stimulates erection of penis or clitoris	reproductive system

groups of neurons in **brain**

sympathetic trunk

Sympathetic outflow

fibres pass to:

sweat glands, smooth muscle, blood vessels } in skin	contracts hair erector muscle, stimulates sweat production
iris of eye	pupil gets larger
heart	heartbeat rate goes up
bronchial muscle	relaxes so breathing tubes open wider
blood vessels of abdomen	blood pressure increases
liver	glycogen changed to glucose and released into blood
adrenal gland	adrenalin hormone secreted
small intestine and colon walls	peristalsis slowed down; secretion of gastric juice slowed down
bladder (urinary system)	decreases output of urine, relaxes the wall of the bladder and contracts the bladder sphincter muscle
reproductive system	stimulates ejaculation

The parasympathetic system is mainly concerned with the production and conservation of energy, (e.g. it slows the heart, increases reabsorption from the gut, etc.)

The sympathetic system prepares the animal for 'fight' or 'flight'

Q4 The transmitter in the sympathetic nervous system is similar to the hormone adrenalin. How are the actions of this system similar to those caused by adrenalin?

Q5 The control of your internal organs is carried out unconsciously. However, there are some organs you learn to control when you are very young. Which are these?

Fetal environment

see science at work

■ **Genetics and Reproduction**
p 10 Conception

□ **How Living Things Work**
p 28 Astronauts and Babies

Embedding the Embryo

A fertilised egg cell takes about a week to travel down the oviduct and reach the uterus. The cell divides many times to make a ball of cells called the **embryo**. The embryo sinks into the soft lining of the uterus (**implantation**). It needs food and oxygen to grow. At first these come directly from the uterus wall. After a couple of weeks an organ starts growing from the tissues of the embryo and the mother. This is the **placenta**.

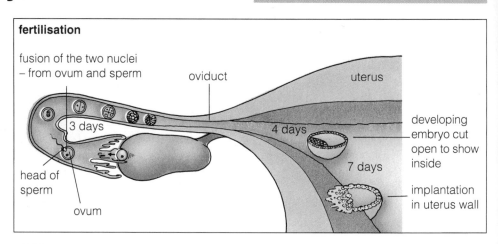

fertilisation

fusion of the two nuclei – from ovum and sperm

oviduct

uterus

3 days

4 days

developing embryo cut open to show inside

7 days

head of sperm

ovum

implantation in uterus wall

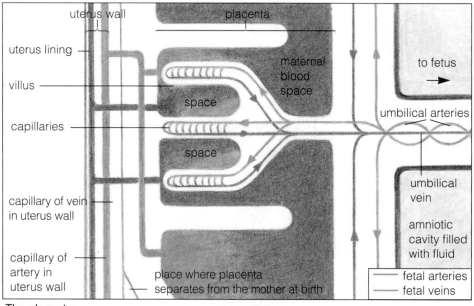

uterus wall

placenta

uterus lining

villus

maternal blood space

to fetus

space

umbilical arteries

capillaries

space

umbilical vein

capillary of vein in uterus wall

amniotic cavity filled with fluid

capillary of artery in uterus wall

place where placenta separates from the mother at birth

— fetal arteries
— fetal veins

The placenta.

The placenta

When the embryo is twelve weeks old, the placenta takes over from the uterus wall as the 'life-support system'. The embryo is now known as a **fetus**. The umbilical cord is the connection between the fetus and the placenta. It contains blood vessels – two umbilical arteries and one umbilical vein. Capillaries from the vein pick up oxygen and food chemicals from the mother's blood. The umbilical arteries take carbon dioxide and other waste chemicals from the fetus to the mother. The blood of the mother and fetus never mix. They are separated by a membrane about 2mm thick. Chemicals, like oxygen, that have small molecules can diffuse across. Larger molecules are transported by mechanisms needing energy. Many dangerous chemicals and microbes cannot cross this barrier, but some can. Examples include the drug thalidomide and the rubella virus. The placenta also helps to protect the fetus from the mother's immune system, so it is not rejected as a transplanted organ might be. It produces hormones too; one (human chorionic gonadotropin) appears in the urine and its presence is used in pregnancy tests.

Q1 If the embryo takes seven days to travel down the oviduct to the uterus, on which day of the menstrual cycle will implantation take place?

Q2 List the jobs of the placenta.

Q3 How do the substances carried in the plasma of the umbilical arteries and veins differ from those carried in the plasma of the mother's arteries and veins?

Q4 Why might the fetus be rejected by the mother's immune system?

Q5 Suggest a reason why the cells in the membranes in the placenta contain many mitochondria.

Q6 Find out what the effects on the fetus are of:
a the drug thalidomide
b the rubella virus.

see further science copymasters
■ **Processes of life**
Hormones, menstrual cycle and pregnancy

Chromosomes and genes

You started life as a single cell, a zygote formed from the fertilisation of one ovum by one sperm. All your tissues and organs have developed from that first single cell. The instructions that decided which cells would develop into muscles, which into nerves and which into skin were all present in that first cell. Also present were instructions about your physical and chemical characteristics. All these instructions were inherited from your parents.

The chromosomes

The cell that forms from the ovum and sperm has a cell membrane, cytoplasm and a nucleus. In the human cell nucleus there are 46 chromosomes. These are thread-like structures made from DNA (deoxyribo nucleic acid). The chromosomes carry all the information that leads to the formation of a new individual.

cytoplasm

nucleus

chromosomes

cell membrane

Chromosomes in the nucleus

6 chromosomes

The chromosomes are in pairs. One chromosome from each pair came from the ovum, and the other from the sperm. The pairs of chromosomes are called homologous pairs.

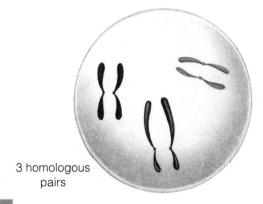

Homologous pairs of chromosomes

3 homologous pairs

The genes

Along the length of each chromosome are genes. Each gene is part of the DNA molecule and is responsible for an activity in the cell. The gene might determine blood group, the ability to manufacture a certain enzyme or contribute to hair colour.

Every plant or animal cell (except gametes) has a full set of chromosomes and therefore a full set of genes. The gene will only be 'switched on' in the cell where it is required. The gene that controls the manufacture of pepsin will be switched on in the stomach cells but not in the skin cells. The gene's instructions are only carried out in the right place.

The diagram represents the genes on a chromosome. In reality there are many more.

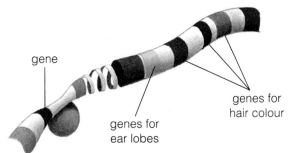

gene

genes for ear lobes

genes for hair colour

Each chromosome in a homologous pair carries genes for the same characteristic. Therefore if the gene controlling blood group is on one chromosome of Pair 9 it will also be on the other chromosome of Pair 9. The gene occupies the same specific site on each chromosome of the pair. The site is called the gene locus. Geneticists are now able to map the sites of many genes.

There are two or more ways a characteristic can be expressed. For example your ear lobes may be attached or unattached, your hair may be blond, brown, black or red. The alternative forms of the gene are called alleles.

If both the alleles for the ear lobe characteristic are the same then the individual is homozygous for that characteristic.

If the two alleles for the ear lobe characteristic are different the individual is heterozygous for that characteristic.

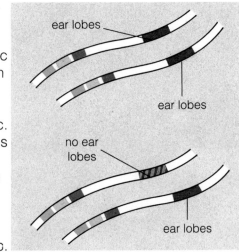

ear lobes

ear lobes

no ear lobes

ear lobes

Chromosomes of different species

Human cell nuclei have 46 chromosomes in 23 pairs. Each species of plant and animal has a specific number of chromosomes. The chromosomes are always in pairs. The number of chromosomes is called the diploid number (2N). Gametes have one chromosome from each pair; they are haploid(N).

Onion   Mosquito   Chicken

Mutations

Mutations are changes to the genetic make-up of the cell. The change might be to a gene, a group of genes or a whole chromosome.

A mutation to the allele controlling the number of toes has led to a group of people having six toes. This mutation has no disadvantage so has been passed through generations of people.

Down's syndrome is a chromosome mutation. The cells all have one additional chromosome.

Mutations occur naturally at random. Many will not be noticed as they do no harm and cannot be seen. Other mutations will be harmful, some are lethal.

If the mutation occurs in the reproductive cells, the young may develop abnormally or may die at an early stage of development. Many miscarriages are of genetically abnormal offspring. Any non-lethal mutation in the reproductive cells will be passed on to future generations.

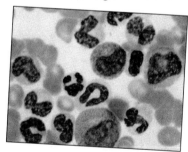

Other mutations occur in the non-reproductive (somatic) cells; these will not be inherited. These mutations could cause uncontrolled growth of the cells and form either benign or malignant tumours (cancer).

Exposure to ionising radiation such as ultra-violet radiation, X-rays and the radiation from radioactive substances as well as certain chemicals can increase the number of mutations. The greater the dose of radiation or chemical, the greater the chance and the degree of mutation.

Mutation can sometimes be beneficial to a species. Horses are subject to intestinal worms. At regular intervals they are treated with drugs to kill the worms.

If the worm mutated to become resistant to the drug it would not be killed and would pass the drug resistance mutation to its offspring. This mutation is beneficial to the worm, as they can now resist the drug.

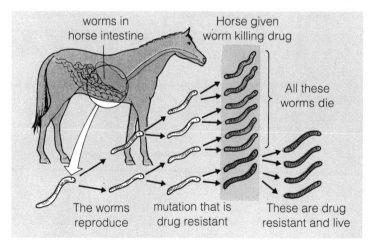

worms in horse intestine — Horse given worm killing drug — All these worms die — The worms reproduce — mutation that is drug resistant — These are drug resistant and live

Q1 Explain these terms:
a homologous chromosomes
b allele c gene locus d mutation

Q2 How many chromosomes are in each mosquito body cell?

Q3 How many homologous pairs of chromosomes are in an onion cell?

Q4 Describe how the mutation of intestinal worms to become resistant to some drugs will be an advantage to the worm and a disadvantage to the horse.

see science at work
■ **Genetics and reproduction**
pp 25–28 Human inheritance

Inherited disorders

Some diseases and disorders are brought about by genes or chromosomes. Down's Syndrome is a condition caused by the presence of an extra chromosome. Colour blindness, cystic fibrosis, sickle cell anaemia, haemophilia and albinism are examples of conditions caused by one or more genes.

Colour blindness and haemophilia are sex-linked. The gene responsible is on the X chromosome. In both cases the normal allele is dominant.

Haemophilia

The gene that controls the production of the blood clotting protein Factor VIII, also called anti-haemophiliac globulin (AHG) is on the X chromosome. The presence of the normal allele **H** leads to normal blood clotting. The presence of the recessive allele **h** means that the blood clotting agent is defective or that amounts present are reduced. The condition is controlled by regular injections of AHG. Unfortunately much of the AHG used in the past was from blood that had not been heat treated. This has led to many haemophiliacs contracting Human Immunodeficiency Virus (HIV).

These are the possible phenotypes and genotypes for the haemophilia gene.

Genotype	Phenotype
$X^H X^H$	Normal female
$X^H X^h$	Normal female but carrier for haemophilia
$X^H Y$	Normal male
$X^h Y$	Haemophiliac male

Queen Victoria was a carrier for haemophilia. The diagram shows how the gene was passed through some of Europe's royal families.

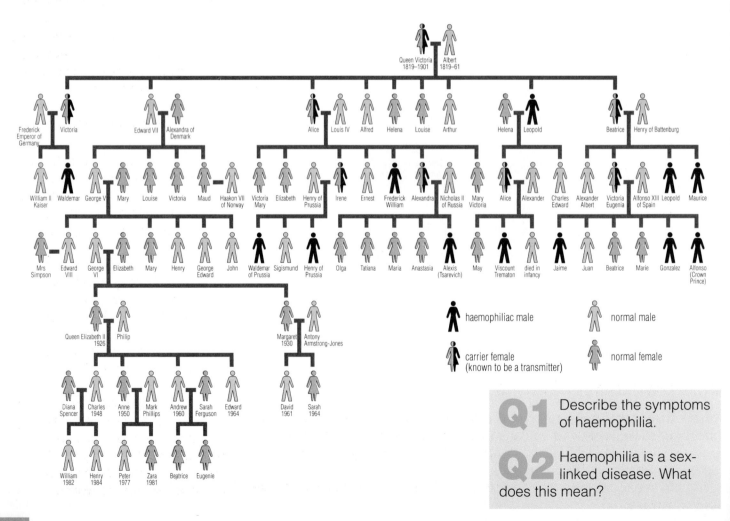

haemophiliac male

normal male

carrier female
(known to be a transmitter)

normal female

Q1 Describe the symptoms of haemophilia.

Q2 Haemophilia is a sex-linked disease. What does this mean?

Cystic fibrosis

This has the highest incidence of any gene inherited disease in Britain (up to one person in 25 is a carrier). It is caused by a recessive allele and so only people who are homozygous recessive for the cystic fibrosis allele will suffer from the disease. Children with cystic fibrosis produce sticky mucus in the lungs and pancreas. This can lead to respiratory and digestive problems. Although there is no cure for cystic fibrosis yet, great progress has been made in the treatment of the symptoms.

The family tree shows the inheritance of cystic fibrosis.

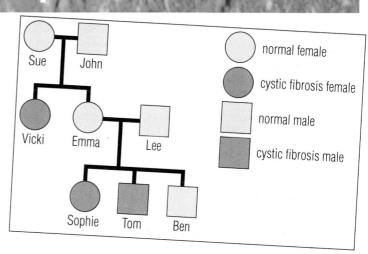

Sickle cell anaemia

In sickle cell anaemia the disc-shaped red blood cells become sickle-shaped.

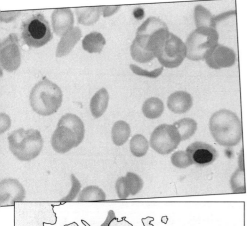

The normal form of haemoglobin is produced by the allele HbA. A slightly altered form, the result of a mutation, is HbS. In low oxygen conditions red cells containing Haemoglobin S become sickle shaped and stick together. Eventually they lose their haemoglobin and this leads to anaemia.

People who are homozygous for HbA will have normal haemoglobin. People who are homozygous for HbS will have abnormal haemoglobin and rarely survive to have children. Because of this it would be expected that HbS would eventually be lost from the population.

However, people that are heterozygous for the haemoglobin gene are not anaemic and are able to live a normal life. These people have a much higher than usual resistance to the malarial parasite, so gain an advantage in malarial regions.

The maps show the distribution of sickle cell anaemia and malaria.

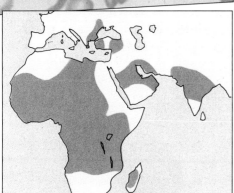

The distribution of sickle cell anaemia.

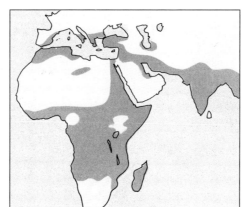

The distribution of malaria.

Q3 Two people who do not have cystic fibrosis marry and have two children. One suffers from cystic fibrosis and one does not. Explain how this happens.

Q4 Two people who are heterozygous for the sickle cell gene marry and have children. What are the possible genotypes of their children and what will the red blood cells of each genotype be like?

Q5 People who are homozygous for sickle cell anaemia rarely survive to produce children. Why has the condition remained so common in some parts of the world?

Huntington's chorea

This is a rare inherited disease of the nervous system; the symptoms are uncontrolled movements. It is caused by a mutant allele that is dominant. Because the allele is dominant, people who are heterozygous for the gene will suffer from the disease.

The disease does not take effect until middle age. There is as yet no cure for the disease.

Mitosis

Cell division is necessary for a plant or animal to grow or replace damaged tissues. Each new cell must contain exactly the same number and type of chromosome as the original cell. The cell division that produces all new cells (except gametes) is called mitosis. The cells produced are non-reproductive or somatic cells.

To understand how the information on the chromosome is passed from cell to cell we need to look at what happens when a cell divides.

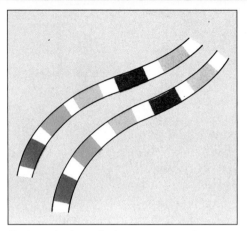

During mitosis each chromosome makes a replicate of itself.

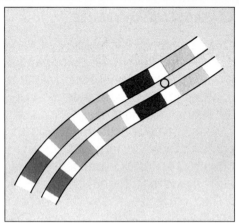

The two replicates are called chromatids and are joined together by a centromere.

This series of diagrams shows the stages that occur in mitosis as a cell divides to produce two new identical cells. The cell shown has four chromosomes.

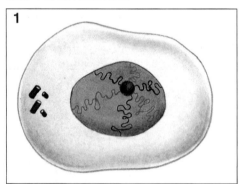

1 Interphase
The chromosomes are long and thin and not visible until just before the cell starts to divide.

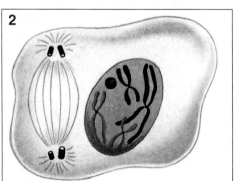

2 Prophase
The chromosomes get short and fat. Each one is made of two chromatids.

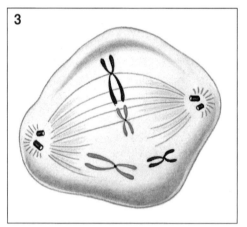

3 Metaphase
The nuclear membrane disappears. A spindle of thin fibres forms. The chromosomes line up at the middle of the spindle.

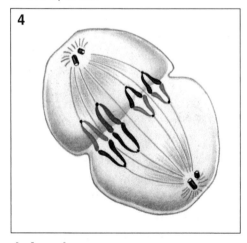

4 Anaphase
The chromatids move apart

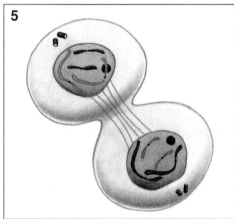

5 Telophase
The chromatids are at opposite ends of the cell. A nuclear membrane forms around each set of chromatids. The cell starts to divide.

6 Cell division is complete. Two daughter cells each identical to the parent cell have formed.

Meiosis

Meiosis is the cell division that leads to the production of gametes. It takes place in the tubules of the testes and in the cell that produces the ovum in the ovaries.

Each gamete must contain only one chromosome from each homologous pair.

The diagrams below show the stages of meiosis in a cell with two homologous pairs of chromosomes. The blue chromosome in each pair is from one parent and the purple chromosome from the other.

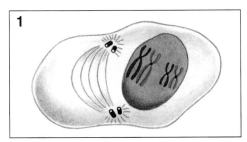

1 Prophase I
The chromosomes get short and fat. Each chromosome is made of two chromatids. Homologous pairs of chromosomes come together.

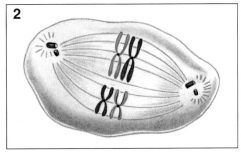

2 Metaphase I
The nuclear membrane disappears. A spindle forms. The homologous pairs of chromosomes line up on the spindle.

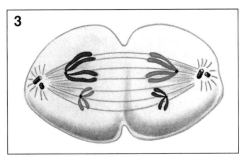

3 Anaphase I
The homologous pairs separate. One chromosome from each pair goes to opposite sides of the cell.

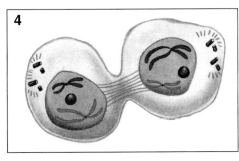

4 Telophase I
A nuclear membrane forms around each set of chromosomes and the cell divides.

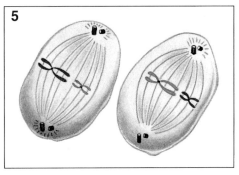

5 Metaphase II
New spindles form. The chromosomes line up on the spindle.

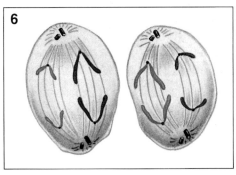

6 Anaphase II
The chromatids move apart.

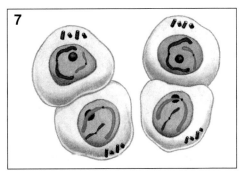

7 Telophase II
The nuclear membrane forms. Four daughter cells have been produced. Each cell has half the chromosome number of the parent cell.

Q1 When a somatic cell with 20 chromosomes divides by mitosis how many chromosomes will there be in each daughter cell?

Q2 A meiotic division of a cell with 40 chromosomes produces 4 daughter cells. How many chromosomes are in each cell?

Q3 Explain the process leading to the production of a sperm cell in the tubule of the testis.

Q4 Copy and complete the chart comparing mitosis and meiosis.

Mitosis
Takes place in _____ cells.
Somatic cells are produced.
Each division produces _____ cells.
The chromosome number is the same.
Both chromosomes from the homologous pair are present.

Meiosis
Takes place in reproductive organs _____ are produced.
Each division produces _____ cells.
There are _____ the number of chromosomes.
_____ chromosome from each homologous pair is present.

Monohybrid inheritance

see science at work
■ **Genetics and reproduction**
pp 14–17, 24 Variation and inheritance

We have seen how our genes have been inherited from our mother and father. Many of our characteristics are controlled by combinations of several genes, and their inheritance is very complicated.

Other characteristics are controlled by single genes.

Remember these words:
- ☐ **Alleles** are the alternative forms of a gene.
- ☐ The **phenotype** is how the characteristic looks.
- ☐ The **genotype** is the genetic make-up for the characteristic.
- ☐ If both alleles are the same the individual is **homozygous** for the characteristic.
- ☐ If the alleles are different the individual is **heterozygous** for the characteristic.
- ☐ A **dominant** allele will show in the phenotype of a person homozygous or heterozygous for the characteristic.
- ☐ A **recessive** allele will only show if the person is homozygous for the allele.

One characteristic that is controlled by a single gene is the ability to tongue roll. There are two possible phenotypes and three genotypes.

Phenotype	Genotype
Tongue roller	RR
Tongue roller	Rr
Non-roller	rr

Genetic crosses can be worked out and used to predict the probability of an individual showing particular characteristics.

The crosses must always be written out clearly and carefully.

Q1 Barry can roll his tongue, but knows he must be heterozygous for the gene because his father cannot roll his tongue, Barry marries Susan who cannot roll her tongue. Use genetic crosses to work out the probability of their children being able to roll their tongues.

Jenny, who is a homozygous tongue roller, marries John who cannot roll his tongue. All their children can roll their tongues. Here is the explanation.

Parents' phenotype	Tongue roller	Non-roller
Parents' genotype	RR	rr
Gametes	R R	r r
Offspring's genotype	Rr Rr	Rr Rr
Offspring's phenotype	All tongue rollers	

Ann, one of John and Jenny's children, marries Alan. Alan can roll his tongue but his father could not. They decide to work out the chances of their children being able to roll their tongues.

This shows a different way to set out the genetic cross.

Parents' phenotype	Tongue roller	Tongue roller
Parents' genotype	Rr	Rr
Gametes	R r	R r

	R	r
R	RR	Rr
r	rR	rr

Offspring's genotype	1RR	2Rr	1rr
Offspring's phenotype	3 rollers		1 non-roller

The offspring are usually referred to as the first generation (F1). If in animals (other than humans) or plants the F1 generation is allowed to mate randomly, the next generation would be the F2 generation.

Many characteristics follow this pattern and this method can be used to predict the inheritance of any characteristic controlled by a single gene with a dominant and recessive allele. The offspring from two heterozygous parents will always show the dominant : recessive characteristic in the ratio of 3 : 1.

In mice, black fur is dominant to brown fur.

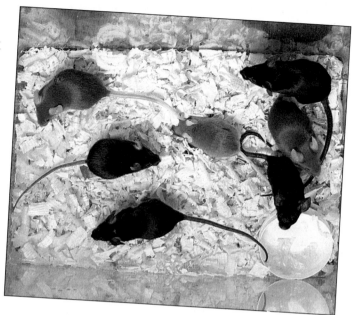

Parents' phenotype	Black	Brown
Parents' genotype	BB	bb
Gametes	(B) (B)	(b) (b)
F1 (allowed to mate randomly)	Bb Bb	Bb Bb
F1 gametes	(B) (b)	(B) (b)
F2 genotype	BB Bb	Bb bb
F2 phenotype	Black	Brown

Black coat colour in labradors is dominant to yellow.

Q2 The black labrador in the photo is known to be homozygous for coat colour. If the two labradors are mated, what colour will the puppies be? Show how you worked this out.

Q3 Two black labradors are mated and have eight puppies. Five are black and three are yellow. What are the genotypes of parents?

Q4 A breeder has a black mouse. She wants to know if it is homozygous or heterozygous for coat colour. How can she find out?

Chromosomes, made of DNA, are found in the nucleus of a cell. They are normally invisible because they are so long and thin. Chromosomes are seen when they condense (shorten and thicken) before cell division occurs. A typical mammalian cell contains about 1·8 metres of DNA.

DNA contains genetic information for controlling all cell activities. It has the code for making all the proteins needed. Proteins, like enzymes and hormones, control chemical activities. Other proteins are important in building structures. Each chromosome consists of units called genes. Genes control the characteristics of an organism like hair colour, eye colour, and blood group. Each gene seems to control the production of a specific protein.

The chemical structure of DNA

DNA consists of two long strands which are joined together, and twisted into a spring-like shape. Each strand is made of basic units called nucleotides. Each nucleotide consists of three molecules: sugar, a phosphate and a chemical base joined together. There are four different bases. They fit together as pairs. Each base has its own special shape and can only fit with one specific partner.

Making more DNA

Special enzymes help DNA to unwind and to separate into two strands. The chemical bonds holding the base partners together are broken. The bases are then exposed and are available to form new bonds with the many free nucleotides in the nucleus. This means that each separated strand of original DNA builds up a new strand joined to itself. The relationship between the bases is highly specific. The final result is two strands of DNA which are identical to each other, and to the original piece of DNA. This process is important when new chromosomes have to be made before cell division; either mitosis or meiosis, occurs.

Q1 What is DNA?

Q2 What do genes control?

Q3 What is a nucleotide?

Q4 What happens when DNA unwinds?

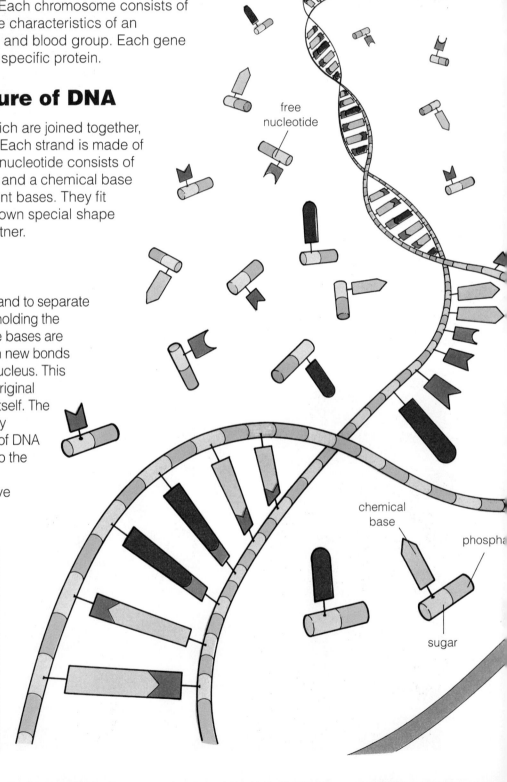

DNA

free nucleotide

chemical base

phospha[te]

sugar

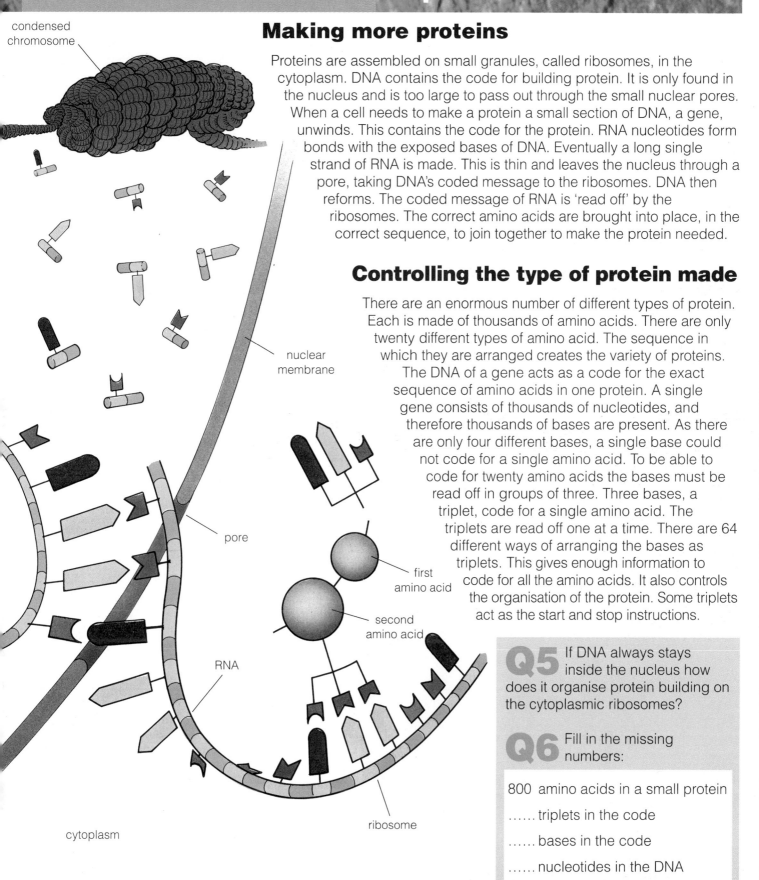

condensed chromosome

nuclear membrane

pore

first amino acid

second amino acid

RNA

ribosome

cytoplasm

Making more proteins

Proteins are assembled on small granules, called ribosomes, in the cytoplasm. DNA contains the code for building protein. It is only found in the nucleus and is too large to pass out through the small nuclear pores. When a cell needs to make a protein a small section of DNA, a gene, unwinds. This contains the code for the protein. RNA nucleotides form bonds with the exposed bases of DNA. Eventually a long single strand of RNA is made. This is thin and leaves the nucleus through a pore, taking DNA's coded message to the ribosomes. DNA then reforms. The coded message of RNA is 'read off' by the ribosomes. The correct amino acids are brought into place, in the correct sequence, to join together to make the protein needed.

Controlling the type of protein made

There are an enormous number of different types of protein. Each is made of thousands of amino acids. There are only twenty different types of amino acid. The sequence in which they are arranged creates the variety of proteins. The DNA of a gene acts as a code for the exact sequence of amino acids in one protein. A single gene consists of thousands of nucleotides, and therefore thousands of bases are present. As there are only four different bases, a single base could not code for a single amino acid. To be able to code for twenty amino acids the bases must be read off in groups of three. Three bases, a triplet, code for a single amino acid. The triplets are read off one at a time. There are 64 different ways of arranging the bases as triplets. This gives enough information to code for all the amino acids. It also controls the organisation of the protein. Some triplets act as the start and stop instructions.

Q5 If DNA always stays inside the nucleus how does it organise protein building on the cytoplasmic ribosomes?

Q6 Fill in the missing numbers:

800 amino acids in a small protein

...... triplets in the code

...... bases in the code

...... nucleotides in the DNA

see science at work
■ **Genetics and reproduction**
pp 31–32 Artificial selection

Changing living things

Selective breeding

Six thousand year old cave paintings, pictures on stone tablets, and ancient writings record details of plant and animal breeding. Early humans domesticated dangerous animals for their own safety on farms. Working dogs were produced from dangerous pack animals, like wolves and hyenas.

Selective breeding is still used today. It involves using individuals with the best characteristics to produce offspring. The best offspring are selected to produce the following generation. Repeating the process many times helps farmers to get the best tasting produce and the highest yields. For example, cows have been successfully bred to produce the most milk (Friesians), the highest butterfat (Jerseys), and the most meat (Herefords). This has taken centuries.

Breeding plants or animals was not easy. Plant breeders had difficulties controlling pollination. They had to wait years for some plants to produce seeds, and some plants failed to produce fruits. In captivity animals often refuse to mate with the partner selected for them. Artificial insemination now overcomes this problem and is successfully used for breeding cattle.

Intensive breeding for special characteristics also caused problems in the past. Breeding grain crops for higher yields produced larger ears, but the stems were too weak to support them. Trying to combine characteristics like high yield with disease resistance and early ripening was disappointing. Unsuitable combinations of characteristics were common. Many plants were diseased, had low yields and ripened late. Animal breeders also had problems. Pigs bred for long backs, for bacon, had weak legs and backs.

Cloning

This is a new method of reproducing identical copies of a gene, cell or simple organism like a bacterium.

Cloning plant cells is successful and cost effective. Small pieces of tissue or single cells are removed from a 'parent' plant. They are then kept in ideal, sterile conditions with essential nutrients and hormones provided. Complete plants soon grow. All are disease-free and genetically identical. Fast production of numerous crop plants with genes for high yields and resistance to disease, herbicides and pesticides is possible.

Animal cells are more difficult to clone. Mammal cells especially are unstable and die quickly. Single cells and simple tissues cannot produce complete organisms, but knowledge about cell function and genetics has improved. Cloning young skin cells has produced successful grafts for treating burns and ulcers. Studies of viruses in cloned animal cells have resulted in successful vaccine production. Soon, cells to produce hormones for blood clotting factors may be cloned and transplanted into people with deficient cells. New methods of drug delivery and cures for baldness may be possible.

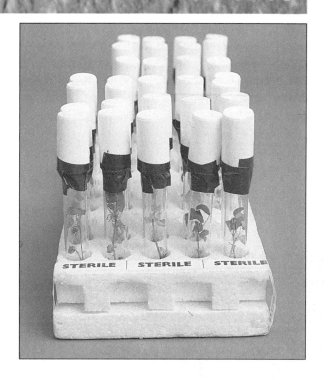

Genetic engineering

A gene, or genes, can be removed from one organism and transferred to another, of the same or different species. Genes can be modified during removal. A new strain of organism, genetically different from the original is created.

Large-scale production of insulin is possible using bacteria with an added human gene. This has saved the lives of thousands of diabetics. Blood transfusions are safe in the UK, but some countries have to use substitute disease-free blood, produced by bacteria, for safety.

Here are some genetically engineered bacteria successes:
    substances to regulate blood calcium
    substances to control blood pressure
    substances to inhibit food poisoning microbes
    interferon to fight viral infections
    red blood cells
    haemoglobin
    anti-coagulants
    growth hormones

Cystic fibrosis can now be detected. This inherited disease is caused by a recessive gene. A single cell is removed from an eight-cell human embryo cultured in laboratory conditions. The DNA of the cell is tested. If the cell is disease-free the embryo is transplanted into the mother to develop into a normal baby. Research continues into genetically caused disease and disease resistance. Hopefully defective genes can be replaced with healthy ones.

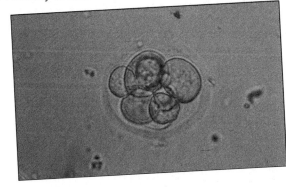

Q1 How is selective breeding carried out?

Q2 What does cloning mean?

Q3 What is meant by genetic engineering?

Q4 Labradors are used as guide dogs for the blind. What characteristics do you think a breeder would select?

Q5 Why is it difficult to clone mammal cells?

Q6 How may genetic engineering help our future health?

Has it always been the same?

The Earth's environment has changed many times. Mountains and continents have appeared and disappeared. Sea levels have changed as ice and desert conditions have alternated. Changes continue today. Polar ice caps slowly change size. Holes in the ozone layer suddenly appear. Natural events, like volcanic activity and earthquakes, cause as much change as human activities like pollution and the removal of tropical rainforests. Organisms have to adapt to the changes to survive.

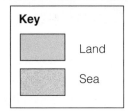

Key

	Land
	Sea

Devonian period, about 360 million years ago.

38°C

43°C

−20°C edge of ice sheet

ice-age coast line

0°C

Ice age, about 20,000 years ago.

The effects of the environment

Charles Darwin wrote about the effect of the environment on living things in 'The Origin of Species' in 1859. He studied finches in the Galapagos Islands. Their seed eating ancestors had arrived thousands of years earlier. Although the present birds looked similar their beaks differed. He thought this was the result of the early competition for food. When seeds became scarce, any bird slightly adapted to eat different food would be better fitted to survive and breed. Specialised beaks for eating leaves, insects, grubs, buds and fruits were evidence of the adaptations that had aided survival.

The peppered moth can be pale or dark. Recent studies show how environmental change affected its survival. When tree trunks were blackened by industrial smoke, predators easily found the pale moths. The well camouflaged dark moths were not eaten. They survived, bred and increased in numbers until the Clean Air Act. Less smoke meant that tree trunks became paler. The dark moths were then more easily seen and eaten. The numbers of surviving pale moths increased.

Environmental change does not directly alter organisms but it does alter their chances of survival. Any change in an organism results from genetic change.

Q1 What has caused the Earth's environment to change?

Q2 What must organisms do to survive environmental change?

Sources of genetic variation

Reshuffling genetic material

In early meiosis crossing over and gene exchange occurs between the chromosome pairs. For the 23 pairs of human chromosomes 50 exchanges are likely. The chromosome pairs are separated and arranged randomly in daughter cells. There are new combinations of genetic material. Gametes are not genetically identical. No new genes are made. The variation is caused by new combinations of existing genes.

What are mutations?

Mendel's work, rediscovered in 1901, showed how genes function. Chromosomes and DNA are usually stable but mutations, sudden changes, can occur and be inherited. Mutations are random, rare events occurring about once in a million cell divisions. Most mutations are caused by changes in a single gene. Loss or addition of bases changes the DNA sequence so a different protein is made. Sometimes part of a chromosome is lost or added on in the wrong place. Down's Syndrome is caused by an extra chromosome.

What are the effects of mutations?

Mutations are important because they alter the normal development of an individual. Sometimes mutations are lethal. Most are harmful. Very few are advantageous. Fortunately most mutations do not affect the population. A mutant gene is unlikely to be present in every gamete, so it may not pass on to the next generation. Many mutant genes are recessive. If inherited they have little effect because they are suppressed by the dominant gene. Harmful or lethal genes are selected against by the environment. Their spread through the population is limited. The rare beneficial mutations spread quickly.

What causes mutations?

Natural sources of mutation include radiation from uranium in the Earth's crust, and cosmic rays (high energy radiation from outer space). Very high temperatures and chemicals like mustard gas and defoliants are other sources. High energy radiation caused by beta, gamma and X-rays are more important. Nuclear weapon testing, atomic bombs, the Chernobyl disaster and small leaks from nuclear power stations, like Sellafield, have released radiation. The long term effects are uncertain and a cause for concern.

Q3 How does reshuffling of genetic material occur?

Q4 An individual inherited chromosomes A, B and C from its mother and chromosomes a, b and c from its father. What combinations of chromosomes are possible in its gametes?

Q5 What is a mutation and why is it important?

Q6 Why do mutations have little effect on the population?

What is evolution?

The relationship between variation, natural selection and reproductive success.

Variation

Any offspring from the same parents show variations. Some are genetic and can be inherited. Some may aid survival. To be valuable, survival time must allow reproduction and ensure a future generation.

Selection

Variations are selected for or against by the environment. Selection is caused by climate, vegetation, the need for food, the need to reproduce, and the effects of predation and competition. Individuals best fitted to survive leave the largest number of offspring. Their advantageous genes are passed on. Beneficial characteristics are selected for and become increasingly common in future generations. Individuals not adapted to the environment are selected against and become rare. They may die without breeding. Their genes are not passed on. 'Natural selection' occurs over millions of years. It limits population size to numbers that the environment can support.

Q1 What causes selection?

Q2 What happens to individuals, and their genes, which are best fitted to an environment?

Q3 What happens to individuals, and their genes, which are not adapted to an environment?

Q4 Why do mammals have more reproductive success than fish?

Reproductive success

Any pair of organisms could potentially produce numerous offspring. This does not occur. Population sizes seem stable. Something limits the growth rate.

Producing large numbers of gametes or offspring does not ensure reproductive success. Any individual produces more gametes than are used. Fish release millions of gametes. External fertilisation is wasteful. Few eggs are fertilised. Very few birds survive from a large brood. They weigh less than those from smaller broods. Parents have more problems providing enough food.

Mammals are more successful. Fewer gametes are needed for internal fertilisation. Few young are produced, often only one. A long period of parental care makes survival to adulthood more likely.

Successful reproduction alone does not guarantee evolutionary success. For all species there is a struggle for existence. Few of the offspring produced become adults. Only those best fitted to survive the environment will grow up and reproduce. These individuals will be of evolutionary importance.

The significance of these relationships to evolution

Evolution results from the accumulation of small changes in a population of related organisms. Fossils and remains of organisms preserved in bogs and ice provide evidence for evolution. All existing species seem to have descended from earlier forms of life. Many generations of modification may produce a new species. Millions of years later the original ancestors may be extinct. Carbon dating has helped to show the timescale.

A single species can be clearly defined. Individuals have the same evolutionary history and stages of development. The members are easily recognised by their similar appearance and have the same ecological needs. The individuals can only breed with each other, not with other organisms. This keeps the species distinct. There is no 'normal' version of an individual. Individuals can be distinguished from each other by small differences, or variations.

Variation can be caused by environmental effects. Evolution

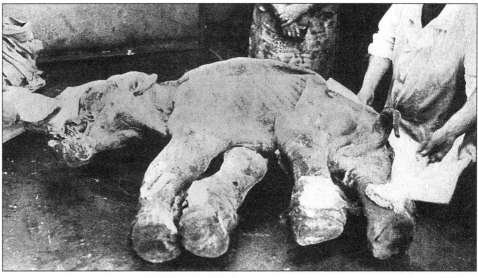

10,000 year old baby mammoth. Found in an excavation in Siberia.

only progresses by selection of genetic variations. It can occur faster if there is a great range of variation. The environment selects for advantageous genes for the next generation. Mutations provide the genetic changes on which selection acts. Favourable mutants survive and reproduce. Unfavourable mutants may disappear, recur many times or remain rare. They may be favoured and become more

common if conditions change or the species migrates to a new environment. New species develop and some become extinct as evolution proceeds.

Millions of species live on Earth today. Not all have been discovered and named. Human activity may cause hundreds to become extinct in our lifetime. Habitat destruction as a result of pollution or land use has disastrous effects. Environmental management of game parks and conservation areas may preserve habitats. Sheltered areas at the side of motorways, railways, and airports form new, safe habitats. In new environments some variations will be advantageous. Selection may allow the development of new species.

Q5 What causes evolution?

Q6 How could human activity alter the course of evolution?

Damaging the atmosphere

see science at work

■ **Pollution**

p 1 What is pollution?
p 25 Smokeless zone
p 31 Lead pollution and the motor car
p 32 Controlling lead pollution

For centuries we have been using the Earth's atmosphere as a giant dustbin. We have been pouring waste gases into the air without a thought for the damage that we may be causing. Since the middle of the 19th century scientists have known that the atmosphere was being altered by pollution.

To begin to understand the issues affecting today's atmosphere we need to look at a little history.

Before the 18th century most people lived and worked on the land or in small towns. Each town or village obtained food and fuel from close by. By 1770 the first small factories had been built in the UK. These were mainly textile mills using Arkwright's newly invented 'Spinning Jenny'. People moved from the countryside into the towns to work in these mills. The populations in the towns grew rapidly. Roads, canals and eventually railways were built to transport the manufactured goods.

The first factories were water-powered and small. They caused relatively little environmental pollution. However bigger factories needed more power to work the machines. Factory owners installed steam engines to drive the machines. The burning of coal to heat the steam engines led to heavy smoke pollution by the middle of the 19th century. Bigger factories meant that more waste was produced and even more people moved to the towns to work in them.

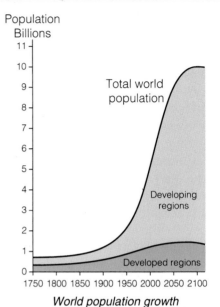

World population growth

Towns grew. People created rubbish, burned more coal for heating and cooking, and sewage disposal became a serious health problem. Lighting in houses used town gas which was made from burning coal. More and more coal was mined, and methane was released from the rotting rubbish and sewage.

The rise in the atmospheric concentration of CO_2 since 1958 as measured at Mauna Loa, Hawaii

Q1 Explain why the amount of carbon dioxide in the atmosphere has increased since the industrial revolution.

Q2 Look carefully at the population graphs and describe the pattern of population growth over that period of time. What evidence is there for a link between population size and the increasing amounts of CO_2 in the atmosphere?

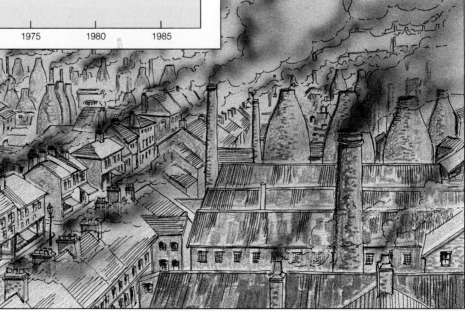

Cars – the great polluters!

In 1885 Karl Benz invented the first internal combustion engine. It had three wheels and a maximum speed of 25 km/h. The engine was powered by gas made from coal. Ten years later Benz and Daimler had invented an engine which would run on petrol. This engine was much more efficient and allowed faster speeds to be reached.

Petrol is a complex hydrocarbon, made from the fractional distillation of crude oil. When it is burned the chemical energy locked up in the fuel is converted into kinetic energy to make the vehicle move. During combustion the engine also produces waste exhaust gases.

During the 20th century people have come to rely heavily on motor vehicles as a form of transport. Pollution from vehicle exhausts is so great in some cities e.g. Tokyo that walking on the street is a health hazard.

**Carbon dioxide
Acid gases
Sulphur dioxide
Nitrogen(I) oxide**

**Poisonous fumes
Carbon monoxide
lead fumes
and *water vapour***

Alternative fuels to drive engines are now being used in some parts of the world.

Methane or biogas is used in China to power tractors. Alcohol, from fermented sugar cane is used to supplement petrol in Brazil. These fuels give off carbon dioxide and carbon monoxide in the same way as petrol, but do not produce harmful acid gases.

Fossil fuels factfile

Mostly formed 300 million years ago.

We are using them faster than they are being formed, so they are described as non-renewable energy sources.

It has been estimated that gas and crude oil reserves will run out early in the 21st century.

Coal reserves may last until the end of the 21st century.

Seven ways to reduce vehicle pollution

1 Fit catalytic converters to reduce exhaust gas emissions.
2 Use lead-free petrol.
3 Limit speed to reduce fuel consumption.
4 Switch from using petrol to diesel. It is more energy-efficient (more km/l).
5 Increase fuel tax, or make a carbon tax to encourage less fossil fuel usage.
6 Improve the performance of internal combustion engines.
7 Use a bicycle or public transport, or share a car.

Q3 Fossil fuels are described as non-renewable fuels; bio-gas and alcohol are described as renewable fuels. Explain the difference between the term renewable and non-renewable using these as examples.

Q4 Many people are now concerned about atmospheric pollution and are taking steps to reduce the amounts they contribute to the problem. Imagine that you were Minister for the Environment. Outline the measures you would take to reduce air pollution in the UK.

The changing atmosphere

see science at work

■ **Pollution**
p 24 Global warming and the greenhouse effect

All life on this planet depends on the atmosphere. Plants use **carbon dioxide** to produce food by photosynthesis. Plants and animals need **oxygen** for respiration. Nitrogen fixing bacteria can turn **nitrogen** into nitrates. Plants use nitrates to make amino acids to build proteins. All these three **gases** are found in the Earth's atmosphere.

The atmosphere acts as a blanket trapping heat energy around the Earth. It is estimated that without the atmosphere the Earth would be about 30°C colder. The warmth of the Earth enables life's enzyme-controlled processes to work at their optimum rates. The atmosphere also protects us from harmful ultra-violet waves from the Sun. Long-term exposure to these can cause cancer of the skin.

light energy

carbon dioxide

oxygen

Sugars made by plants provide food for the whole food web of life on Earth

Photosynthesis

$$6H_2O + 6CO_2 + light\ energy \xrightarrow{chlorophyll} C_6H_{12}O_6 + 6O_2$$

water   carbon dioxide   light energy   glucose oxygen

Gases in the atmosphere

Gas	Amount	
Nitrogen	78%	Stable
Oxygen	21%	Stable
Argon	0.94%	Stable
Carbon dioxide	0.04%	Increasing
Neon, Krypton, Xenon	small traces	Stable
Helium, Hydrogen	small traces	Stable
Methane	small traces	Increasing
Ozone (O_3)	small traces	Decreasing
Nitrogen (I) oxide	small traces	Increasing
Sulphur dioxide	small traces	Increasing
CFCs	small traces	Increasing
Water vapour	varying amounts	

The Earth's atmosphere has built up over 2000 million years and the recycling of carbon dioxide and oxygen has reached a delicate balance. However the increase in the burning of fossil fuels and amount of agriculture and industry has altered this balance.

160 km

UPPER ATMOSPHERE

130 km

Meteor burn up (often call shooting stars)

80 km

Temperatu uniform

STRATOSPHERE

Ozone abs ultra-violet from the s

16 km

Jet plane

TROPOSPHERE

Weathe

8 km

Temperat decreases height

←13000km→
EARTH

The structure of the atmosphere

Increasing carbon dioxide

Since the Industrial Revolution, the combustion of fossil fuels in ever-increasing amounts has increased the amount of carbon dioxide in the air around us by 30%. Every year 20 000 million tonnes of carbon dioxide are added to the atmosphere. At this rate we will double the amount of CO_2 in the air by the end of the century. A certain amount of carbon dioxide is soaked up by the oceans, but the rest remains in the air. This problem is being added to as we clear more forest land for growing food and to make profit from the timber. This is destroying vast amounts of plant life, especially trees, that use up a lot of CO_2. So human activity has altered the balance of gases in the atmosphere.

Carbon dioxide is a greenhouse gas.

Increasing methane

Methane is released when rotting vegetable material is broken down anaerobically (without oxygen) by microbes. The process works best in warm damp places. Bogs and swamps can release small amounts of methane gas. However, growing human populations have made increasing amounts of refuse and sewage, both of which release methane as they rot down. Increasing amounts of methane are being given off from rice fields and from cattle.

Methane is a greenhouse gas.

Surface ozone

Ozone is a form of oxygen. It has three atoms of oxygen instead of the more usual two. Ozone is formed at ground level when sunlight hits the waste gases from factories and vehicles. It **adds to the greenhouse effect**.

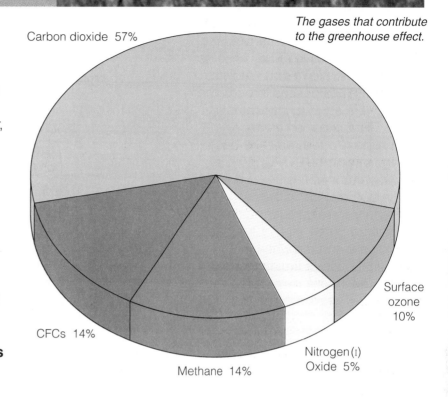

The gases that contribute to the greenhouse effect.

Carbon dioxide 57%

CFCs 14%

Methane 14%

Nitrogen (I) Oxide 5%

Surface ozone 10%

Increasing CFCs

CFCs (chlorofluorocarbons) are gases made in factories, and are used to cool down fridges, to make plastic foam packaging and aerosols. Until this century they were unknown in the atmosphere. They are known to break down the ozone layer of the upper atmosphere. This layer absorbs a lot of the Sun's harmful ultra-violet rays. Scientists have found holes in the ozone layer above the polar regions; the layer above Australia has become very thin and there is evidence that the ozone above Europe is getting less.

The amount of CFCs in the atmosphere are growing by about 4% a year.

As well as damaging the ozone layer, **CFCs are greenhouse gases.**

Increasing sulphur dioxide and nitrogen (I) oxide

Fossil fuels are the remains of prehistoric plants and animals that lived about 300 million years ago. The remains have been broken down by the action of microbes into a series of hydrocarbons contaminated with sulphur and nitrogen molecules from their proteins. When we burn these fossil fuels to release energy, we release sulphur and nitrogen compounds as well. These two gases are thought to be responsible for acid rain. This causes extensive damage to both plant and animal life in the areas affected by it.

Nitrogen (I) oxide in the air is also increasing, by 0.3% each year, because of the ploughing of land and the increasing use of nitrogen fertilisers.

Nitrogen (I) oxide is a greenhouse gas.

Q1 List four ways in which the atmosphere is important to life on Earth.

Q2 Many of Britain's power stations burn fossil fuels. Name two acid gases that these power stations may release into the air.

Q3 What problem do these gases cause in the environment?

Q4 How can we reduce the amounts of CFCs we release into the air?

Q5 How is the ozone layer in the upper atmosphere useful?

Global warming

see science at work

■ **Earth science and atmosphere**
p 40 People and climate

■ **Pollution** p 24 Global warming and the greenhouse effect

All the Earth's energy comes from the Sun, apart from a little released from the radioactive decay of some minerals. Shortwave solar radiation that reaches us passes through the atmosphere and warms up the Earth. The Earth then emits longwave infra-red radiation back into the atmosphere. Much of this longwave radiation is soaked up by the carbon dioxide in the atmosphere. A little escapes back into space. Some is reflected back down to the surface when it reaches the top of the atmosphere. Other greenhouse gases also trap the longwave radiation on the Earth's surface.

The overall effect of trapping increasing amounts of energy in the atmosphere is that the global temperatures are slowly rising.

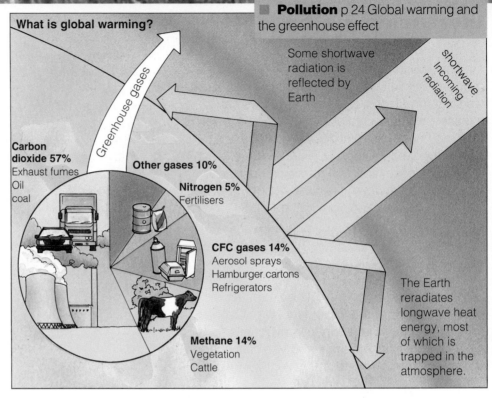

What is global warming?

Greenhouse gases

Some shortwave radiation is reflected by Earth

Shortwave Incoming radiation

Carbon dioxide 57%
Exhaust fumes
Oil
coal

Other gases 10%

Nitrogen 5%
Fertilisers

CFC gases 14%
Aerosol sprays
Hamburger cartons
Refrigerators

Methane 14%
Vegetation
Cattle

The Earth reradiates longwave heat energy, most of which is trapped in the atmosphere.

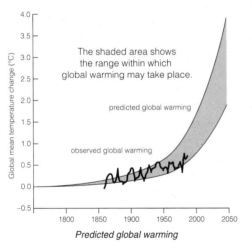

The shaded area shows the range within which global warming may take place.

predicted global warming

observed global warming

Predicted global warming

Changes in the world's global climate are not new phenomena. There have been several ice ages and tropical ages in the past. The difference this time is that the process appears to be caused by mankind and is out of control. If we take severe steps now to control the emission of greenhouse gases it may take a long time for the global climate to stabilise.

To reduce pollution will require international cooperation. Steps towards this have been taken with the Montreal Protocol of 1989. One of its achievements was to reach limited agreement on reducing the use of CFCs. There have also been two world climate conferences and scientists have now presented their evidence to politicians to decide on international action. However, progress is slow, as so many different countries are involved in trying to reach an agreement about the best course of action to limit the release of excess greenhouse gases.

Each country has its own arguments as to why it cannot take action now.

Q1 Global warming is an international problem. It affects all the world. Why might different countries not wish to take action to reduce the release of greenhouse gases and slow down the problem now? What sorts of arguments could they give against them taking action?

Discuss your ideas with others in your class and then write them down.

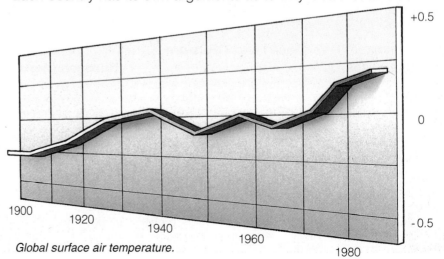

Global surface air temperature.

Why worry

■ **Ecosystems**
The CFC man

You may actually like the idea of living in a warmer world; you may think that there is not a lot that you personally can do about global warming; so why worry?

A rise in temperature of 1°C in a century does not sound a lot. It is less than the temperature difference between day and night or between the seasons. Yet it has caused a drop in rainfall in the subtropical regions of the world, which in turn has contributed to the famines in Northern African countries and the spread of the African deserts.

Changes in rainfall patterns have caused flooding in parts of the world. In Bangladesh there have been floods over a number of years, killing people and animals, destroying towns and villages and ruining farming; all this in an area where the people are already very poor. Recently there has also been bad flooding in Europe, hitting areas such as Southern France and the south of England.

Extra warmth in the summers may bring drought. This will affect the way that plants grow. Crops may fail to grow and there will be an ever-increasing chance of famine. Farmers will have to start growing different varieties or different types of crops.

Extra warmth in the summer will also improve the conditions for insect pests and plant diseases. Different pests may thrive, and new techniques will have to be developed to deal with them. All of this will cause extra expense to farmers.

Temperature changes will affect the global patterns of winds. We have already experienced this in Britain with the Great Storm of 1987 when there was unexpected and extensive damage to property and to trees.

There has also been an increasing number of violent hurricanes all around the world over the last decade.

Increasing global temperatures will gradually melt the Polar ice caps and release the water locked up in the ice. This will lead to a rise in the level of the sea. Scientists have predicted that present sea levels will rise by 30–60 cm by the middle of the next century. In Britain cities like London, Hull, Liverpool and Southampton could be flooded, even with the building of further expensive flood barrier schemes. On a worldwide level whole countries could be threatened: much of Southern France, most of Florida, and the entire countries of Holland and Bangladesh.

Activities

1 Using an atlas and a blank copy of a world map, plot the areas which are likely to become flooded if the sea rises by a few metres.

2 Make a list of the major coastal cities of the world that could be affected by the rise in sea level.

Microbes and sewage

see science at work

■ **Body maintenance** p 1–5
Reacting to changes
Extension sheet 1

■ **Pollution**
p 3 Biodegradable waste
p 4–5 Dealing with waste

Most of us never give a second thought for the waste we flush down the toilet. Everyday millions of litres arrive at Britain's sewage treatment plants. It is taken there by a vast underground network of sewers, some large enough to drive a train through!

Sewage works range from simple septic tanks for small villages, to giant works that treat the effluent from our large cities.

The role of the sewage works is to cleanse the waste material that we pour into the drains and sewers and make it 'safe' to put back into the environment. In doing so they produce sludge that can be used as a fertiliser and may collect enough methane to heat the treatment plant and generate the electricity that it needs.

Microbes are a vital ingredient in the whole process of making sewage 'safe'.

Q1 What does the word aerobic mean?

Q2 Why does warming the sewage to 30°C speed up the decay process?

Q3 How is sewage treatment paid for?

Q4 An efficient sewage works is able to recycle many of its products. How does this keep down the costs of processing?

Q5 What environmental problems may arise as a result of dumping processed sludge at sea?

1 Screening
As the effluent enters the sewage works it is passed through a series of strainers to take out the larger solids such as paper and plastics and cloth. If this was not done these materials would clog up the machinery further along the process.

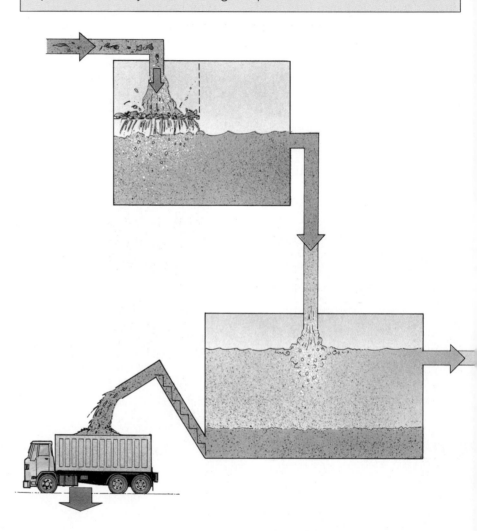

2 Settlement
In this stage the speed of flow of the sewage is reduced. This allows the heavy particles of sand and grit, suspended in the sewage, to settle to the bottom. The liquid that is left is mainly water mixed with faecal remains, detergents and other dissolved pollutants.

4 Water purification

The liquid left after biological treatment may look clean, but it often still contains many environmental pollutants. These may be high levels of nitrates, which will affect aquatic plant growth, or detergents which can poison water animals or a variety of other harmful dissolved substances. The liquid needs further processing to remove these before it can be discharged into the environment. Scientists at sewage works are needed to carefully monitor the effluent (outflow) water quality.

Not all Britain's sewage disposal is of the highest standard. Many coastal towns still discharge raw untreated sewage into the sea. They rely on the action of the tides and the waves to break the sewage down. However, this is not always effective. Consequently, many of our beaches are contaminated with raw sewage and harmful, pathogenic, bacteria. The E.E.C. have set standards for reducing the bacterial contamination of beaches. The British water authorities have now started a programme of investment to try to reach these standards. The problem is not only a British one, but can be found in many coastal areas where there are large numbers of people. Many Mediterranean beaches also have very high levels of bacterial contamination.

Q6 Find out what the Blue Flag Scheme is.

Q7 Find out which British seaside towns have 'clean' beaches and which don't.

Q8 Why is the bacterial contamination of beaches a serious health hazard, and who is likely to be at greatest risk?

Q9 Why is it not reasonable to expect water authorities to immediately stop pumping raw sewage into the sea?

Q10 What effect will raw sewage have on marine life, particularly plants?

3 Activated sludge treatment

The activated sludge treatment uses microbes to decay sewage. Sewage is mixed vigorously with air and then kept at 30°C. This encourages aerobic microbes to rapidly decay the organic remains in the sewage. As this happens methane gas is released which can be used as a fuel to heat the sludge tanks, and to make electricity to power the machines being used to aerate the sewage. The sludge left at the end is either processed to be sold to agriculture or is dumped at sea.

Natural cycles

There has been a lot of publicity over recent years about recycling. Maybe in your house you save newspapers and glass bottles and take them to paper or bottle banks. Some of you will also save steel and aluminium cans and even plastic bottles. We have discovered that it saves energy and natural resources if we use materials again and again.

In some parts of the country all the rubbish has to be sorted into different bins and it is all recycled or burned to generate electricity or provide heating.

These ideas are not new. Nature has been recycling its energy and materials for as long as there has been life on this planet. The most important cycles are probably the carbon, nitrogen, oxygen and water cycles. Many other elements are also constantly being recycled in smaller amounts.

This chart shows the main elements found in living organisms. The units are measured in kilograms per hectare of land surface. Living organisms constantly recycle all these elements and others in even smaller amounts.

Carbon cycle

All living things on the Earth contain carbon. We simply borrow carbon from the planet as we grow and develop. We constantly exchange it with our surroundings while we are alive. When we die our carbon all goes back to the environment.

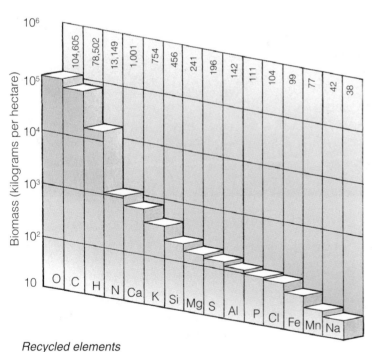

Recycled elements

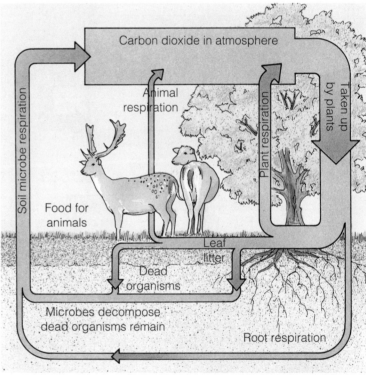

Q1 What can you recycle at home or at school?

Q2 Why is it wise for us to recycle as much material as possible?

Q3 Design a poster to encourage young people to save and recycle things like paper, glass, plastic bottles and aluminium cans. Include information about where you can take things to be recycled locally.

Q4 Make a key to identify the elements shown in the bar chart.

Nitrogen cycle

▶ Nitrogen is important in the formation of amino acids which build up into proteins. The nitrogen cycle is more complex than the carbon cycle. Only a few types of bacteria can directly use nitrogen from the atmosphere. This is then converted into nitrates that can be taken up by plants. Each step of the cycle depends on different microbes. When organisms die their remains are then decayed into a re-usable form.

The reactions in this cycle depend upon the action of microbes in the soil.

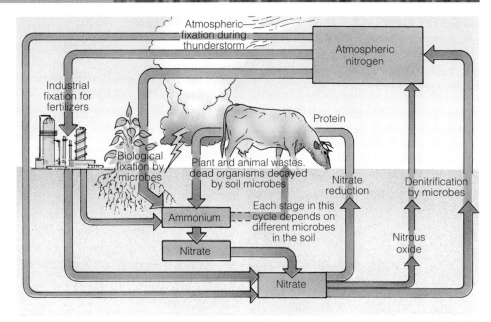

Oxygen cycle

▶ Oxygen is needed by most living organisms to release energy inside cells. This is called aerobic respiration. During respiration plants and animals use oxygen to break up complex organic food molecules like glucose. Carbon dioxide and water are formed, and energy released from the breaking up of the chemical bonds. The process is exothermic as some heat energy is released. The process is reversed during photosynthesis when plants use light energy to build

Respiration
Glucose + Oxygen ⟶ Energy + Carbon dioxide + Water

Photosynthesis
Carbon dioxide + Water + Light energy ⟶ Glucose + Oxygen

up complex organic molecules. The energy is used to make chemical bonds. Photosynthesis is an endothermic reaction as it needs light energy to take place.

Water cycle

◀ Water is an important component of most living organisms. The cytoplasm of living cells is mainly made of water. All the biochemical reactions that are needed to keep things alive take place in solution in the cytoplasm. Without water most living things will quickly die.

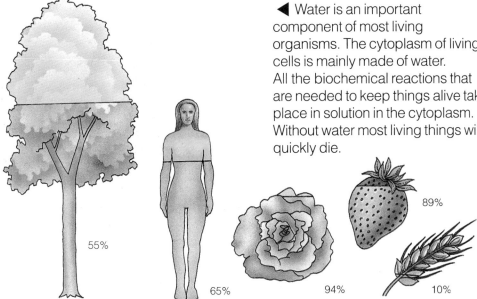

Water content of living things

Q5 Why are minerals and energy recycled in nature?

Q6 Which elements are found in all organic molecules?

Q7 Which element is needed to make amino acids?

Q8 In which two cycles are microbes very important?

Q9 Some organisms are able to respire anaerobically. What does the word anaerobic mean?

Q10 Respiration is an exothermic reaction. What does this mean?

Q11 Why do all living things need water? Explain your answer in detail.

Earth structure 1

Scratching the Earth's surface

The deepest drill holes on Earth are only nine kilometres deep so only a small part, less than 0.2% of its depth, has been directly sampled. The average density of the Earth is 5500 kg/m³. The rocks at the surface have an average density of 2700 kg/m³, so there are much denser materials below the surface. As we can only 'scratch the Earth's surface' we have to rely on indirect evidence to tell us about the sorts of materials and the processes taking place below the surface.

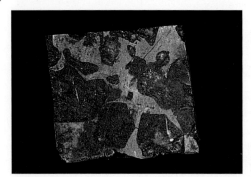

A meteorite sample

Evidence that we can use includes:
● the increase in temperature down mine shafts
● rock samples from the deepest boreholes
● meteorite samples which land on the Earth's surface
● the few rock samples found on the surface which are thought to be from the Earth's **mantle** (The part of the Earth's interior between the crust and the core.)
● the study of the Earth's gravity
● the study of earthquakes as they travel through the Earth
● the study of the Earth's magnetic field.
The last two kinds of evidence have provided the most information.

Exploring the Earth using earthquakes

Earthquakes happen when rocks suddenly fracture and move. The energy makes the ground vibrate and these vibrations travel as earthquakes away from the **focus** where the rocks fracture. The energy moves in three types of wave called P, S and L waves. These can be picked up by detectors called **seismometers**. Each type of wave has different properties that give us information about the materials through which they have passed.

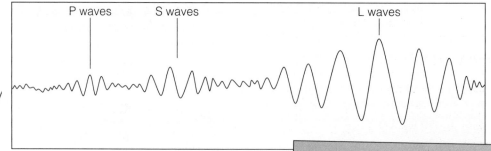

P waves   S waves   L waves

Seismograms record the vibrations picked up by seismometers. They clearly show the three main types of wave.

shake → S wave direction

push → P wave direction

P waves are the fastest and the first to be recorded. They are push and pull waves or primary waves. P waves are longitudinal and are able to travel through the interior of the Earth, through both solids and liquids.

S waves travel more slowly than P waves. They are shake or secondary waves. S waves are transverse and can only move through solids.

L Waves travel most slowly and are the last to be recorded. They are also transverse waves but can only travel near to the Earth's surface. These are the waves that cause most damage when an earthquake occurs.

Q1 What does the increase in temperature in mine shafts tell us?

Q2 What sort of earthquake wave causes the most damage?

Q3 Write down the order in which earthquake waves are received by a seismometer.

Evidence for a liquid core

Earthquake rays (lines at 90 degrees to the waves) are refracted as they pass through the Earth in the same way that light is refracted as it passes from one medium to another. P and S waves from an earthquake are not received all over the Earth and this is used as evidence that part of the Earth's interior is liquid.

P waves are not recorded between 103 and 142 degrees away from the focus of an earthquake. These waves are slowed down on their way through the Earth as they pass through a core of different composition. No S waves are recorded beyond 103 degrees from the focus because S waves cannot travel through liquids. This is taken as evidence that part of the core of the Earth is liquid.

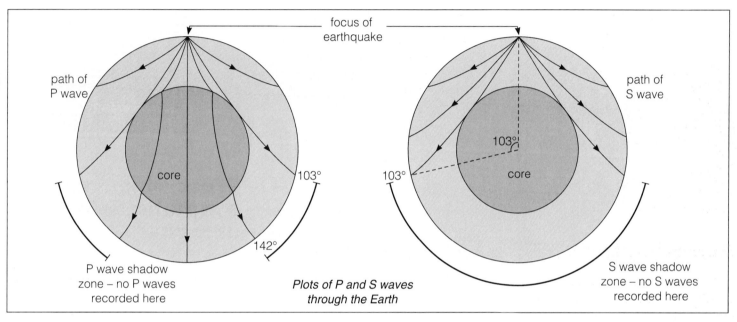

Plots of P and S waves through the Earth

Evidence for a layered structure

The velocities of P and S waves within the Earth change as the waves pass through different layers. On the basis of velocity-depth curves the Earth is divided into four layers: crust, mantle, outer core and inner core.

These equations give some idea of the reasons the velocities of P and S waves are affected by the properties of the materials they pass through. ▶

$$P_v = \sqrt{\frac{K + \frac{4}{3}N}{D}} \qquad S_v = \sqrt{\frac{N}{D}}$$

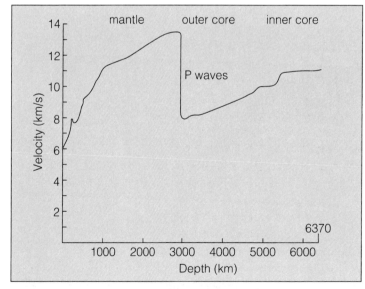

D = density
N = rigidity modulus
  (the resistance to change of shape without change of volume)
K = bulk modulus
  (the resistance to change of volume without change of shape).
  (N is zero for liquids)

Q4 You are watching a seismometer when an earthquake takes place. You see P and L waves but no S wave recorded. Why do two waves reach you but not the other?

Q5 How do we know that there are different distinct layers in the Earth's structure?

Q6 Why is the rigidity modulus (N) zero for liquids?

What is the Earth's magnetic field?

When we use a magnetic compass, the compass needle comes to rest in a position pointing north-south. This is because there is a magnetic field. When we look at the pattern of the Earth's magnetic field it is shaped as if there was a large bar magnet in the centre of the Earth. This magnet seems to be lying at an angle of 11 degrees to the axis of the Earth. The magnetic field is not uniform over the surface of the Earth and changes slightly each day. There is some evidence that the Earth's magnetic field has changed over time.

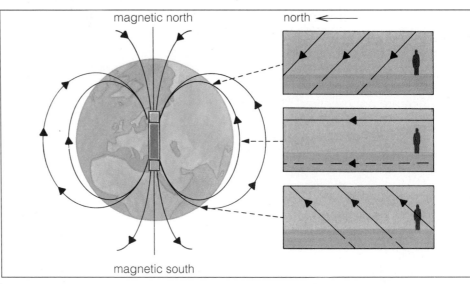

magnetic north

north ←

magnetic south

crystals in an igneous rock

north ←

sea

grains in a sedimentary rock

inner solid core

outer liquid core

mantle

crust

Preserving Earth's magnetic field in rocks

When rocks form they become magnetised in the same direction as the Earth's magnetic field. This happens when lava flows cool and the iron oxide minerals crystallise, 'freezing' the magnetism in. Magnetic mineral grains similarly collect in sediments on the sea floor, lying parallel to the Earth's magnetic field. In these ways igneous and sedimentary rocks may preserve a record of the Earth's magnetic field when they were formed.

Evidence for a liquid core

What does a study of the Earth's magnetic field tell us about the Earth's interior?

One of the most important results of a study of the Earth's magnetic field is that the outer core of the Earth appears to be made of liquid iron. Heat destroys the magnetism in magnets and the core of the Earth is thought to be very hot. Because of this there cannot actually be a permanent bar magnet at the Earth's centre. The most likely cause of the magnetic field is the liquid iron outer core. This liquid is rotating and is an electrical conductor. It has been suggested that it acts as a dynamo which makes its own magnetic field. The original cause of the flow of electric current in the core is not known at present.

Q1 What does the pattern of the Earth's magnetic field look like?

Q2 How is a record of magnetism preserved in rocks?

Q3 If the centre of the Earth is very hot, why cannot the core be a permanent magnet?

Ancient magnetism

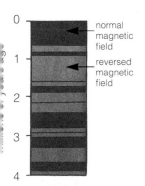

Polarity time scale for the last 4 million years

Studies of ancient magnetism in volcanic rocks have shown that some rocks have been magnetised in a direction opposite to that of the present magnetic field (**reversed polarity**). Others have been magnetised in a direction parallel to the present field (**normal polarity**). This shows that the Earth's magnetic field has changed or reversed its polarity in the past. It appears that there has been a sequence of regular reversals over the past 8.5 million years. One suggestion is that these reversals have been caused by the dynamo in the core reversing the electric current.

Aeromagnetic surveys of the world's ocean ridge systems can pick out **magnetic banding patterns** running parallel to the ocean ridges. These give evidence for sea floor spreading. Symmetrical bands of igneous rock with normal or reversed polarity can be picked out on each side of the ocean ridge. As new igneous rock is formed at the ridge it is magnetised in the direction of the Earth's field at the time. It is then pushed to each side as newer material forces its way along the crack on the ridge axis. By using polarity time scales it has been possible to work out the spreading rates of the ocean ridges. The North Atlantic ridge is spreading at about one centimetre a year on each side.

The magnetic banding patterns can be further explained by **mantle convection**. This is possibly the mechanism for moving the rigid plates of the Earth over the Earth's surface.

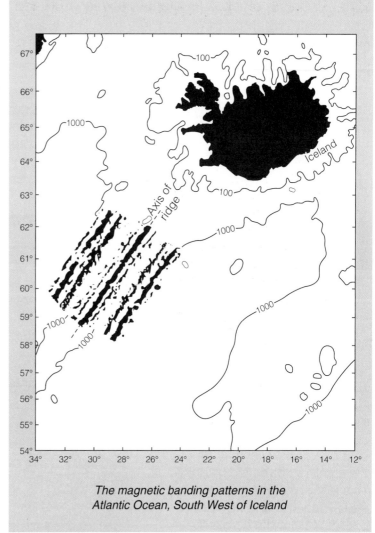

The magnetic banding patterns in the Atlantic Ocean, South West of Iceland

Q4 How do we know that the Earth's magnetic field changes?

Q5 How can magnetism be used to show that the sea floor is spreading at the middle of the Atlantic Ocean?

Q6 What would we notice (in Britain) if another reversal of polarity took place?

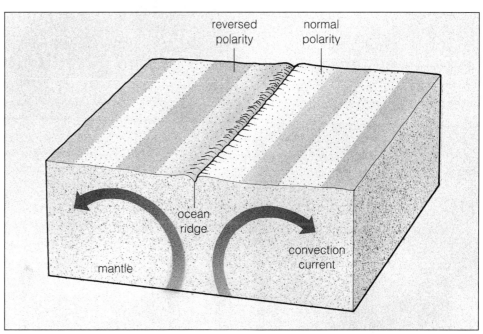

The theory of plate tectonics

Plates are rigid blocks of material between 100 and 150 kilometres thick which make up the surface of the Earth. There are six major plates and a number of smaller ones. The plates may be made up of continental crust and/or oceanic crust.

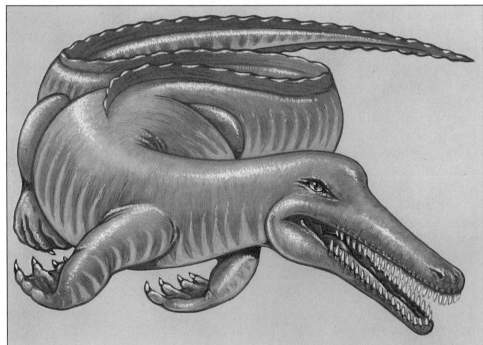

Plate tectonics is the theory of plate movements which has been generally accepted since the mid-1960s. It explains how plates move and slide over less rigid material below them. The theory neatly brings together the earlier ideas of sea floor spreading and continental drift and helps to explain why they occur. It had taken a long time for early theories to be changed through advances in several fields of science and technology.

Evidence for the theory of plate tectonics

The matching fit of the coastlines of Africa and South America on either side of the Atlantic has been known for centuries. As early as 1915, Alfred Wegener published his ideas on **continental drift**. The theory was not widely accepted because there was no mechanism to explain it. At this time most geologists believed that the Earth was still cooling and contracting from a mass of molten material.

The distribution of some fossil plants and animals provides further evidence to support the theory of continental drift. One 280 million year old fossil which can be used is the small reptile called Mesosaurus. This fossil is found in South America and Africa. It is unlikely to have been able to swim across the Atlantic. It is found in both continents because, at the time the creature lived, the continents were joined together. Many Victorian geologists believed that land bridges existed across the oceans to account for such fossils.

There are other examples of fossils that can be used to suggest that South Africa, South America, Australia and Antarctica were close together in the past.

Certain rock types only form in particular climates and so provide further evidence. Glacial deposits form today in cold climates and so it is surprising to find sedimentary rocks in South Africa which must have been deposited by glaciers. There is no reason to suggest that the ancient climates have changed. We conclude that the continent has moved to its present position from one close to the South Pole over the last 300 million years.

Plate movements causing continental drift have also affected the distribution of coal, one of the Earth's most important physical resources. Coal was formed in tropical swamps but coal-bearing layers are now found in the temperate regions of Europe and North America.

The patterns in rocks, which have been affected by fold mountain building movements, can be matched up in South America and Africa, if the two continents were joined together. Similar evidence can be seen in Britain. The fold mountain chain that runs through

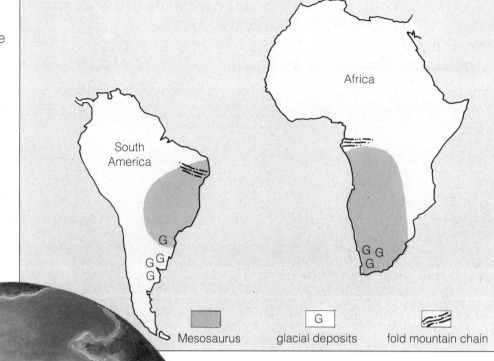

Mesosaurus | glacial deposits | fold mountain chain

Scotland can be linked to the mountain chains which run down through Scandinavia and through the Appalachians in the USA.

The present day distribution of active volcanoes, earthquakes and young fold mountain ranges shows that activity is largely confined to narrow zones of intense activity around the Earth. Most of these zones of activity are a few hundred kilometres wide but extend over thousands of kilometres in length. It is possible to divide the Earth's surface into a number of plates whose edges are marked by these narrow zones of activity.

Other evidence includes:
- surveys of heat flow
- palaeomagnetic surveys
- dating of the ocean crust.

Reconstruction of the original continent called Gondwanaland

Q1 Why is the best fit between continents made by not using the present coastlines?

Q2 If the Atlantic Ocean has widened by 2 metres in the last 100 years how far apart have North America and Britain moved since you were born?

Q3 Why were early ideas of continental drift not generally accepted?

Q4 How do coal deposits, found in this country, show that continents have moved?

Q5 What does the distribution of active volcanoes around the world tell us?

Q6 What kinds of evidence would you look for to see if two continents had ever been joined?

see science at work

■ **Earth science and atmosphere**
p 11 Plates
pp 12–13 Moving rocks

Plates meet along edges called **plate boundaries**. There are three types of plate boundaries: **constructive**, **destructive** and **conservative**. Which type of boundary is present is defined by the relative movement between the plates.

constructive plate boundary
conservative plate boundary
destructive plate boundary
direction of plate movement (length of arrow is proportional to the rate)

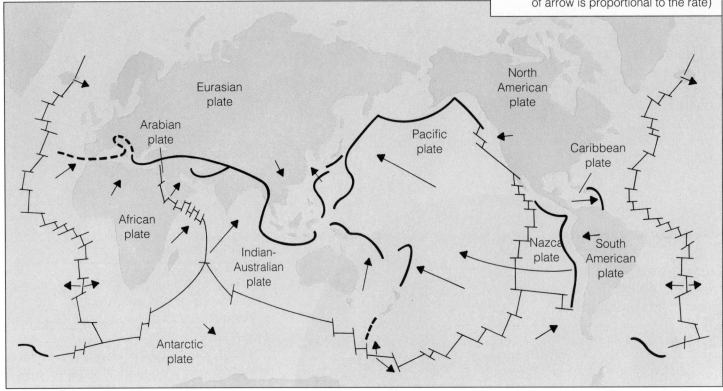

Eurasian plate

Arabian plate

North American plate

Pacific plate

Caribbean plate

African plate

Indian-Australian plate

Nazca plate

South American plate

Antarctic plate

Types of plate boundaries

Constructive plate boundaries are where the plates are moving apart. New ocean plate material is created at this type of boundary and is added to the edges of the plates as they move apart. Ocean ridges form along these plate boundaries. The mid-Atlantic ridge is an example. ▼

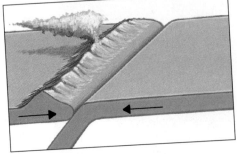

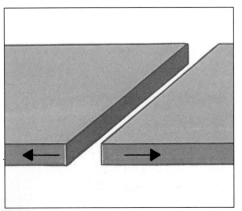

▲ Destructive plate boundaries are where plates move towards each other. Ocean plate material is destroyed at this type of boundary by the process called **subduction** as the plate is pushed deep into the mantle. Different types of collision may happen at these boundaries and ocean trenches, island arcs and fold mountain ranges may form here. Examples are the Andes and the Peru Trench in South America.

Conservative plate boundaries are where plates simply slide past one another. Material is neither created nor destroyed at these boundaries. Transform faults form along these boundaries as the plates move past each other. The San Andreas Fault in America is an example. ▼

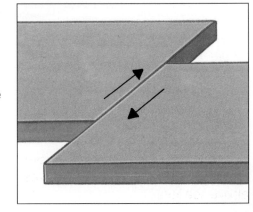

The reasons for plate movements are not fully understood. It is thought that the driving mechanism may be convection currents within the mantle. These convection currents rise at ocean ridges where new ocean crust is formed at constructive plate boundaries and sink at destructive plate boundaries. These convection currents may occur throughout the whole of the mantle or may be confined to the upper part of it. It is likely that more than one process is operating, but the heat to drive the convection currents in the mantle would be created by the decay of radioactive isotopes in the Earth.

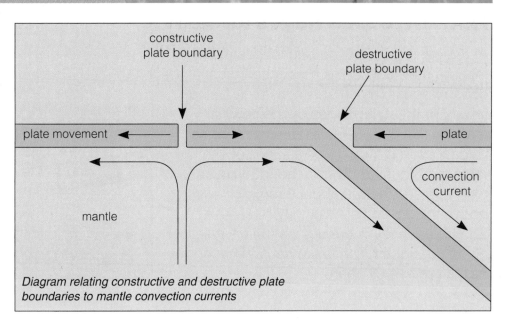

Diagram relating constructive and destructive plate boundaries to mantle convection currents

The effects of plate movement

Ocean trenches and ocean ridges
One of the effects of plate movement is that in some parts of the Earth new ocean crust is being created at ocean ridges. As this happens plates move away from the ridge and so the width of the ocean floor is increasing. Elsewhere ocean floor is being destroyed at the same rate. This happens at ocean trenches as plate material is subducted into the mantle.

Fold mountains
Another effect of the plate movement is that continental crust is not destroyed by being subducted into the mantle. This is because continental crust has a lower density than ocean crust and cannot sink. Where the two plates meet the continental crust is simply compressed, folded into **anticlines** and **synclines** and thickened to form a fold mountain range similar to the Andes.

If two continental plates meet the effect is to form fold mountains similar to the Himalayas. This type of fold mountain range has no volcanoes or deep focus earthquakes. It is even more surprising to find that the rocks near the summit of of Mount Everest are sedimentary rocks containing fossil sea shells. These creatures were formed under the sea and have been pushed more than 8800 metres above sea level.

The Himalayas, a great mountain chain formed by two continental plates colliding

Earthquakes
Most earthquakes are created by the different types of movement along the three types of plate boundaries. Movements along conservative plate boundaries like the San Andreas fault produce great earthquakes such as the 1906 San Francisco earthquake. Deeper focus earthquakes formed at depths below the surface between 300 and 700 kilometres are found along subduction zones along destructive plate boundaries. These earthquakes are common in Japan. Shallower focus earthquakes are formed at spreading ocean ridges.

Q1 Where are most constructive plate boundaries found?

Q2 Where are the rates of spreading highest?

Q3 Why do most active volcanoes form around the edges of the Pacific Ocean?

Q4 Why is Britain unlikely to experience a major earthquake?

Q5 Explain why the original fossils in many limestones found in fold mountain ranges can no longer be seen.

Q6 How does the theory of plate tectonics help to explain the rock cycle?

How are ocean ridges formed?

At the constructive plate boundaries molten magma rises and forms new ocean crust at the ocean ridges. The crust is constantly being forced apart at the ridges by the newest material rising up. The rising magma forms volcanoes and triggers off a series of shallow focus earthquakes. The linear ridges usually form a raised feature about three kilometres above the ocean floor but they rarely rise above sea level. There are central rift valleys along the ridges. These are caused by tension as the plates pull apart.

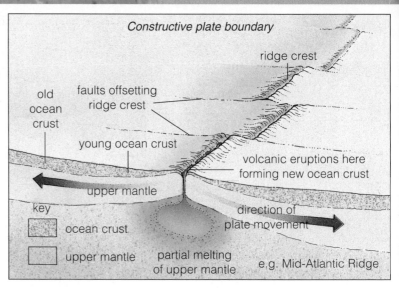

Constructive plate boundary

e.g. Mid-Atlantic Ridge

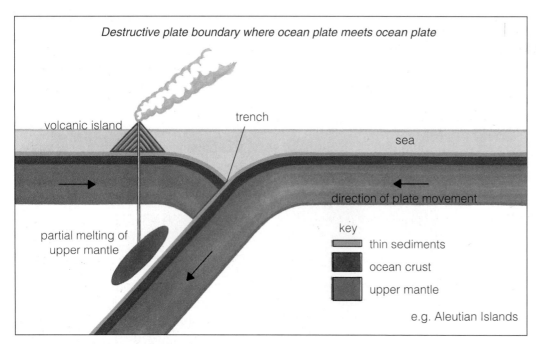

Destructive plate boundary where ocean plate meets ocean plate

e.g. Aleutian Islands

How are ocean trenches formed?

Ocean trenches form at destructive plate boundaries where two ocean plates collide or a continental plate collides with an oceanic plate. The ocean trench is formed on the sea bed marking the actual boundary between the two colliding plates. The deepest ocean trench, the Marianas Trench in the Pacific, is over eleven kilometres deep.

How are volcanoes formed?

Volcanoes at the ocean ridges are mainly submarine volcanoes. The magma is poured on to the sea floor as lava which cools and hardens quickly in contact with the sea water. Globules of lava form pillow lava structures on the sea floor. Iceland is one of the few places on the Earth where the ocean ridge rises above sea level.

Volcanic eruptions cannot be predicted accurately but by keeping a close watch on volcanoes we now recognise events which occur before an eruption. These include:
● small earthquakes
● animals behaving strangely
● snow and ice melting on volcanic cones
● land bulging
● ground cracking
● changes in groundwater temperatures.

Volcanoes do not only form at constructive plate boundaries. They are also formed at destructive plate boundaries. The denser plate at these boundaries is forced into the mantle. As it reaches the lower parts of the mantle parts of the plate melt and form magma. In the case of two ocean plates colliding this rises to form volcanoes which build up a chain of volcanic islands known as a volcanic island arc.

How are mountain ranges formed?

Mountain ranges form at destructive plate boundaries where ocean crust collides with continental crust. The leading edge of the continental plate suffers great distortions, folding, faulting and uplift as well as volcanic activity. The Andes were formed in this way.

Where two continental plates meet neither is dense enough to be forced into the mantle and so they grind against one another. The sedimentary rocks formed at the edges of the continents are uplifted into fold mountains. The Himalayas were formed as the Indian Plate collided with the Asian Plate.

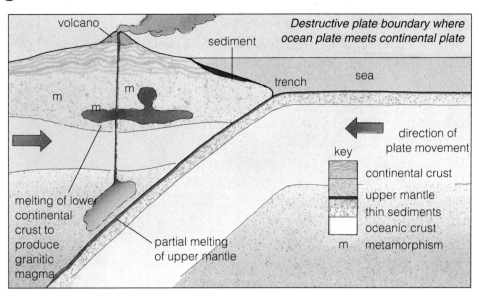

Destructive plate boundary where ocean plate meets continental plate

volcano
sediment
trench
sea
direction of plate movement
key
continental crust
upper mantle
thin sediments
oceanic crust
m metamorphism
melting of lower continental crust to produce granitic magma
partial melting of upper mantle

How are earthquakes formed?

The mechanism which explains how earthquakes occur along plate boundaries is illustrated here. The stress builds up and the rocks bend until the blocks finally move and energy is released from the focus of the earthquake.

Earthquakes are difficult to predict with accuracy. They are such hazardous events that it would be useful to forecast when they will occur. So far a number of events which may occur before an earthquake have been noted. These include:
● unusual animal behaviour
● release of radon gas
● swelling of rock
● slight changes in land levels.

stress builds up: rocks bend like a bow

fault stuck after last movement

earthquake: rocks spring back and vibrate

Q1 Ocean floor material is less than 200 million years old everywhere on the Earth. Explain why this is.

Q2 Why do lava flows forming on Iceland form flat sheet-like structures rather than pillow lava structures?

Q3 Groundwater temperatures increase before a volcanic eruption. What other changes in the groundwater might you expect to see at the same time?

Q4 Suggest reasons why animals may behave strangely before earthquakes or volcanic eruptions.

Q5 Explain why the suggestion to get rid of radioactive waste material by dumping it in ocean trenches was not a good idea.

Q6 The remains of ancient fold mountains are found in Britain. What does this tell us about the pattern of plate boundaries in the past?

Evolution of the atmosphere

What was the early atmosphere like?

It was very different from the Earth's atmosphere today. The atmosphere was probably made up of carbon dioxide, carbon monoxide, nitrogen, water vapour and hydrogen. An oxygen-poor environment like this is described as anaerobic. It was a **reducing** environment rather than today's **oxidising** environment. Small amounts of oxygen would have been released by water vapour being broken down into its elements by energy from ultraviolet (UV) light. This is called **photo-dissociation**.

The early atmosphere was formed by volcanoes erupting and releasing gases from the Earth's interior. Studies of gases given off by modern volcanoes give us clues as to the likely composition of the early atmosphere.

We know the atmosphere has changed from evidence in ancient rocks. The oldest rocks discovered so far are 3800 million years old.

About 3500 million years ago the first simple organisms appeared. The most important of these were the cyanobacteria. These built up layered, domed structures called **stromatolites**. Stromatolites still form today. Primitive animals did not appear until about 650 million year ago, suggesting that an aerobic environment similar to today's took a long time to develop.

In a few places we can find ancient sedimentary rocks containing the mineral called **uraninite**. These rocks are one of the most important sources of uranium. Uraninite does not form in sediments collecting today because the mineral breaks down in an oxidising environment. The last uraninite deposits are found in layers about 2300 million years old. Calculations suggest that the oxygen content of the atmosphere then was less than one hundredth of its present level.

Gas composition of a modern volcanic eruption (% volume)	
Water	77.0
Carbon dioxide	11.5
Sulphur dioxide	6.5
Nitrogen	3.0
Hydrogen	0.5
Carbon monoxide	0.5
Sulphur vapour	0.3
Other gases	0.7

Q1 Why is there no evidence for the composition of the Earth's atmosphere more than 3800 million years ago?

Q2 What processes produce oxygen in the atmosphere?

Living stromatolites

How has the atmosphere changed?

The cyanobacteria give off oxygen during the day. It appears that these organisms were very important in helping to increase the oxygen levels in the atmosphere. As this happened other life forms were able to evolve. When oxygen levels increased to about one tenth of their present value **ozone** layers in the upper atmosphere were built up. The ozone layers helped to absorb harmful UV radiation and so started to protect the life forms living on the planet's surface.

The earliest land plants appeared about 430 million years ago. Once they had evolved they quickly spread. The process of photosynthesis soon produced oxygen levels in the atmosphere close to those of today.

Further evidence from rocks

Banded iron formations are found in rocks more than 1700 million years old. These are sedimentary rocks rich in the iron mineral called **haematite**. In the sea today iron is quickly oxidised and is not deposited. Ancient iron deposits must have formed in an oxygen-poor environment. About 1700 million years ago the environment changed and became aerobic so banded iron formations did not occur again.

Banded iron formation

Red beds

Red beds (red sedimentary rocks) appeared as the banded iron formations disappeared. These beds indicate the presence of free oxygen in the atmosphere.

What is the atmosphere like now?

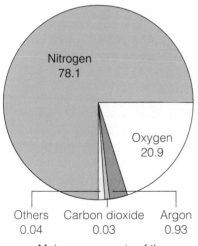
Nitrogen 78.1
Oxygen 20.9
Others 0.04
Carbon dioxide 0.03
Argon 0.93

Major components of the Earth's atmosphere (% volume)

The atmosphere has a very simple composition. It is made up almost entirely of two elements. There is evidence that the atmosphere is beginning to change now, for example, as people burn more fossil fuels and produce more carbon dioxide.

The effects of oxygen build up in the atmosphere and hydrosphere are:

● a great variety of life forms have appeared
● rocks weather because most weathering processes involve oxidation
● ozone has increased in the upper atmosphere to form a protective shell to shield the Earth's surface from harmful UV radiation
● different sediments have been deposited at different times in the Earth's history.

Q3 How has the oxygen level in the atmosphere changed over time?

Q4 Make a list of ways in which the atmosphere is beginning to change.

Q5 How has the changing oxygen level in the atmosphere affected the nature of the Earth's surface?

Balance in the atmosphere 1

see science at work

■ **Pollution**
p 1 What is pollution?
p 24 Global warming and the greenhouse effect

Changing but staying the same

Everything on the Earth is in a state of change. Chemicals are combining and recombining to give new compounds. Gases are evaporating from lakes and oceans. Rain is carrying chemicals back to the land. If, however, we look at the whole Earth over a period of time the amount of any chemical in the atmosphere will be steady. This is because there is a balance between the amount leaving and entering the atmosphere. This pattern is called a **cycle**.

Carbon dioxide

burning fossil fuels

photosynthesis

plants

solution into seas

respiration

animals

evaporation

decaying matter

The carbon cycle

ocean ⟹ plants

decaying matter

sediments—coal and oil

Carbon is gained by the atmosphere in the form of carbon dioxide, by animals breathing, by burning fuels and by evaporation from lakes and seas. It is lost from the atmosphere by photosynthesis in plants.

Some parts of the cycle are changing rapidly like burning fuels and breathing. Some are changing very slowly like carbon dioxide dissolving in the oceans. Because some parts of the cycle are changing at different rates it is hard to see if the balance is being kept. We do know, however, that until the beginning of the twentieth century the balance was well maintained.

With the increase this century of industrialisation the amount of carbon dioxide in the air has increased. This is not only because factories and power stations have burnt fossil fuels, but also because transport has improved and we are demanding better heating in our homes.

The situation has been thrown further off-balance by the clearing of large areas of trees in this century. This has happened not only to use the wood but also to make space for people to live in and to grow crops. On a timescale that is short compared with the life of the Earth, it

seems that human activities have had an effect on the balance.

Q1 What sort of actions need to be taken to put the carbon in the atmosphere back into balance?

Q2 What effects would a rise in sea level have on a part of Britain like East Anglia?

Q3 How might industry save energy to become more efficient and produce less carbon dioxide?

Maintaining the balance

Industry

In North America and Western Europe it has been possible for industry to become more efficient in its use of energy and to provide new sources of energy that do not rely on burning carbon fuels. In these parts of the world the amount of carbon dioxide produced has levelled off or even fallen in the last few years. In developing countries however the amount of carbon dioxide produced has continued to increase as their industries have begun to grow.

Global warming

When the balance of carbon gases in the atmosphere is altered it has an effect. The increasing levels of carbon dioxide, CFCs (chlorofluorocarbons – better known for their effect on the ozone layer) and methane gas from rubbish dumps and animal dung are holding in more of the Earth's heat. The exact amount of this and the effects it will have are still being argued about by scientists. It is clear that there is likely to be a slight increase in the average temperature of the Earth. The prediction is that by the end of the next century the Earth will be 1 to 4°C warmer. Although this may have benefits for some parts of the world, other areas are likely to suffer if the ice caps partially melt causing the sea level to rise by up to a metre. The changes produced in weather patterns would also cause great problems in some parts of the world.

Transport

Cars and lorries produce carbon dioxide, carbon monoxide and nitrous oxide from their exhausts. Trains burn diesel fuel or consume electricity (made in power stations). Governments have to balance the demands for goods and for people to be moved against the effects that transport has on the environment.

Climate report confirms worst fears of experts

Paul Brown
Environment Correspondent

One area of increased concern is the disappearance of snow cover over much of the northern hemisphere in the last few years and the melting of the permafrost in the tundra.

Analysis of satellite snow data shows northern hemisphere snow at record low levels since the middle of 1987 with the largest drop being in the Spring. Canadian and Russian Arctic tundra have melted causing landslides, which dammed streams and damaged water quality.

Methane one of the important contributors to global warming, which is trapped in the frozen ground, is then being released. The report says this effect has probably been underestimated.

(Source: *Independent* June 1992)

Q4 A quarter of the carbon dioxide in Britain is produced in heating homes. How could this be reduced?

Q5 You are the leader of a European Community country. How could you help a developing country with large rain forests?

Q6 How could Britain's transport facilities be rearranged to make the best use of energy resources in the future?

see science at work

■ **Pollution**

p 22 Acid rain

Nitrogen – the commonest gas

Where do we find nitrogen?
- 80% of the atmosphere is nitrogen
- Farmers use nitrogen fertilisers to improve crop yields
- Nitrous oxide (NO) is emitted by factory chimneys and car exhausts
- Plants and animals use nitrogen in making proteins
- Electric storms make ammonia (NH_3) from nitrogen in the air
- The soil has large reserves of nitrogen as nitrates
- Farm and human waste produces ammonia and nitrogen
- Bacteria play an important part in moving nitrogen about.

The nitrogen cycle

As with other processes in the atmosphere, the nitrogen is in a complicated cycle. This means that nitrogen and its compounds are both leaving and re-entering the atmosphere. Some parts of the cycle of movement are quick and some are very slow indeed. Bacteria play an important part in transporting nitrogen around the cycle, converting it into other compounds. As nitrogen plays an important part in the make-up of both plants and animals it is very useful that bacteria can help to make nitrogen available to growing structures.

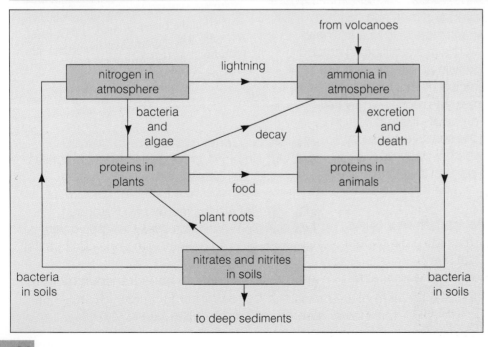

Drinking water

When farmers use large amounts of nitrogen fertiliser, there is a danger that the nitrates which will dissolve in water can reach the water supplies. The rainfall on the farmland washes some of the fertiliser down through the soil. Too much nitrate in drinking water can cause illness. The maximum legal European limit is 50 milligrams per litre of water. Many farming areas across Europe fail to meet that level. Nitrates in water also act as a fertiliser for plants in rivers and lakes. The enrichment by fertiliser of the water can lead to sudden growth of plants that can choke out the normal species and alter the balance of aquatic life.

Acid rain

Nitrous oxide from engines' exhausts and power station chimneys rises high in the atmosphere and combines with water droplets to make nitric acid. Similarly, sulphur dioxide combines to make sulphuric acid. When this water falls as rain or snow it falls as acid, sometimes thousands of miles from where it entered the atmosphere. On lands where this acid water is held by soils it affects the roots of slow-growing plants like trees. Snow containing oxides of nitrogen and sulphur releases large amounts of acidic water when it melts. If this flows into lakes it may affect insect life that cannot survive in very acid waters, thus breaking food chains.

Some of the sulphur dioxide in the atmosphere comes from eruptions of volcanoes and this is beyond human control. This makes it even more important to control the emissions from power stations, boilers and cars.

Q1 What is acid rain?

Q2 Why can nitrogen fertilisers have a harmful effect?

Q3 What gases have nitrogen in them?

Q4 What organisms are affected by acid rain?

Q5 Why is it important to control sulphur dioxide and nitrous oxide emissions?

Q6 Where might the ammonia produced by volcanoes come from?

Processes in the atmosphere

see science at work
■ **Earth science and atmosphere**
pp 35–38 Weather systems: 1–4

Clouds – and what comes out of them

Cool air holds less water vapour than warm air. As air cools, tiny droplets of water appear like mist on a cold window or dew on grass. The temperature when this occurs is called the **dew point**. When warm air rises, the pressure on it gets less and it cools down until it cannot hold its water vapour. Droplets of water form on dust in the air. These cloud droplets are very small – it takes millions to make one raindrop.

Air can be made to rise for different reasons. It can meet some cold air and rise over it. It can be forced to rise over hills. It can pass over warm ground. How it is formed determines the shape of the cloud.

The circulation of water vapour in the atmosphere is controlled by many variables. Air that has travelled over an ocean will contain more water vapour than if it has been across a desert. The air pressure and temperature changes will also affect how the air circulates. The damage that is caused by storms is an indication of the amount of energy that is carried by moving air masses. The number and complexity of the variables makes forecasting the weather very difficult.

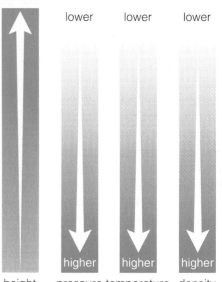

lower   lower   lower

higher higher higher

height   pressure temperature density

Q1 How is a raindrop formed?

Q2 What are the differences between how a hailstone is formed and how a snowflake is formed?

Q3 Why does fog form in low-lying areas and in dips in the ground?

Q4 What fixes where the bottom of a cloud begins?

Q5 Why do low pressure zones produce unsettled weather?

Q6 In a cloud, what links are there between:
a height and temperature?
b air pressure and air density?

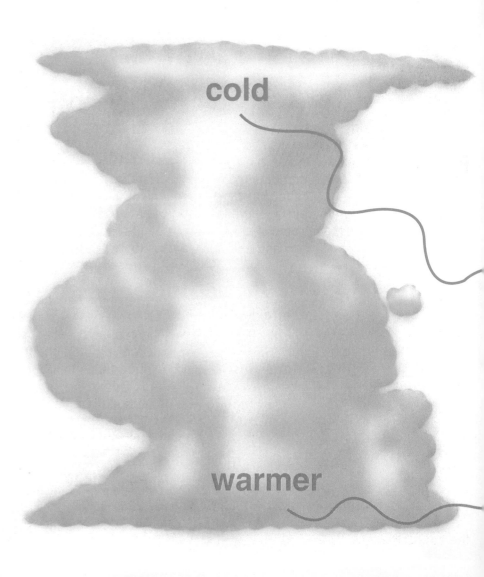

cold

warmer

Wind

In a high pressure area, the air will be pushing down towards the Earth. Winds blow outwards from the middle of the **high** with a clockwise twist (in the northern hemisphere) because of the Earth's rotation. In a low pressure zone the air will be drawn in to replace the warm air that is rising. High pressure zones tend to give dry settled weather while **lows** give unsettled stormy conditions.

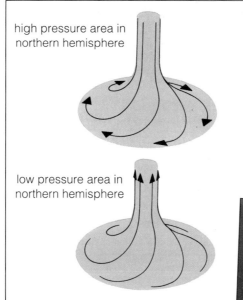

high pressure area in northern hemisphere

low pressure area in northern hemisphere

Fog

Fog forms when still air is cooled below the dew point. The tiny droplets of water that condense are too small to fall and hang in the air. On clear nights, the air and ground temperatures fall rapidly so fog is more common especially in damp areas. The air being cold tends to flow downhill to form fog in pockets.

Hail

The tiny droplets in a cloud are rising and falling in air currents. They start to join together into bigger drops and when they rise, they cool and may freeze. Falling through the cloud allows the drop to warm and melt. Hailstones are formed by repeated freezing and melting as drops are swirled in turbulent storm clouds. Each time the hailstone falls it gains another layer of water on the outside which then freezes as the hailstone rises. In extreme conditions hailstones of over 500 grams can fall from storm clouds.

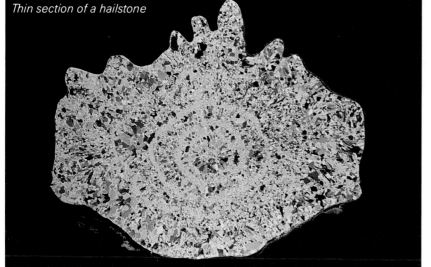

Thin section of a hailstone

Snow

The top of clouds may be as cold as – 40°C. In very cold conditions like this the water vapour in the air will form crystals directly. The symmetrical patterns in snowflakes show that the water molecules have had time to arrange themselves and so snowflakes are formed slowly. Many clouds may have snowflakes inside them but it only snows when the base of the cloud nearest the ground is cold enough. Heavy snow falls happen when the cloud is just below freezing because very cold air does not contain much water vapour.

Rain

If the base of the cloud is warm then any water that falls out will be in the form of raindrops. The size of the drops will depend on how many of the small droplets have joined together. Most water leaves the atmosphere as rain.

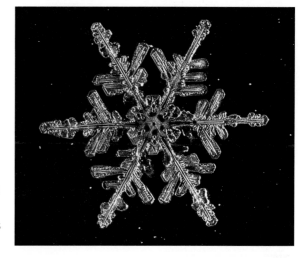

see science at work
Earth in space
pp 8–9 Gravity

Gravity and satellites

Gravity is a force of attraction between all pieces of matter. The gravitational force between two things depends on their masses and how far apart they are.

Your weight is the force of gravity between you and the Earth. It depends on your mass, the mass of the Earth, and how far away from the centre of the Earth you are. The gravitational force between two masses can be calculated using the formula:

$$F = \frac{GMm}{r^2}$$

Where G is a constant called the universal constant of gravitation, M and m are the two masses, and r is the distance between them.

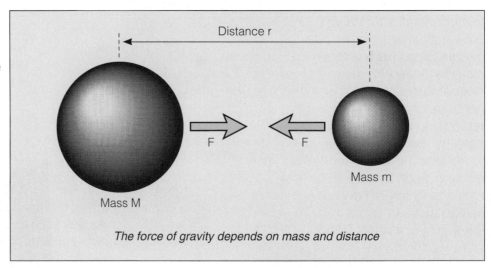

The force of gravity depends on mass and distance

We can use this formula to calculate the force of gravity on a one kilogram mass on the surface of the Earth. (G is equal to 6.7×10^{-11} Nm² kg², the mass of the Earth is 6×10^{24} kg and its radius is 6.4×10^6 m.)

$$F = \frac{6.7 \times 10^{-11} \times 6 \times 10^{24} \times 1}{(6.4 \times 10^6)^2} = 9.8 \text{ N}$$

So the gravitational force at the surface of the Earth is 9.8N for every kilogram of mass. The gravitational force gets less as the object gets further from the Earth. For instance, if a satellite was orbiting 600 kilometres above the surface of the Earth its distance from the centre of the Earth would be 7×10^6 metres, and the gravitational force would be 8.2 N/kg.

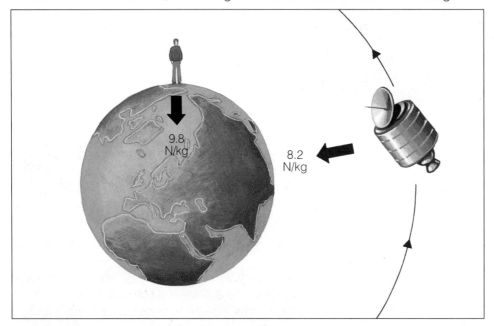

Gravity stops the Earth's atmosphere from escaping into space. Without gravity there would be no life on the Earth, because there would be no air to breathe.

Tides

There is a gravitational force between the Earth and the Moon, which causes the tides. As the Earth spins on its axis the direction of this force changes, and pulls the seas upwards. The seas also bulge up on the side of the Earth opposite the Moon. The gravitational force between the sun and the Earth also has an effect on the tides.

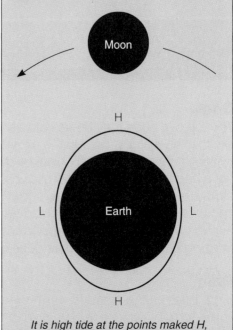

It is high tide at the points maked H, and low tide at the points marked L

Moving in circles

It is the force of gravity that keeps the Earth and the other planets moving around the Sun, and keeps the Moon orbiting the Earth.

A stationary object above the Earth would just fall until it hit the ground. If the object is moving, it will fall to Earth along a curved path. If it is moving fast enough, it will carry on falling around the Earth – it will be in orbit. If it is moving even faster it will escape from the Earth altogether and fly off into space.

Most satellites go around the Earth in almost circular orbits. Satellites in low orbits travel fast, and can orbit the Earth in a couple of hours. Some satellites are put into special orbits called **geosynchronous orbits** – these satellites take exactly 24 hours to go around the Earth.

The Earth is turning on its axis once every 24 hours as well, so these satellites always stay above one spot on the Earth. Geosynchronous orbits are useful for TV satellites, or satellites that relay telephone calls or watch the weather

The planets travel around the Sun in **elliptical** orbits. When books refer to the distance between the Sun and a planet they usually mean the *average* distance. Comets travel through the Solar System in very elliptical orbits.

Some comets, like the famous Halley's comet, are in regular orbits and we can predict when we will see them again.

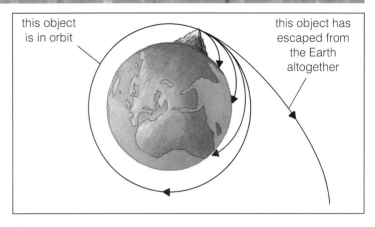

this object is in orbit

this object has escaped from the Earth altogether

How the Sun affects tides

When the Sun and Moon are pulling in the same direction the tides are higher. These high tides are called **spring tides** and happen twice a month.

When the Sun and Moon are pulling at right angles the tides are lower. These low tides are called **neap tides** and happen twice a month.

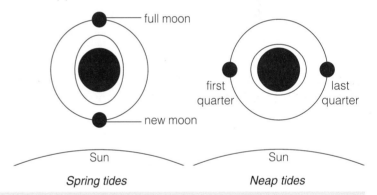

full moon

new moon

first quarter

last quarter

Sun

Sun

Spring tides   *Neap tides*

You will need to use the data sheet in the copymasters to answer some of these questions.

Q1 Use the information in the data sheet to calculate the gravitational pull of each planet at its surface.

Q2 Calculate the gravitational force on a 1000 kilogram satellite in an orbit:
a 100 kilometres above the Earth.
b 100 kilometres above Mars.

Q3 Calculate the gravitational force between an astronaut (mass 150 kilograms) and his spaceship (mass 900 tonnes) if they are 100 metres apart.

Q4 **a** Calculate the gravitational force on a 100 kilogram object and a 1 kilogram object near the surface of Mercury.
b Calculate the acceleration of each object towards the centre of Mercury (Hint: you will need to use the equation F = ma.)
c What can you say about the acceleration of the two objects? If they were dropped at the same time, which one would hit the ground first? Would the same thing apply for objects of any mass?
d On the Earth, heavy objects like hammers often seem to fall faster than light objects like leaves. Explain why.

Q5 Astronauts in orbit feel 'weightless'. Because they feel weightless, astronauts have to do many ordinary things (like moving around, eating and drinking) in a different way. Find out about some of the difficulties that astronauts have, and how they overcome these difficulties.

The solar system

The Solar System consists of the Sun, nine planets with their moons and rings, and a collection of asteroids, meteorites and comets. There are two different theories to account for the formation of the Solar System – the **nebular theory** and the **catastrophic-event theory**.

The nebular theory was first proposed in the eighteenth century. The idea behind this theory is that a flat, disc-shaped cloud of dust and gas gradually shrunk and condensed. As it condensed gaseous rings were thrown off. Each ring condensed to form a planet and the centre of the disc contracted to become the Sun. ▶

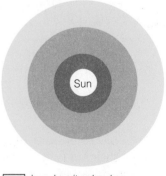

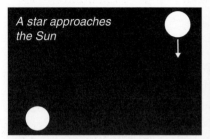
A star approaches the Sun

Both stars are distorted by gravity

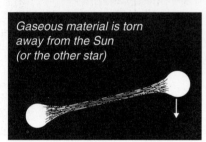
Gaseous material is torn away from the Sun (or the other star)

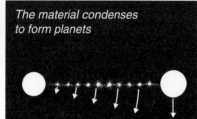
The material condenses to form planets

◀The catastrophic-event theory was first proposed at the beginning of the twentieth century. This theory assumes that another star came close to the Sun, and the gravitational force between the two stars pulled away a sausage-shaped stream of gases. These gases spread out around the sun and eventually condensed to form the planets.

Both these theories say that the planets condensed from a cloud of gas and dust – the difference between the two theories is how the cloud of dust and gas got there in the first place.

Inner and outer planets

Look carefully at the Solar System data sheet. You should see that the planets can be divided into the **inner planets**, Mercury Venus, Earth and Mars, and the **outer planets**, Jupiter, Saturn, Uranus and Neptune (we will ignore Pluto for now). The inner planets are all much smaller and denser than the outer planets. The inner planets are rocky, and have only a few moons. Mars even has volcanoes, just like Earth, except that the Martian volcanoes are no longer active. The outer planets probably have rocky or icy cores, but are mainly made of gases such as hydrogen, helium, ammonia and methane, and have rings and lots of moons. Let us see whether the differences between the two groups of planets can be explained by the idea that they condensed from a cloud of dust and gas.

The 'pre-planetary' cloud of dust and gas *might* have been like this. If the Sun had already started to shine the heat would have made the light gases move away from the centre, leaving behind the more dense rocky fragments nearer to the centre. Mercury would have formed from the densest part of the cloud. Venus, Earth and Mars would have

formed from the high-density part, and the outer planets would have formed from the low-density part. As each planet began to condense, its gravity would have increased, and it would attract more and more particles and molecules to it.

Olympus Mons (on Mars)– the biggest known volcano anywhere in the Solar System

low density cloud, forming the outer planets

high density cloud, forming the inner planets

very high density cloud, forming Mercury

see further science copymasters

■ **Earth and space**
Does the Sun go round the Earth?
Exploring the Solar System

Earth and space

The Earth may originally have had an atmosphere like Jupiter's. Because the Earth is nearer to the Sun than Jupiter, the Earth is warmer, and so light molecules like hydrogen or helium could escape from the atmosphere. Jupiter and the other outer planets are cooler than the Earth, and their gravitational pull is greater, so they have kept the light gases in their atmospheres.

A crater caused by a meteorite hitting the Earth

Asteroids

There are about 40 000 asteroids orbiting between Mars and Jupiter. They are like very small planets – lumps of rock that never joined up to make a planet. Some astronomers think that there was a planet between Mars and Jupiter and that this planet broke up to give the asteroids. Some asteroids do not have nice, circular orbits, but wander across the Solar System. When these rocks hit the Earth's atmosphere they are heated by friction with the air and burn up. They are known as **meteorites** or 'shooting stars'. Sometimes they do not burn up completely, and they hit the Earth. A good time to look for shooting stars is at the beginning of August each year.

Planets and moons

Other lumps of rock or ice were captured by the outer planets and became their moons. Many astronomers believe that Pluto and its moon, Charon, were once in orbit around Neptune. Pluto's orbit actually comes closer to the Sun than Neptune at one point, so Pluto is not always the furthest planet from the Sun.

Some of the moons of the outer planets are bigger than the Earth and some even have active volcanoes.

This is Io, one of Jupiter's moons photographed by Voyager 1. Each of the dark circular features is a recently active volcano.

Q1 Why do you think the outer planets have rings and more moons than the inner planets?

Q2 What are 'shooting stars'? Are they really stars?

Q3 Choose a suitable scale and draw a scale diagram of the Solar System to show how far each planet is from the Sun. You will need a very long piece of graph paper. Can you see any connection between the sizes of the planets and the distance between their orbits?

Q4 Asteroids are bits of rock that never joined up to make a planet. Use the data table and any other information you can find out to predict:
a what radius the planet would have
b what mass it would have
c what its gravitational pull would be
d what its surface temperature would be
e what its day and year lengths would be.

Q5 This diagram shows three comets just entering the Solar System. Explain why the three comets follow different paths through the Solar System.

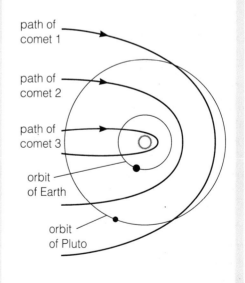

path of comet 1

path of comet 2

path of comet 3

orbit of Earth

orbit of Pluto

Q6 You may need to use a library to find out the answers to this question.
a Jupiter has a Red Spot, which is visible through telescopes from Earth. Find out what this Red Spot is.
b Find out why the surface of Venus is hotter than the surface of Mercury, even though Venus is further away from the Sun.

Exploring space

Space was first explored by men and women who used their eyes to observe the sky. Many people in ancient civilisations watched the stars, and gave names to constellations. They also observed five 'wandering stars' that we now know to be some of the planets of our solar system (Mercury, Venus, Mars, Jupiter and Saturn).

In 1609 an Italian scientist called Galileo heard of a new invention – the telescope. Galileo made his own telescope and started to observe the stars and planets. He observed the rings of Saturn, and Jupiter's moons. Other astronomers also used telescopes and in 1781 William Herschel discovered Uranus. Neptune was not discovered until 1846.

When photography was invented astronomers could take photos through their telescopes and analyse them instead of having to draw what they saw. Pluto was discovered in this way in 1930. Today astronomers use large optical telescopes to observe the sky and explore the distant parts of the universe.

Light telescope, at the Crimean Astrophysical Observatory at Simeiz, USSR

Stars emit electromagnetic radiation at lots of different frequencies. Optical telescopes are used to observe visible light, and astronomers use radio telescopes, like the one at Jodrell Bank, to observe the radio waves emitted by stars.

Space Travel

The first person to travel in space was a Russian called Yuri Gagarin, who orbited the Earth in 1959. The first person to land on the moon was Neil Armstrong, from the USA, in 1969. So far the Moon is the only part of the Solar System that humans have visited. More of the Solar System has been investigated using spacecraft, without astronauts at the controls.

Spacecraft have visited Venus and Mars, and two Voyager spacecraft have flown past the outer planets taking photographs and measurements. When it leaves the Solar System, Voyager 2 will be heading towards the star Sirius, but it will take nearly 300 000 years to get there.

Travelling to other stars

The stars are so far away from the Earth that astronomers use a special unit for measuring distance. A **light-year** is the distance that light travels in one year (approximately 9.5×10^{15} metres).

The nearest star to the Earth is Alpha Centauri, and it is over four light-years away. Even if spaceships could be developed which travelled near the speed of light it would take four years to get there. Spaceships like this are not likely to be developed for a very long time. Because the stars are so far away, explorers would not know what they were like until they got there. We do not even know if any stars have planets.

Some stars are in pairs orbiting around each other. They are called **binary stars**. This painting shows what the view might look like from a planet orbiting a binary star.

Some stars are surrounded by rings of glowing gas. This is an artist's impression of the view from a planet orbiting the Ring Nebula in Lyra.

Some stars are clustered together.

The sky would look very strange to us if we managed to reach other parts of our galaxy, or if we managed to travel to other galaxies.

Q1 Why is it very difficult to observe planets around other stars? You should be able to think of two reasons.

Q2 Voyager will take 300 000 years to get to Sirius. How fast is it travelling compared to the speed of light? (Use the data table, included in the Earth and space copymasters, to help you work out the answer.)

Q3 If a spacecraft could be built which travelled at one tenth of the speed of light, how long would it take to reach:
a Alpha Centauri
b Betelgeuse
c the nearest star in Andromeda?

Q4 Fictional starships, like the USS Enterprise, use special drive systems that let them travel faster than the speed of light. Engines like these do not exist, but if they did how fast would the Enterprise have to travel to go from Earth to Betelgeuse in three days?
(The speed of light is 3×10^8 m/s, and a light-year is 9.5×10^{15} metres.)

Q5 Look at the picture of an imaginary planet orbiting a binary star. How many shadows would you have if you stood on this planet?

The Beginning

Time (in 1000 million years) ⟶

0   1   2   3   4   5   6   7

galaxies
begin to form

stars begin
to develop

The Big Bang Theory

Most scientists now believe that the matter in the Universe is expanding. It started expanding **15 000 million** years ago after a huge explosion called **'The Big Bang'**. It is thought that all the matter that exists in the Universe was once together in a very small and extremely hot lump – as separate electrons, neutrons and protons. When it exploded hot gases spread out in all directions and particle combinations started to take place. As the matter cooled, the galaxies, stars and planets were formed. Galaxies are still moving outward from the point of initial explosion. Some of them are receding (moving away from us) at almost the speed of light.

Other theories

The Oscillating Universe

The oscillating theory is similar to the Big Bang theory. The differences that some scientists believe that the expansion will slow down, eventually stop and then be pulled back by gravity. Finally the galaxies would collide and there would be another huge explosion, which would cause the Universe to start expanding again. Scientists believe that the cycle would be repeated every 80 000 million years.

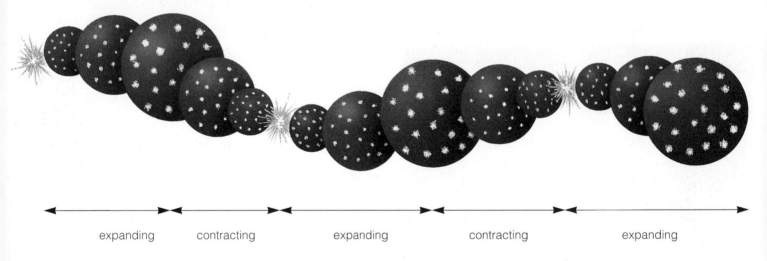

expanding   contracting   expanding   contracting   expanding

Q1 List the three main theories of the Universe.

Q2 Explain the meaning of the Big Bang.

The Steady State Universe

In the case of the steady state Universe scientists believe that new galaxies are being formed at the centre of the Universe, to replace those that are moving outwards. This is like the idea of people in a city – some are being born, some are dying – but the total number of people in the city stays the same.

```
8        9        10        11        12        13        14        15
                  our solar   oldest    first     single cell         Earth's      Now
                  system      known     plant     animals live        atmosphere   i.e.
                  forms       rock      life      in sea              similar to   15 000 000
                                                                      today        years since
                                                                                   Big Bang
```

```
                  0        2        4        6        8        10
                  14 900                                       15 000
                  million                                      million

                  first animals              rabbit           Homo
                  with pouches               rodents          erectus

                      ↓                                        (1 million
                  marsupials                 early primates    years ago)
                                             (monkeys etc.)
                                                               Modern
                                                               people

                                                               14 000 years ago
```

The Red Shift

Most stars and galaxies show something called a **red shift** when they are viewed through a **spectrometer**. The red shift is the lengthening or 'stretching' of light waves from a source which is moving away from us. The amount of shift represents the size of the recessional velocity of the star. A big red shift means the star is moving away at a very fast speed. The red shift effect is further evidence in support of the expanding (or Open) Universe theory.

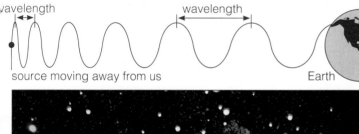

wavelength   wavelength

source moving away from us   Earth

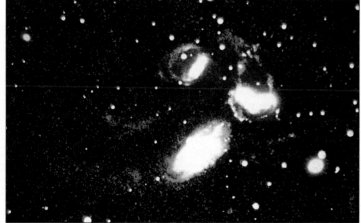

Stefan's Quartet group of galaxies – red shift is clearly visible. The blue areas are sources which are travelling at a slower speed.

Hubble's Constant (H)

$$H\ (s^{-1}) = \frac{\text{Recessional velocity (m/s)}}{\text{distance (m)}}$$

Hubble believed that the speed of recession increases with increasing distance. Whether H is truly constant or not is still open argument. The value for H ranges from $1.6 \times 10^{-18}\ s^{-1}$ — $3.2 \times 10^{-18}\ s^{-1}$. If this theory is correct then there would comes a time when some stars would be moving away from us at the full speed of light. These stars would be right out at the 'edge' of space – i.e. some of the very first matter emitted from the Big Bang explosion. No visible light could reach us from these stars as it would be shifted entirely out of the visible spectrum into the radio – such stars would be detected with radio telescopes.

The Hubble telescope is able to look in to very deep space

Q3 What does the term 'red shift' mean?

Q4 What can we find out from the red shift?

Q5 Assuming some stars are recessing at the speed of light, use Hubble's equation to determine the radius of the Universe.

Q6 Use Hubble's equation to give an upper and lower limit for the age of the Universe.

see science at work

■ **Materials and their uses**
Extension sheet 11 John Dalton's
atomic theory

The changing idea of atoms

The idea of atoms is an old one. It probably occurred first in Ancient
Greece during the period 450–400 B.C. Modern atomic theory began with
John Dalton in 1805. Since then, our ideas about atoms have changed
several times.

Dalton's model of the atom
Date: 1805

Atoms of different elements have different masses.

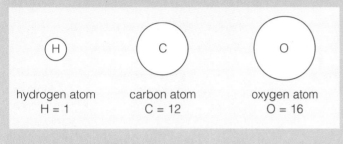

hydrogen atom   carbon atom   oxygen atom
H = 1   C = 12   O = 16

Atoms cannot be broken up.
Atoms are like billiard balls.

Dalton explained the differences between elements by
saying that their atoms had different masses.

Problems with Dalton's theory

1 In 1896 **radioactivity** was discovered. It showed
   that atoms can break up: during radioactive decay,
   heavy elements break up into light ones.
2 In 1897, J. J. Thomson, a Cambridge scientist,
   discovered the **electron**. It is a particle much lighter
   than an atom and is found inside all kinds of atom.

Thomson suggested another model of the atom: the
'plum pudding' model.

Thomson's 'plum pudding' model
of the atom
Date: 1900

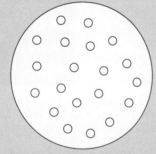

Electrons are dotted throughout the atom like plums
in a pudding.
Electrons carry negative charge. The rest of the
atom is positive.

Problems with Thomson's model

In 1911, Ernest Rutherford, a New Zealander working
in Manchester, proposed the 'nuclear atom', which
contradicted Thomson's model. Rutherford's
experiments showed that the atom was mostly empty
space, with a tiny nucleus at its centre. The nucleus
contained almost all the mass of the atom.

The nuclear atom
Date: 1911

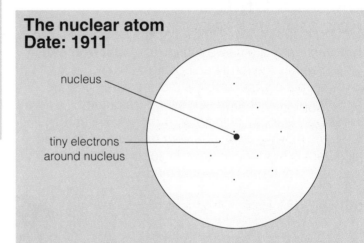

nucleus

tiny electrons
around nucleus

The nucleus is at the centre. It is tiny, but has a large
mass and is positively charged.
Very tiny electrons are negatively charged and exist
around the nucleus.

Rutherford proposed that the nucleus contained
positive particles called **protons**. He could not
explain the mass of atoms solely in terms of protons,
so he found that he had to invent another particle. As
this had to be neutral, he called it the **neutron**. It was
eventually discovered in 1932. Protons and neutrons
have the same mass, equal to that of the hydrogen
atom.

Sub-atomic particles

Particle	Relative mass	Relative charge	Where found in atom
proton	1	+1	in nucleus
neutron	1	0	in nucleus
electron	$\frac{1}{1840}$	-1	around nucleus

Atomic number and nucleon number

Atoms of elements are defined by two numbers called the nucleon number (A) and the atomic number (Z). Sodium has a nucleon number of 23 and an atomic number of 11:

$$^{23}_{11}\text{Na}$$

← nucleon number (mass number)
← atomic number (proton number)

atomic number = number of protons
= number of electrons
nucleon number = number of nucleons
(protons plus neutrons)

Both numbers are shown in the Periodic Table. The atomic number tells us which element it is and the nucleon number tells us the mass of the atom.

Example: $^{238}_{92}\text{U}$, uranium

The atomic number is 92. Uranium atoms contain 92 protons and also 92 electrons.

The nucleon number is 238. We know that 92 nucleons are protons. The rest, 238 – 92 = 146 are neutrons.

Isotopes of elements

In 1913 Thomson discovered that some elements could have atoms with different masses. They are called isotopes.

Isotopes are atoms of the same element which have different numbers of neutrons.

Example

Hydrogen has three isotopes ▶

The existence of isotopes explains why most relative atomic masses are not whole numbers.

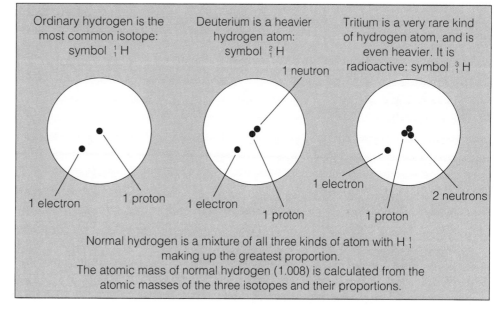

Ordinary hydrogen is the most common isotope: symbol ^1_1H

Deuterium is a heavier hydrogen atom: symbol ^2_1H

Tritium is a very rare kind of hydrogen atom, and is even heavier. It is radioactive: symbol ^3_1H

1 neutron
1 electron
1 proton
1 electron
1 proton
1 electron
1 proton
2 neutrons

Normal hydrogen is a mixture of all three kinds of atom with H $^1_1$ making up the greatest proportion.
The atomic mass of normal hydrogen (1.008) is calculated from the atomic masses of the three isotopes and their proportions.

The relative atomic mass of chlorine

Chlorine has two isotopes: $^{35}_{17}\text{Cl}$ and $^{37}_{17}\text{Cl}$. Natural chlorine gas is a mixture of both kinds of atom. They exist in the following proportions: 75% of $^{35}_{17}\text{Cl}$ and 25% of $^{37}_{17}\text{Cl}$.

The relative atomic mass of chlorine is the *average* mass of a chlorine atom. This is calculated below.

In 100 chlorine atoms, 75 are ^{35}Cl and 25 are ^{37}Cl.

Total mass of 100 atoms $= (75 \times 35) + (25 \times 37)$

$= 2625 + 925$

$= 3550$

Average mass of one atom is $3550 \div 100 = 35.5$

Relative atomic mass of chlorine is 35.5

Q1 What are the main differences between Thomson's plum pudding atom and Rutherford's nuclear atom?

Q2 Why are protons and neutrons known as nucleons?

Q3 Which came first, the idea of neutrons or their discovery?

Q4 Atomic number Z is sometimes called proton number. Why?

Q5 Nucleon number A is sometimes called mass number. Why?

Q6 What are the sub-atomic particles in $^{39}_{19}\text{K}$?

see science at work
■ **Making new materials**
p 32 Nuclear reactions

Radioactivity

Some isotopes are radioactive. They have unstable atomic nuclei which decay and give off radiation. The radiation can be of three types.

Radiation

alpha (α) radiation consists of helium nuclei: $^4_2\text{He}^{2+}$

beta (β) radiation consists of electrons

gamma (γ) radiation is short wavelength (high energy) electromagnetic radiation

The properties of radiation

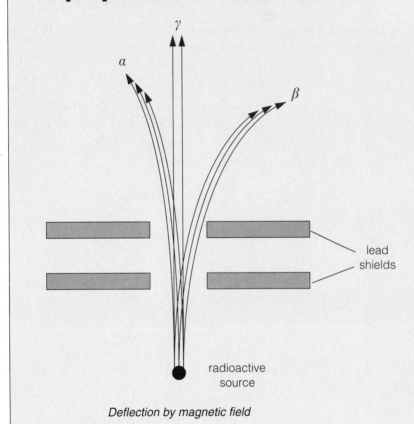

Deflection by magnetic field

Range in air
α rays: a few centimetres
β rays: a few metres
γ rays: a few kilometres

Penetrating power
α rays can pass through only 0.01 mm of metal
β rays can pass through 1 cm of metal
γ rays can pass through about 15 cm of metal

Radioactive decay is a natural *nuclear* reaction. Some radioactive elements decay quickly, others very slowly. The rate of decay is measured by the **half-life** of the isotope. Half-life is the time taken for half the atoms in a sample of radioactive material to decay. Different isotopes decay by emitting different types of radiation. Most radioactive isotopes eventually change into the element lead.

α-decay

An unstable nucleus can decay by α-decay by losing a helium nucleus $^4_2\text{He}^{2+}$. For example:

$$^{238}_{92}\text{U} \rightarrow \,^{234}_{90}\text{Th} + \,^4_2\text{He}$$

During α-decay, the nucleon number falls by 4 units and the proton number falls by 2 units.

β-decay

An unstable nucleus can decay by β-decay by losing an electron from the nucleus. The electron is provided when a neutron decays to a proton and an electron:

$$^1_0\text{n} \rightarrow \,^1_1\text{p}^+ + \,^{0}_{-1}\text{e}^-$$

An example of β-decay:

$$^{234}_{90}\text{Th} \rightarrow \,^{234}_{91}\text{Pa} + \,^{0}_{-1}\text{e}^-$$

During β-decay, the nucleon number remains unchanged but the proton number increases by one.

Some half-lives

Radioactive isotope	half-life
$_{92}^{238}$U (uranium)	4.5 billion years
$_{6}^{14}$C (carbon)	5700 years
$_{38}^{90}$Sr (strontium)	28 years
$_{53}^{131}$I (iodine)	8 days
$_{84}^{214}$Po (polonium)	0.00015 s

Graph showing radioactive decay

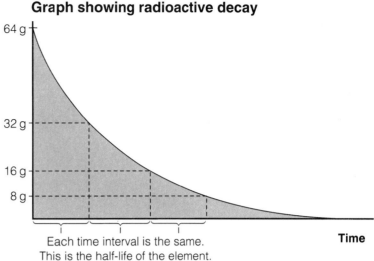

Mass of radioactive isotope

64 g, 32 g, 16 g, 8 g

Time

Each time interval is the same.
This is the half-life of the element.

Nuclear fission

Nuclear fission is an artificial nuclear reaction. 'Fission' means splitting up. Nuclear fission can yield huge amounts of energy and is the process used in nuclear power stations.

If a uranium-235 atom gains an extra neutron it splits:

$$_{92}^{235}U + _{0}^{1}n \rightarrow _{56}^{144}Ba + _{36}^{90}Kr + 2_{0}^{1}n + ENERGY!$$

Two neutrons are produced, which cause two more ^{235}U atoms to split, *each* of which produces two more neutrons.

This is a **chain reaction**: a controlled version is used in nuclear reactors; an uncontrolled version is used in nuclear bombs.

Some nuclear reactors produce radioactive waste with long half-lives. This has to be carefully disposed of to avoid polluting the environment for a long time.

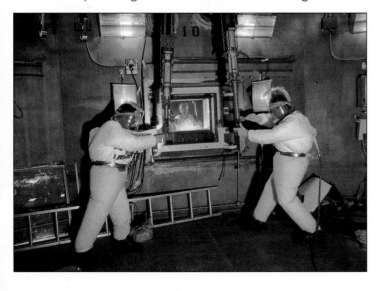

Nuclear fusion: The Holy Grail

Fusion is the opposite of fission: it means 'squeezing together'. A nuclear fusion reaction in which hydrogen nuclei fuse to produce helium occurs in the Sun. Vast amounts of energy are produced.

$$4_{1}^{1}H \rightarrow _{2}^{4}He + 2_{-1}^{0}e + \gamma\,rays$$

Since the late 1940s scientists have tried to produce a fusion reactor. A successful reactor would produce vast quantities of very cheap and non-polluting energy. Despite forty years of research, scientists have not yet managed to satisfy this quest.

Q1 Name each type of radiation and its associated electric charge (positive, negative or no charge).

Q2 α rays are deflected less by an electric field than β rays. What does this suggest about the relative masses of α and β particles?

Q3 Which type of radiation is most dangerous?

Q4 What differences are there between nuclear reactions and chemical reactions?

Q5 Explain how bombardment of uranium-235 leads to a chain reaction.

Q6 Why is nuclear fusion described as 'The Holy Grail'?

Organising the elements

Ask your teacher for a copy of the Periodic Table. It can be found in
SAW Copymasters 1.

Elements in the Periodic Table are listed in order of their atomic number
(proton number) and placed into groups of similar elements. Scientists
believe that the arrangement of electrons in an atom explains similarities
between elements. The atomic number of an element gives us the number
of electrons in an atom of the element as well as the number of protons.

Energy level structure

Electrons are arranged around the nucleus in **energy levels** or **shells**.
The shells or energy levels are numbered from the inside outwards.

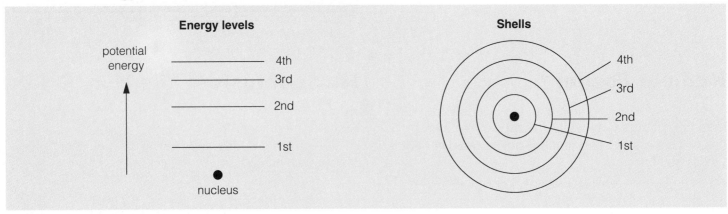

Each shell can only contain up to a certain number of electrons.

The first shell can contain up to **2** electrons.

The second shell can contain up to **8** electrons.

The third shell can contain up to **8** electrons.

Examples: chlorine and sodium

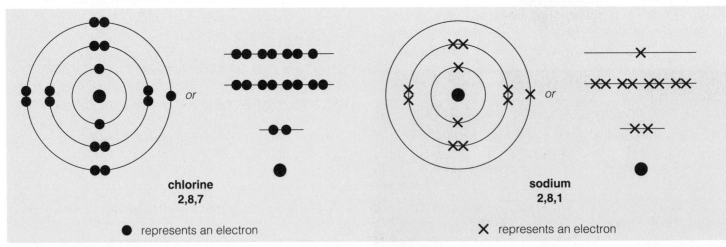

Diagrams like these complete our model of the atom. It has a nucleus
which contains protons and neutrons, and is surrounded by electrons
arranged in energy levels or shells. It is wrong to imagine electron shells as
being like the orbits of planets around the Sun. In reality, the movements of
electrons are much more complicated than the movements of planets.

Atoms of elements in the same group of the Periodic Table
have similar chemical properties.

The noble gases: Group 0

Element	Atomic number	Electron arrangement
helium	2	2
neon	10	2, 8
argon	18	2, 8, 8
krypton	36	2, 8, 8, (10), 8

The alkali metals: Group 1

Element	Atomic number	Electron arrangement
lithium	3	2, 1
sodium	11	2, 8, 1
potassium	19	2, 8, 8, 1
rubidium	37	2, 8, 8, (10), 8, 1

Reactivity and electron arrangement

The noble gases (Group 0) are unreactive elements: they are **stable**.
Their outer electron levels are full. Chemical stability seems to be related
to complete shells of electrons.

The alkali metals (Group 1) are all reactive. They have only one electron
in their outer level.

Group 7 elements are reactive non-metals. They have seven electrons in
their outer level: one electron less than a full shell.

The magic of chemistry

2Na + Cl$_2$ → **2NaCl**

Sodium and chlorine are very different, dangerous elements. When mixed
together and heated gently, sodium and chlorine react. A bright orange
flame is seen. All that remains after the reaction is a white powder called
sodium chloride.

The white powder, common salt, is not dangerous. In fact, in small
quantities, it is essential to life.

The theory of the atom and its electrons must be able to explain:
● why sodium and chlorine are reactive
● why they react with each other
● why sodium chloride is so different to the separate elements
● why sodium chloride is stable
● how sodium and chlorine stay together in sodium chloride.

Q1 **a** How many elements
are there in period 1?
How many electrons are needed
to fill the first energy level or shell?
b How many elements are there
in periods 2 and 3? How many
electrons are needed to fill the
second and third energy levels
or shells?

Q2 Look at the electron
arrangement of
rubidium and find rubidium
(atomic number 37) in the
Periodic Table. Why are ten
electrons shown in brackets?
Write out an electron arrangement
for bromine (atomic number 35).

Q3 In what ways are the
Group 1 elements (the
alkali metals) similar? How can
electronic arrangements explain
the similarities?

Q4 Draw diagrams of the
following atoms,
showing nucleon numbers and
electron arrangements:
a $^{7}_{3}$Li **b** $^{24}_{12}$Mg **c** $^{16}_{8}$O **d** $^{20}_{10}$Ne

How Chlorine and Sodium found love and stability

(this story first appeared in a national tabloid newspaper)

A story of true love at sub-atomic level

Chlorine TRUE LOVE Sodium

By our Daily Atom reporter

ONCE UPON A time there was an atom called Chlorine. Now, you might have thought that she was the happiest atom in the world – she had a slim attractive nucleus with only 17 protons and 18 neutrons in it (not like her tubby sister iodine who had 53 protons and 74 neutrons). Around this nucleus she had 17 electrons beautifully arranged in three energy levels – two in her first layer, eight in her second and seven in her third. Yet, for some reason she was never happy. She always felt excitable and on edge, as if she was missing something. Why, oh why, did she feel like this? Other atoms, like her next door neighbour Argon always seemed so relaxed and calm.

'Why are you so stable, Argon?' asked Chlorine one Friday night as they sat having a drink in a down town Quark bar. 'No matter what I do, I can never seem to settle down'.

'What you need' replied Argon 'is a good metal'.

'What do you mean, a good metal?' exclaimed Chlorine. 'I haven't noticed you running after any of them!'

'Ah' said Argon in her usual superior way, 'that's because I have a full outer energy level. You only have seven electrons in yours. That's why you feel the way you do. Now, any decent metal will sort out your problems for you. Personally, I've always had a soft spot for the alkali Metals. They're so exciting and reactive.'

Chlorine said nothing, but thought long and hard about what Argon had said to her. The next

Friday, she plucked up her courage, arranged her electrons as well as she could, and headed for the local singles bar. Sure enough, later that evening, in walked Sodium. She already knew him by sight: he was one of the wilder elements of the neighbourhood. He too

---

He looked around the bar, their eyes met … it was love at first sight!

---

was feeling restless – could it be because of his single outside electron?

He looked around the bar, their eyes met … it

The next Friday … she headed for the local singles bar.

was love at first sight! They rushed out into the night together, and Sodium gave Chlorine his outer shell electron! 'At last, my darling!' she sighed as she gratefully accepted the electron. Now, they both felt so stable, relaxed and happy.

Suddenly, they both realised that they had acquired an electric charge. Chlorine found that she had a negative charge, and Sodium found that he had a positive charge. They were puzzled, but not too worried since it seemed to bring them closer together.

So, off they went together into the sunset, under their married name of Sodium Chloride. They lived together in a commune with many other sodium and chloride ions for many years. Nothing changed the stability of their relationship until one day a stranger called Sulphuric Acid came amongst them – but that's another story.

After publication of the article, sodium and chlorine considered suing the newspaper for intrusions into their private lives. However, their lawyers decided that the newspaper had published the truth. Moreover the Government decided that this was a suitable romance for study by students at Key Stage 4!

The reaction between sodium metal and chlorine gas

Argon is an unreactive element because it has a *full* outer level of electrons.

Reactive **sodium** and reactive **chlorine** both become stable when they react with one another. **Sodium chloride is stable**.

Let us examine the electrons in sodium and in chlorine:

sodium, Na: 2,8,1
chlorine, Cl: 2,8,7

Neither sodium nor chlorine has a full outside shell. But if sodium were to *lose* one electron it would have the same electron arrangement as neon. If chlorine could *gain* one electron it would have an electron arrangement like argon. Thus both sodium and chlorine *could* have stable electron arrangements if sodium gave one electron to chlorine.

We believe that this *is* what happens when sodium metal is heated in chlorine gas. We have a theory which explains why, and what happens when, sodium reacts with chlorine.

Theory

Atoms react to become more like noble gases.

Atoms react to get full outer shells of electrons.

Electron transfer and ionic bonding

Study the diagram carefully.
The results of electron transfer are charged atoms called **ions**.

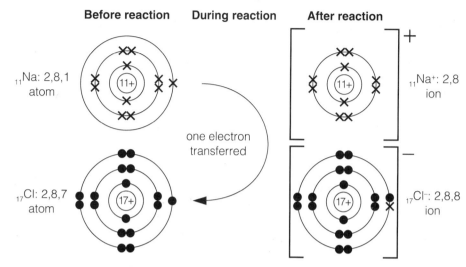

A shorthand diagram (only outer electrons shown)

$$Na× \quad + \quad :\overset{\cdot\cdot}{\underset{\cdot\cdot}{C}}l\cdot \quad \Rightarrow \quad [Na]^+ \quad [:\overset{\cdot\cdot}{\underset{\cdot\cdot}{C}}l\overset{\cdot}{×}]^-$$

$$\begin{matrix} (2,8,1) & (2,8,7) & (2,8) & (2,8,8) \\ \text{sodium atom} & \text{chlorine atom} & \text{sodium ion} & \text{chloride ion} \end{matrix}$$

Millions of positive sodium ions and negative chloride ions are formed during a chemical reaction. The resulting compound, sodium chloride, is made up of Na+ and Cl- ions:

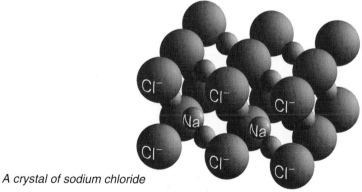

A crystal of sodium chloride

Sodium chloride is an **ionic** compound.

Q1 What are the outer electron levels of noble gases like?

Q2 Name two other elements which could react together by exchanging one electron.

Q3 Explain why a sodium ion has an overall charge of +1 but a sodium atom has no overall charge.

Q4 Explain why a chloride ion has an overall charge of −1 but a chlorine atom has no overall charge.

Q5 **Name a** an element which is likely to form an ion with two positive charges
b an element which is likely to form an ion with two negative charges.

Chemical bonding 2

Introduction

Ionic bonding takes place when electrons are transferred from one atom to another to make charged atoms, or ions. Removing electrons from atoms *always* requires energy. Adding electrons to atoms usually also requires energy.

Carbon's problem

Carbon atom: $^{12}_{6}$C, electron arrangement 2,4

For carbon to gain a stable noble gas electron arrangement it needs to lose four electrons or to gain four electrons. Both transfers require too much energy. In fact carbon does not form ions or ionic compounds. Carbon, however, *does* form many compounds, but using a different kind of bonding – **covalent** bonding.

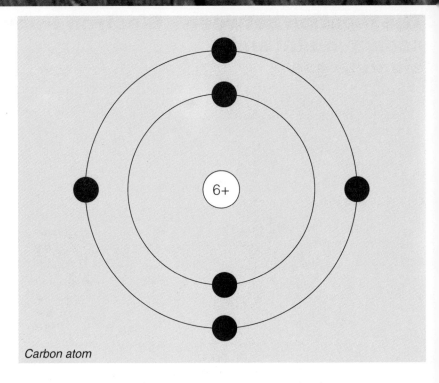

Carbon atom

Hydrogen fluoride

To understand covalent bonding let us look at the way hydrogen gas and fluorine gas react together. In fact, they react so readily that they explode. Look at the arrangement of electrons in each atom:

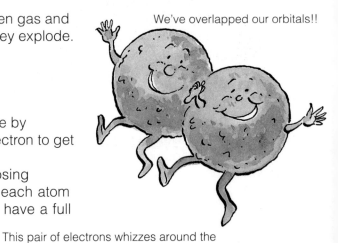

We've overlapped our orbitals!!

       hydrogen,   H : 1
       fluorine,   F : 2,7

We cannot explain the bonding between hydrogen and fluorine by transfer of electrons because both atoms need to gain one electron to get a full outer shell and become like noble gases.

   We can explain how hydrogen fluoride is formed by proposing another kind of bonding which involves **electron sharing**. If each atom shares one of its electrons with the other atom then both will have a full outer level of electrons.

This pair of electrons whizzes around the hydrogen nucleus and the fluorine nucleus. It forms the covalent bond.

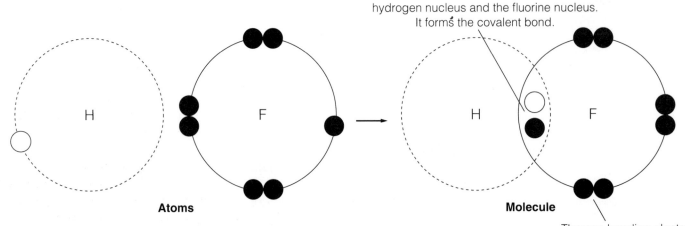

Atoms

Molecule

The non-bonding electrons s around the fluorine nucleus

A bond formed like this from a shared pair of electrons is called a **covalent bond**.

Molecules

When hydrogen and fluorine share an electron in this way they make a neutral **molecule** of hydrogen fluoride. In a chemical reaction between hydrogen and fluorine, many millions of hydrogen atoms will pair up with many millions of fluorine atoms to form many millions of *separate* hydrogen fluoride molecules.

The shared pair of electrons, or covalent bond, forms a negative electron cloud which pulls both positive atomic nuclei towards it. It is this *strong* force which holds molecules together.

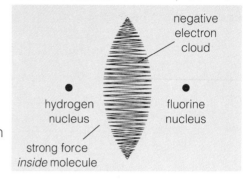

negative electron cloud

hydrogen nucleus

fluorine nucleus

strong force *inside* molecule

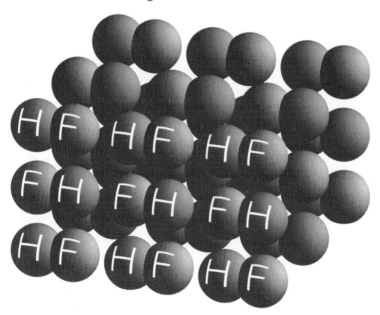

Molecular compounds

Covalent bonding, or electron sharing, makes molecules. Molecules are neutral. When they are packed tightly in solid compounds, molecules are only weakly attracted to one another.

Molecular compounds have *low* melting points and boiling points. Many are liquids and gases at room temperature. Molecular compounds are formed when non-metals bond together.

Many non-metallic elements form molecules, for example O_2, H_2, N_2, Cl_2.

Multiple covalent bonds

Oxygen, O_2

An oxygen atom has six outer level electrons.

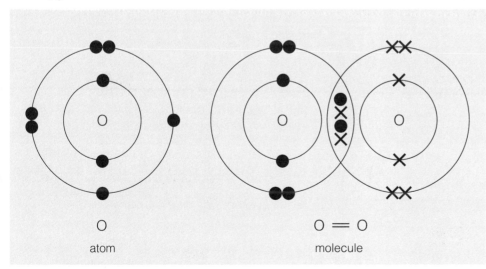

O

atom

O $=$ O

molecule

Two atoms can form a molecule if they share two pairs of electrons. This is called a double covalent bond.

Q1 Carbon is a Group 4 element. Which other groups contain elements which would form ions with difficulty?

Q2 What holds atoms together in a molecule?

Q3 Why are molecules neutral?

Q4 Why are molecules only weakly attracted to one another?

Q5 A nitrogen molecule, N_2 is held together by a triple covalent bond. Draw its electronic structure showing outer electrons only.

Structures of materials

see science at work
■ **Materials and their uses**
pp 5–8 What are materials like?
pp 13–21 Solids, liquids and gases
Extension sheets 1–7

How materials are put together

The properties of materials can be explained by looking at the kinds of particle they are made of and how those particles are put together.

We have seen two structures: ionic compounds and molecular compounds. Many materials have these structures.

Structure	Particle	How particles are held together in solid
ionic	ions (positive and negative)	strong electrostatic attraction
molecular	molecules	weak attraction

Some melting points of ionic and molecular materials

Material	Melting point/°C	Material	Melting point/°C
sodium chloride, NaCl	808	potassium chloride, KCl	767
water, H_2O	0	carbon dioxide, CO_2	–56
oxygen, O_2	–219	copper chloride, $CuCl_2$	498
glucose, $C_6H_{12}O_6$	146	ethanol, C_2H_5OH	–117
lead bromide, $PbBr_2$	370		

Q1 Which of the materials in the table are ionic and which are molecular? What patterns in melting point can you see? Can you explain these patterns in terms of forces between particles?

Reminder: Compounds formed from a metal and a non-metal are often ionic.
Compounds formed from a non-metal with another non-metal are molecular.

Ionic materials have high melting points and are solids at room temperature. Molecular materials have low melting points and are mostly gases and liquids at room temperature.

Electrical conductivity and structure

Theory

For a material to conduct electricity, it must contain charged particles which are free to move. These can be ions or electrons.

Sodium chloride is ionic, glucose is molecular and copper is metallic.

Material	Electrical conductivity
sodium chloride	poor
sodium chloride solution	good
molten sodium chloride	good
glucose	poor
glucose solution	poor
molten glucose	poor
copper	good
molten copper	good

Ionic materials are poor conductors when solid. They are good conductors when liquid or in aqueous solution.
Molecular materials are poor conductors under all conditions.
Metals are good conductors when liquid and solid.

Q2 Look at the table. What links can you see between structure and electrical conductivity? Can you explain any links with the Theory statement?

Explanations
Molecular materials are made out of neutral molecules and so cannot conduct electricity.

Ionic materials cannot conduct when solid because the ions can only vibrate about fixed positions. However when molten or in aqueous solution, ions become free to move and electrical conduction is possible.

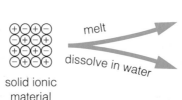

solid ionic material

melt

dissolve in water

liquid ionic material: ions free to move

aqueous solution: ions free to move amongst water molecules

The metallic structure

How can we explain that metals can conduct electricity when solid, and that they have high melting points?

Metal atoms are packed tightly together. Each atom gives up its outer level electrons to an 'electron cloud'. These electrons are free to move. Atomic cores are held strongly by negative electrons between them.

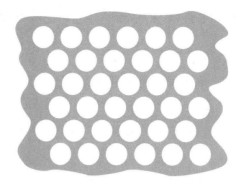

A solid metal structure: atomic cores surrounded by a cloud of mobile electrons

Q3 What properties of metals are explained by their structure?

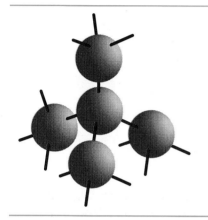

A tiny part of a diamond crystal showing one atom covalently bonded to four others. Every atom in the crystal is similarly bonded.

Another kind of structure: macromolecules

Diamond, which is pure carbon, has a very high melting point but does not conduct electricity under any conditions. It is also the hardest known natural material.

In diamond crystal containing millions of carbon atoms, each atom is covalently bonded to four others. The entire crystal is a single molecule held together by strong covalent bonds.

Q4 What properties of diamond are explained by its structure?

Plastics are a major class of material made out of macromolecules. Polythene, for example, is made of very long hydrocarbon macromolecular chains, called **polymers**. The arrangement of chains determines the properties of the plastic, as shown in the diagrams.

Fibres are another major class of material made out of long, polymer macromolecules. There are several different types: some are natural and some synthetic.

Glass has a complex structure. It is essentially a mixture of calcium and sodium silicates, which are ionic. Different kinds and different colours of glass are produced by different additives.

Polythene with tangled chains – low density, useful for carrier bags

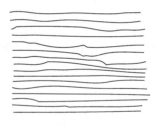

Polythene with tightly packed chains – high density, useful for rigid containers

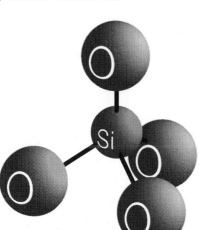

Ceramics also have a complex structure involving both ionic and covalent bonding. Ceramics are made from clays which contain silicon dioxide (SiO_2), aluminium oxide (Al_2O_3) and varying amounts of other oxides.

Ceramics have a crystalline structure built out of silicon–oxygen units.

Some ceramics, like asbestos, are made of rings or chains of silicon–oxygen units joined at two corners. Units joined at three corners produce sheets or planes; mica has this structure. Quartz is an example of a ceramic made out of units joined at four corners.

Glass is essentially a type of ceramic, but one which does not have a crystalline structure.

Properties/uses of materials

see science at work

■ **Materials and their uses**
pp 5–12 What are materials like?

Properties can be measured and given a number – they are **quantifiable**. Properties of a particular class of material will show a range of values; for example, all metals conduct electricity, but some are better conductors than others.

Table 1 shows the **electrical resistivity** of some metals, which is measured in $\Omega\,m$ (ohm metres). The smaller the electrical resistivity, the better the metal is at conducting electricity. Electrical resistivity is given the symbol ρ_e.

Material	Resistivity ρ_e ($\times 10^{-8}\,\Omega\,m$)
Al	2.45
Ag	1.50
Cu	1.56
Fe	8.9
Sn	11.5
U	4.9
Au	2.04

Table 1 Electrical resisitvity of some metals

Q1 Which metal is the best conductor?.

Q2 Which metal has the highest electrical resistivity?

Q3 What do you think is meant by electrical resistivity?

We can compare the electrical resistivity of metals with that of other materials. Look at Table 2.

Name of material	Type of material	$\rho_e \times 10^{-8}\,\Omega\,m$
electrical porcelain	ceramic	$10^{18} - 10^{20}$
bakelite	plastic	10^{22}
vitreous silica	glass	10^{11}

Table 2

Q4 Which is the best insulator of the materials in Table 2?

Q5 Suggest a use for this material.

Q6 Why is a range of values given for electrical porcelain?

When choosing a material for a job, it is not usually sufficient to consider just one property. A range of properties must be looked at, and the best combination found.

Name of material	Density $g\,cm^{-3}$	Tensile strength $MN\,m^{-2}$	Compressive strength $MN\,m^{-2}$	Moisture expansivity $\times 10^{-3}$	Combustibility	Moisture resistance VG = very good G = good F = fair P = poor
high tensile steel	7700	340 (yield strength)	340	–	melts at 400°C	–
timber (oak)	720	21 (parallel to grain)	15	0.4–0.5	burns	F
plywood	600–700	8–16	5–8	0.7–3.4	burns	F
plasterboard	700–1300	2–5	–	0.1–0.7	weakens	P
common brick	1500–1800	depends on joints	7–70	0.1	does not burn	VG
concrete	2200–2400	cracks unless reinforced	20–35	0.2–0.6	stable	VG
rigid plastic	1250–2500	40–60	40–60	–	melts at 200°C	VG

Table 3 Properties of building materials

Table 3 shows some of the many properties which must be considered when choosing building materials. Appearance, cost and safety are all important factors, as well as the performance of the materials under different conditions.

Use the information in the table to answer the questions.

Q7 What is meant by
a tensile strength
b compressive strength?

Q8 Which material expands most on exposure to moisture?.

Q9 Select three properties which it would be important to consider when choosing a material for external walls. Explain your choices.

Q10 How might your choices be different if you were choosing a material for an internal wall?

Changing the properties of materials

It is often necessary to modify the properties of material to make them more suitable for a particular job. There are many ways that this can be done. In **Materials and their uses**, you saw that the tensile strength of materials could be improved by using them to produce composite materials. For example concrete cracks unless it is reinforced by steel rods (see Table 3).

Metal	Density $\rho\,\mathrm{mg\,cm^{-3}}$	Resistance to corrosion
Al	10.50	very good
Cu	8.94	good
Au	19.32	excellent
Ag	2.70	very good
Sn	7.31	v good
Fe	7.86	poor

Table 4

Properties of metals can be changed by physical means, for example **heat treatment**, **coldworking** and **alloying**.

Coldworking involves rolling, drawing or otherwise deforming a metal at room temperature.

Heat treatment has several forms. **Tempering** means suddenly cooling a metal from a high temperature. **Precipitation hardening** also involves sudden cooling from a high temperature, but it is followed by reheating to a lower temperature. Precipitates form in the metal, which increase its hardness.

Alloying involves mixing metals in fixed proportions. There are hundreds of different alloys.

Objects made of metal alloy

Cold working, a steel milling machine

Moles 1

see science at work

■ **Materials and their uses**
p 33 More about the Periodic Table of elements
Extension sheet 11 John Dalton's atomic theory

How many oranges?

How many atoms?

It is easy to count a number of large 'particles' like oranges, but it is impossible to count the number of sulphur atoms simply by looking at the photos. Atoms (and ions, molecules and electrons) are too small to count. Yet there are many times, for example in medicine, pharmacy, and the food industry, when scientists need to know how many particles of a material they have. Although we cannot count these tiny particles, we *can* calculate how many there are. The idea of moles allows us to do this. To understand this idea, try doing this 'thought experiment'.

A thought experiment

Begin with two familiar elements: hydrogen and carbon. Take one atom of each.

Question
How many times heavier is the atom of carbon than the atom of hydrogen?

Answer: 12 times heavier

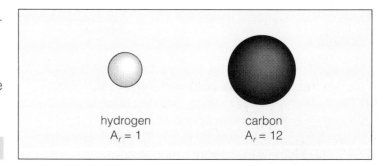

hydrogen
$A_r = 1$

carbon
$A_r = 12$

Now take 10 hydrogen atoms and 10 carbon atoms. The mass of 10 hydrogen atoms is 10, and the mass of 10 carbon atoms is 120.

Question
How many times heavier than the hydrogen atoms are the carbon atoms?

Answer: 12 times heavier

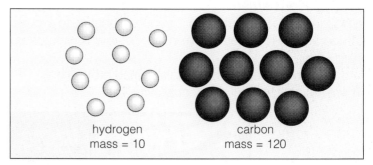

hydrogen
mass = 10

carbon
mass = 120

Now take 100 hydrogen atoms and 100 carbon atoms. The mass of 100 hydrogen atoms is 100 and the mass of 100 carbon atoms is 1200.

Question
How many times heavier than the hydrogen atoms are the carbon atoms?

Answer: 12 times heavier

You can see that if we take the *same number* of hydrogen atoms and carbon atoms, the carbon atoms will always be *12 times* heavier than the hydrogen atoms.

Suppose we now take enough hydrogen atoms to make 1g of hydrogen. If we take the same number of carbon atoms the mass of the carbon will be … 12g!

A **mole** of any material contains as many particles as there are in exactly 12g of carbon.

A mole of particles is an extremely large number called 'Avogadro's constant'. It is given the symbol L. Avogadro's constant $L = 6.02 \times 10^{23}$ = 602 000 000 000 000 000 000 000

1 mole of hydrogen atoms contains 6.02×10^{23} atoms and has a mass of 1g.

1 mole of carbon atoms contains 6.02×10^{23} atoms and has a mass of 12g.

If a mole of a material is measured out in grams, this quantity is called its **molar mass**. The molar mass of any element is its relative atomic mass in grams (g).

Although we have so far used atoms of elements as our examples, we have been careful to mention other particles. It is not only atoms that are 'counted' in moles – molecules, ions, and electrons are too.

If the material to be 'counted' is a compound we use **relative molecular mass** instead of relative atomic mass.

Water has a relative molecular mass of 18.

1 mole of water contains 6.02×10^{23} molecules and has a mass of 18g.

Molar masses of some elements

1 mole of sodium chloride (58.5 g)

1 mole of sodium chloride has a mass of 58.5g. It contains 6.02×10^{23} sodium ions and 6.02×10^{23} chloride ions.

Electrons can also be counted in moles. 1 mole of electrons has a charge of 96 500 coulombs (1 Faraday). This idea is used in work on electrolysis.

The idea of the mole is important because it allows us to calculate the number of particles in a material from its mass.

$$\text{Number of moles} = \frac{\text{Mass of material}}{\text{Molar mass}}$$

In the next section we look at why this is so useful.

Q1 How many particles are there in 2 moles of atoms?

Q2 What is the molar mass of
  a lithium
  b nitrogen
  c lead?

1 mole of ice (18 g)

Moles 2

1 Combining atoms

When sodium metal and chlorine gas react together, millions of sodium atoms react with millions of chlorine molecules to make sodium chloride, NaCl.

For every mole of sodium atoms that reacts, a mole of chlorine atoms also reacts. The formula of sodium chloride shows this: NaCl.

The formula of a different compound, magnesium fluoride, is MgF_2. This shows us that every mole of magnesium atoms combines with two moles of fluorine atoms. If we know the masses of materials that react together, we can use moles to work out the formula of the compound. When atoms combine, they do so in **fixed proportions**.

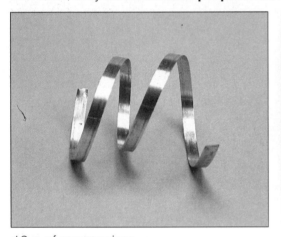

12 g of magnesium … reacts with 8 g of oxygen … making magnesium oxide

0.5 moles of magnesium react with 0.5 moles of oxygen
We change the fractions to a **whole number ratio**.

> 0.5 moles Mg: 0.5 moles O
> = 1 mole Mg : 1 mole O

The formula of magnesium oxide is MgO.

2 Moles in gases

It is usually easier to measure the volume of a gas than its mass. The idea of moles allows us to calculate the number of particles of a gas from its volume. In **Materials and their uses**, you found out that the volume of a gas varies with temperature and pressure. When we measure the volume of a gas, we must specify the temperature and pressure at which the measurements are made. Volumes are usually quoted at **standard temperature and pressure** (s.t.p.) which is 0°C (273K) and 1 atmosphere.

The volume of one mole of a gas is called its **molar volume**.

oxygen 32g   hydrogen 2g   chlorine 71g   xenon 131g

Information

Volumes of gases, solutions and pure liquids are measured in **cubic decimetres, dm^3**.

1 litre = $1 dm^3$ = $1000 cm^3$

At s.t.p. the molar volume of any gas is 22.4 dm^3.

$$\text{Number of moles of a gas} = \frac{\text{volume of gas (dm}^3\text{)}}{22.4 \ dm^3}$$

see further science copymasters

■ **Chemical changes**
Finding the formula of copper oxide
Finding the formula of zinc iodine □ Moles and formulae
Reacting mass calculations

Chemical changes

3 Moles in solution

Many chemical reactions take place in solutions. This means the materials are dissolved in water or some other solvent. To allow us to calculate the number of particles in these reactions, we use the idea of a **molar solution**.

A molar solution contains 1 mole of a material dissolved in 1 dm⁻³ of solution.

The molarity of a solution tells us its concentration, or how many moles are dissolved in one dm^3 of solution.

A solution of copper sulphate which contains 1 mole of copper sulphate (250 g) dissolved in 1 litre of solution has a concentration of $1 mol dm^{-3}$.

A solution of copper sulphate which contains 5 moles of copper sulphate (1250 g) dissolved in 1 litre of solution has a concentration of $5 mol dm^{-3}$.

Number of moles of solute = molarity of solution ($mol\ dm^{-3}$) × volume of solution (dm^3)

The idea of molar solutions is used in analysis.

0.02 m   1 m   5 m

Q1 What is meant by s.t.p.?

Q2 Why is it necessary to quote volumes of gases at s.t.p?

Q3 Volumes of gases and liquids are measured in dm^3. How many cubic centimetres (cm^3) are there in $1 dm^3$?

Q4 What is meant by a molar solution?

Q5 A solution of copper sulphate is made with two-hundredths of a mole of copper sulphate and 1 litre of water.
a What is the weight of two-hundredths of a mole of copper sulphate?
b What is the concentration of the solution?

see science at work

■ **Making new materials**
Extension sheet 4
Symbols, formulae and equations

Formulae and equations

In **Moles 2** you saw that the formula of a material gives the ratio of the number of atoms of each element combined in the material. It is not always convenient (or possible) to find out formulae by carrying out experiments.

A quick and convenient method of writing formulae uses the idea of **valency**.

Valency theory

In the **Materials** module you can learn that when atoms combine they gain, lose or share electrons. The numbers of electrons an atom gains, loses or shares when it combines is called its valency. Atoms usually (but not always) get a full outside shell of electrons when they combine.

The valencies of some elements can be worked out from the Periodic Table. For example, sodium in Group I (electronic configuration 2.8.1) loses one electron to gain a full outside shell, forming a sodium **ion** (electronic configuration 2.8). The valency of sodium is therefore **1**.

The table shows how valency is linked to group number in the Periodic Table.

Group number	I	II	III	IV	V	VI	VII	0
Valency	1	2	3	4	3	2	1	0

Some elements have more than one valency. If this is the case, the valency is written after the name. For example,

copper (I) oxide … copper has a valency of **1**.

copper (II) oxide … copper has a valency of **2**.

Q1 What is the valency of the following elements?
a fluorine
b calcium
c oxygen
d phosphorus
e sulphur in sulphur (IV) oxide
f sulphur in sulphur (VI) oxide

Q2 Use the 'crossover' rule to find the formulae of these compounds:
a calcium fluoride
b aluminium oxide
c iron (III) chloride
d iron (II) chloride
e sodium oxide.

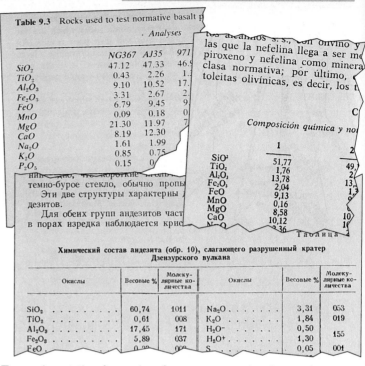

To work out the formula of a compound using valency theory, follow these simple steps:

Write the name of the compound.	⟹	magnesium chloride
Write the symbol of each element.	⟹	Mg Cl
Write the valency of each element underneath its symbol.	⟹	2 1
Cross over the valencies.	⟹	1 2
The crossed over valencies tell us the number of moles of each element in the compound.	⟹	1 mole of magnesium 2 moles of chlorine

The formula of magnesium chloride is Mg Cl$_2$

More examples of the 'crossover' rule can be found in Copymaster *Using the 'crossover' rule to find formulae* and *Writing balanced symbol equations*.

Writing chemical equations

You are familiar with the use of equations to represent chemical reactions. An equation tells us which materials react together (the **reactants**), and the new materials that are made (the **products**).

Equations can be written as words or as symbols. Like formulae, symbol equations can be found by experiment, or they can be worked out!

When materials react, bonds between atoms in the reactants are broken. These atoms then combine in a different way, forming new chemical bonds. See the **Energy in chemistry** section.

Reactants and products have the same number of each type of atom. They are simply combined in different ways.

A simple example shows this. When carbon burns in oxygen, carbon dioxide is made. Both reactants and products have a total of one carbon atom and two oxygen atoms, combined in different ways. $C + O_2 \Rightarrow CO_2$

Writing a symbol equation

A familiar reaction is the combustion of methane. We will write a balanced symbol equation for this reaction.

Step 1 Write the word equation for the reaction.

Methane + oxygen ⇒ carbon dioxide + water

Step 2 Write the formula for each material involved in the reaction (use the crossover rule if necessary).

$$CH_4 + O_2 \Rightarrow CO_2 + H_2O$$

Step 3 Count the total numbers of each atom in the reactants and in the products.

You can see that there are not equal numbers of each type of atom. The equation is not balanced.

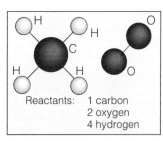

Reactants: 1 carbon
             2 oxygen
             4 hydrogen

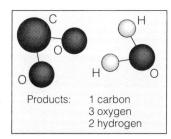

Products: 1 carbon
            3 oxygen
            2 hydrogen

Step 4 Alter the number of molecules of reactants and /or products until there is an equal number of atoms on each side of the equation.

There will probably be some trial and error involved here!

The diagrams show how this can be done for the combustion of methane. We have added one molecule of oxygen to the reactants, and one molecule of water to the products. There are equal numbers of carbon, oxygen and hydrogen atoms on each side. The equation is balanced.

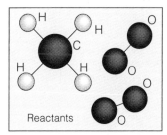

Reactants

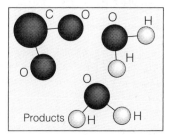

Products

Step 5 Write the symbol equation, showing the number of moles of each reactant and product.

$$CH_4 + 2O_2 \Rightarrow CO_2 + 2H_2O$$

A chemical equation can also show us whether each material is a solid, a liquid, a gas, or dissolved in water. This is done by putting a **state symbol** after each formula.

State symbols	
(g) gas	(s) solid
(l) liquid	(aq) in aqueous solution
	(dissolved in water)

Step 6 Add state symbols to the equation.

$$CH_4(g) + 2O_2(g) \Rightarrow CO_2(g) + 2H_2O(g)$$

The equation tells us that:
1 mole of methane gas reacts with 2 moles of oxygen gas, making one mole of carbon dioxide gas and 2 moles of water vapour.

You can see that the equation is a much more concise way of describing the reaction!

Electrolysis

see science at work
■ **Making new materials**
p 22 Extracting metals using electricity

The manufacture of sodium by electrolysis

Sodium is extracted from molten sodium chloride by electrolysis. Sodium chloride is an ionic compound which conducts electricity when molten because its ions can move.

During electrolysis, positive ions are attracted to the cathode and negative ions are attracted to the anode.

Electroplating

Electrolysis can be used to form a very thin coating of a metal on the surface of another metal. The surface must be made the cathode of an electrolytic cell.

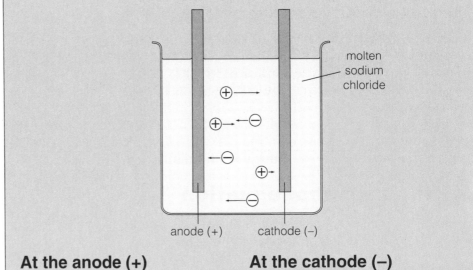

molten sodium chloride

anode (+)   cathode (−)

At the anode (+)
Cl⁻ ions arrive and lose their extra electron to the anode. Chlorine gas is formed.

$$2Cl^- - 2e^- \Rightarrow Cl_2$$

chloride ions — electrons to anode — chlorine molecule

At the cathode (−)
Na⁺ ions arrive and gain an electron from the cathode. Sodium metal is formed, as atoms.

$$Na^+ + e^- \Rightarrow Na$$

sodium ion — electron from cathode — sodium atom

Copper plating by electrolysis

Q1 Positive ions are called **cations** and negative ions are called **anions**. Explain why this is so.

Q2 Write anode and cathode equations like those above for the electrolysis of molten aluminium oxide. See **Making new materials**, p.22. Aluminium oxide contains the ions Al^{3+} and O^{2-}. Aluminium metal is produced at the cathode and oxygen gas O_2 is produced at the anode.

Q3 Write anode and cathode equations for the electrolysis of brine. See **Making new materials**, p.25. Brine is sodium chloride solution: it contains the ions Na^+, H^+, Cl^-, and OH^- in which H^+ and OH^- come from water.

Quantitative electrolysis

1 Measuring the quantity of electricity required to deposit one mole of silver

Experiment
An electric current is passed through silver nitrate solution. The mass of silver deposited is measured. The current flowing is measured with an ammeter and the time allowed for the experiment is noted.

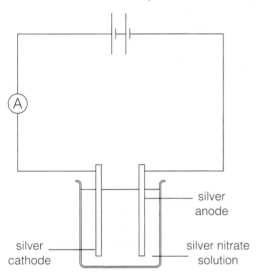

silver anode
silver cathode
silver nitrate solution

Results
Increase in mass of silver cathode = 0.403 g
Current = 0.1A
Time = 1 hr

Cathode reaction
$Ag^+ + e^- \Rightarrow Ag$

Calculation
The calculation assumes that the charge carried by silver ions is +1. The cathode reaction equation shows that 1 mole of electrons will be required to deposit one mole of silver.

Step 1
Total charge passed (coulombs) = current (amps) × time (s)
$$= 0.1 \times 3600 \, C$$
$$= 360 \, C$$

Step 2

0.403 g silver was deposited by 360 C

1 g silver would be deposited by $\dfrac{360}{0.403}$ C

108 g silver (1 mole) would be deposited by $\dfrac{360}{0.403} \times 108 \, C = 96\,500 \, C$

> The quantity of electricity 96 500 C
> is known as 1 Faraday (1 F).
> 1 Faraday is the charge carried by 1 mole of electrons.

2 Using electrolysis to measure the charge carried by copper ions in copper sulphate

Experiment
A similar experiment to the previous one is carried out.

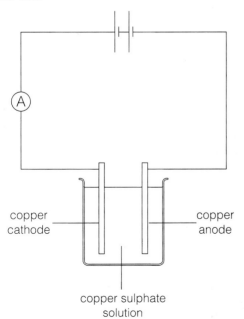

copper cathode
copper anode
copper sulphate solution

Results
Increase in mass of copper cathode = 0.179 g
Current = 0.2A
Time = 45 minutes

Cathode reaction
$Cu^{n+} + ne^- \Rightarrow Cu$ where n is a number to be found out

Calculation
The calculation assumes that the charge carried by 1 mole of electrons is 1 Faraday (96 500 C). The number of moles of electrons required to deposit 1 mole of copper is calculated.

Step 1   Total charge passed = 0.2 × 45 × 60 C
$$= 540 \, C$$

Step 2   0.179 g of copper was deposited by 540 C

1 g of copper would be deposited by $\dfrac{540}{0.179}$ C

64 g (1 mole) of copper would be deposited
by $\dfrac{540}{0.179} \times 64 \, C = 193\,073 \, C$

Step 3 $193\,073 \, C = \dfrac{193\,073}{96\,500} F = 2F$

2 moles of electrons are required to deposit 1 mole of copper. The charge carried by the copper ion is +2.

Energy in chemistry

see science at work
■ **Making new materials**
pp 3–13 Chemical reactions

Chemical reactions involve **energy changes**.

Some chemical reactions release energy to the surroundings as light, heat and sound. These reactions are **exothermic**. Other reactions *take in* energy from the surroundings. In the reaction shown on the far right, the tube becomes cold as ammonium nitrate is added to water. This type of reaction is **endothermic**.

Burning methane

A familiar exothermic reaction, the combustion of methane, can be used to explain these energy changes.

We can represent the energy changes during this reaction on an energy level diagram.

For an exothermic reaction, the reactants (methane and oxygen) contain more energy than the products (carbon dioxide and water). The difference is produced as heat (and some light).

As the reactants change to products, energy is released to the surroundings. This energy is called the **heat of the reaction** or the **enthalpy change of the reaction**. It is given the symbol ΔH.

Reactants
$CH_4(g) + 2O_2(g)$

Products
$CO_2(g) + 2H_2O(g)$

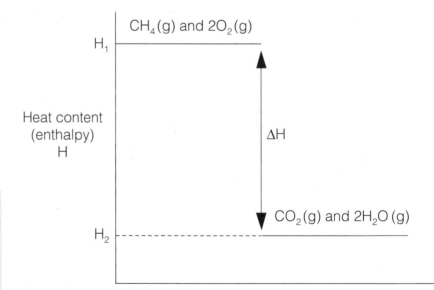

Heat content (enthalpy) H

H_1 — $CH_4(g)$ and $2O_2(g)$

ΔH

H_2 — — — $CO_2(g)$ and $2H_2O(g)$

Q1 The formation of ammonia from hydrogen and nitrogen is an endothermic reaction:
$3H_2(g) + N_2(g) \Rightarrow 2NH_3(g)$
a Which will have the greater heat content: the product (ammonia) or the reactants (hydrogen and nitrogen)?
b Sketch an energy level diagram for this reaction. Show ΔH on your diagram.
c Is the value for ΔH positive or negative? Explain your answer.

The enthalpy change of a chemical reaction is defined as:

$$\Delta H = \frac{\text{heat content}}{\text{of products}} (H_2) - \frac{\text{heat content}}{\text{of reactants}} (H_1)$$

The units of ΔH are kilojoules per mole, $kJ\,mol^{-1}$. For any exothermic reaction, such as the combustion of methane, ΔH is *negative* because the heat content of the products is *lower* than that of the reactants.

Breaking and making bonds

In *all* chemical reactions, bonds between atoms in the reactants must be
broken. Breaking bonds requires energy. New bonds are then made as
the products are formed. When bonds are made, energy is released.

The difference between the energy released when making new bonds
and the energy used when breaking old bonds is the overall enthalpy
change of the reaction.

In an **endothermic reaction** more energy is used to break the bonds
than is released by making them, so energy has to be added to the system.

In an **exothermic reaction** less energy is used to break the bonds than
is released by making them, so energy is released from the system.

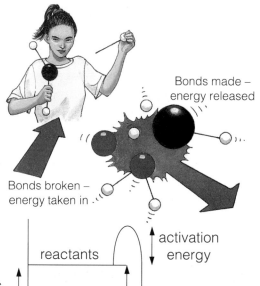

Bonds made –
energy released

Bonds broken –
energy taken in

Starting reactions

A mixture of methane and oxygen is stable. No reaction takes place until the
mixture is ignited (a spark may be sufficient). Many other exothermic reactions
require an initial input of energy to start them. This is called the **activation
energy** of the reaction. It is shown on an energy diagram as a 'hill'.

The energy put in to start the reaction is released once the reaction
begins. It does not affect the overall enthalpy change, ΔH. The idea of
activation energy can explain how catalysts alter the rate of a chemical
reaction. A catalyst lowers the activation energy of a reaction, allowing it to
take place at a lower temperature.

activation
energy

reactants

H

ΔH

products

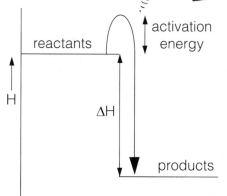

Electrical energy from chemical energy

Copymaster *Measuring the enthalpy change of a reaction* outlines an
experiment in which zinc powder is added to copper sulphate solution.

The reaction is exothermic – energy is released, and the temperature of
the solution rises. In a displacement reaction like this, it is possible to
obtain *some* of the energy released as electrical energy. This is what
happens in an electrical cell (several cells make a battery).

We can write an ionic equation for this reaction:
$Zn(s) + Cu^{2+}(aq) \Rightarrow Zn^{2+}(aq) + Cu(s)$

and (theoretically) separate it into two halves:
$Zn(s) \Rightarrow Zn^{2+}(aq) + 2e^-$ and $Cu^{2+}(aq) + 2e^- \Rightarrow Cu(s)$

In this reaction, electrons are transferred from zinc atoms to copper ions.
If the two halves of the reaction are separated, and the electrons allowed
to pass from zinc to copper through a wire, we have an **electrical
current**. The reaction produces **electrical energy**.

To understand why electrons flow from zinc to copper, think about the
activity series for metals:

Zinc is more reactive than copper.
It loses electrons more readily than copper.
It forms ions in solution more readily than copper.

So $Zn \Rightarrow Zn^{2+} + 2e^-$ takes place more readily than $Cu \Rightarrow Cu^{2+} + 2e^-$.

Q2 Name two reactions
which need activation
energy to make them go at
room temperature.

Q3 Use the idea of activation
energy to explain why
glucose must be heated to make it
react with oxygen in the laboratory,
whereas respiration takes place at
body temperature.

Q4 Use the idea of
activation energy to
explain why chemical reactions
go faster at higher temperatures.

Equilibrium

Reversible reactions

Some chemical reactions are reversible. Many are not; think of trying to 'uncook' an egg!

If blue copper sulphate is heated, white anhydrous copper sulphate and water are made.
$$CuSO_4 \cdot 5H_2O \Rightarrow CuSO_4 + 5H_2O$$

If water is added to anhydrous copper sulphate, blue hydrated copper sulphate reforms.
$$CuSO_4 + 5H_2O \Rightarrow CuSO_4 \cdot 5H_2O$$

These two reactions can be represented by one equation. The symbol $\rightleftharpoons$ shows that the reaction is reversible.
$$\underset{\text{blue}}{CuSO_4 \cdot 5H_2O} \rightleftharpoons \underset{\text{white}}{CuSO_4 + 5H_2O}$$

Now let us look at an example where both parts of a reversible reaction take place at the same time.

Heating copper carbonate

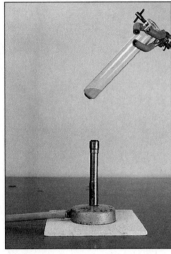 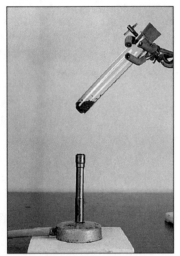

If green copper carbonate is heated in an open container, carbon dioxide gas and black copper oxide are made:
$$CuCO_3 \Rightarrow CuO + CO_2$$
The reaction goes to completion: all the copper carbonate is changed to copper oxide and carbon dioxide.

If copper carbonate is heated in a *closed* container, the carbon dioxide cannot escape. Some of the carbon dioxide reacts with some of the copper oxide, making copper carbonate. A point is reached where all three materials are present.

$$\underset{\text{green}}{CuCO_3} \rightleftharpoons \underset{\text{black}}{CuO + CO_2}$$

Both reactions take place at the same time. If we do not change the external conditions of the reaction (the pressure, temperature or amounts of materials) both reactions will eventually go at the same rate.

The amounts of each material will be fixed. The reaction is said to have 'reached equilibrium'.

The stages of reaching equilibrium are summarised on the right.

Reaching equilibrium

Start $A+B \longrightarrow$ Lots of A and B: fast forward reaction

Later $A+B \rightharpoonup\!\!\leftharpoondown\; C+D$ Less A and B, some C and D: slower forward reaction, backward reaction beginning.

Later still $A+B \rightleftharpoons C+D$ Less A and B, more C and D: forward reaction slower still, backward reaction rate increasing.

At equilibrium $A+B \rightleftharpoons C+D$ Rates of forward and backward reactions equal. Amounts of A, B, C and D *fixed* though not necessarily *equal*.

Changing the position of equilibrium

Dinitrogen tetroxide is a colourless gas which dissociates to brown nitrogen dioxide. Molecules of nitrogen dioxide will reform dinitrogen tetroxide:

$$N_2O_4 \rightleftharpoons 2NO_2$$
colourless   brown

It is important to recognise that energy changes associated with reactions are also reversible.
For this reaction $\Delta H = 57 \, kJ \, mol^{-1}$
By convention, the energy change for the forward reaction ($N_2O_4 \Rightarrow 2NO_2$) is given.

In this example, the positive enthalpy change means the forward reaction is endothermic. The energy change for the opposite reaction ($2NO_2 \Rightarrow N_2O_4$) is therefore $-57 \, kJ \, mol^{-1}$ and exothermic.

The flask on the left contains an equilibrium mixture of dinitrogen tetroxide and nitrogen dioxide.

equilibrium mixture   equilibrium after warming

Changing the temperature of the reaction

If the flask is gently warmed, the colour becomes darker. More NO_2 and less N_2O_4 must now be in the flask. The position of equilibrium bas changed. It has moved to the right.

Q1 Explain in your own words what is meant by dynamic equilibrium.

Q2 Carbon dioxide gas and hydrogen gas will react to make methanol. The reaction is reversible:
CO_2 (g) + $2H_2$ (g) $\rightleftharpoons$ CH_3OH (g) $\Delta H = -92$ kJ
State and explain what will happen to the concentration of methanol, CH_3OH at equilibrium if:
a the temperature is increased
b the volume of the container is made smaller
c more hydrogen is added to the container.

Changing the pressure of the reaction

The pressure is increased by pushing in the plunger. The colour becomes momentarily darker as molecules are squashed together. The next instant the colour lightens as more dinitrogen tetroxide is made. The equilibrium position changes; it moves to the left.

This shows that we can alter the amounts of materials present at equilibrium (in other words the position of equilibrium) by changing the external reaction conditions. The equilibrium position can also be changed by altering the amounts of materials.

Changes in equilibrium systems such as these were described by the French chemist Le Chatelier.

Le Chatelier's Principle

If the external conditions of a chemical reaction are changed, the position of equilibrium is also changed. The position of equilibrium moves to *oppose* the change in conditions.

The table summarises the equilibrium changes observed in the reaction $N_2O_4 \rightleftharpoons 2NO_2$, and uses Le Chatelier's Principle to explain them.

Change in conditions	Equilibrium move	Explanation
temperature increased	to the right	The reaction $N_2O_4 \Rightarrow 2NO_2$ is *endothermic*. As the equilibrium shifts in this direction, heat is *taken in* to oppose the temperature increase.
pressure increased	to the left	$N_2O_4 \rightleftharpoons 2NO_2$ $2NO_2$ takes up twice as much room as N_2O_4. Increased pressure can be opposed by decreasing the number of particles in a given space. The equilibrium shifts towards N_2O_4.

Materials from oil

From this...

to all this and more!

Crude oil is transformed by separation techniques and chemical reactions into a wide range of products.

There are three main stages involved in making oil more useful: separation, cracking, and synthesis.

Separation

Crude oil is a mixture of compounds called **hydrocarbons**. Hydrocarbons contain only the elements hydrogen and carbon. These can be separated by **fractional distillation**.

Many of the hydrocarbons in crude oil belong to a 'family' of compounds called **alkanes**. The alkanes form an **homologous** series of compounds.

An homologous series is a group of compounds with similar chemical and physical properties.

Successive members of a series differ in their formulae by CH_2.

Alkanes all have the same general formula C_nH_{2n+2}. Here, n represents any number from 1 onwards – some of the largest alkanes contain hundreds of carbon atoms. The simplest alkane is methane, CH_4.

Alkanes, especially the 'lighter' fractions (those with fewer carbon atoms) burn well. They are used as fuels because their reactions with oxygen are very exothermic.

Alkanes are compounds of hydrogen and carbon in which all the bonds between carbon atoms are **single covalent bonds**. Such compounds are described as **saturated**.

Some of the heavier fractions are used for road making; the remainder are converted to smaller, more reactive molecules by a process called cracking.

Cracking

Cracking involves heating large hydrocabon molecules to very high temperatures, or using a catalyst to break them down into smaller molecules. The **alkenes** are a common product of cracking. They have a general formula C_nH_{2n}. They all contain a **double covalent bond** between *one* pair of carbon atoms. The simplest alkene is ethene, C_2H_4.

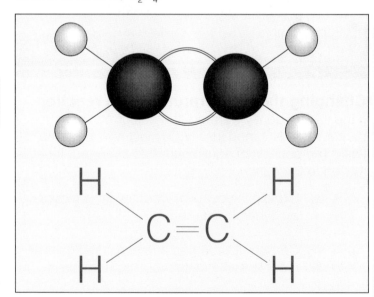

Ways of representing the structure of ethene

Alkenes differ from alkanes in a very important way. Although alkanes burn easily and well, they undergo very few other reactions. Alkenes are much more reactive, and so can be used to make many more new materials.

Synthesis

The smaller, more useful products of cracking such as ethene, are used in many different chemical reactions.

Let us look at some of the reactions of ethene.

If ethene is shaken with bromine in tetrachloromethane, the red-brown colour of the bromine disappears. Bromine molecules are able to add on to ethene molecules, making a saturated compound. This type of reaction is called an **addition reaction** and is shown in the diagram on the right. Addition reactions are characteristic and very useful reactions of alkenes. Alkenes react with many other molecules in a similar way.

Ethene molecules will add to each other if they are heated with a suitable catalyst. They form a giant molecule of **poly(ethene)**, (polythene). A molecule of poly(ethene) contains thousands of ethene molecules. This type of giant molecule, made from identical repeating units, is called a **polymer**. The individual ethene units are called **monomers**.

$$C_2H_4 \quad + \quad Br_2 \quad \Rightarrow \quad C_2H_4Br_2$$

We can represent the polymerisation reaction by an equation:

The symbol n represents a very large number. We cannot say exactly how many molecules of ethene take part in the reaction.

A model of a poly(ethene) molecule

Q1 Another homologous series of compounds is the alcohols.

The first three members of the series are methanol, ethanol and propanol. Alcohols have the general formula $C_nH_{2n+1}OH$.

Write the name and formula of the fourth member of the alcohols.

Q2 Propene reacts with chlorine in tetrachloromethane.

Write an equation for this reaction. Give the name and the structural formula of the product.

Resistance

Resistance is calculated using:

$$\text{Resistance} = \frac{\text{Voltage}}{\text{Current}} \qquad R = \frac{V}{I}$$

The SI unit of resistance is the ohm. The symbol for ohm is Ω.

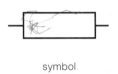

symbol

Resistor colour codes

number	colour
0	black
1	brown
2	red
3	orange
4	yellow
5	green
6	blue
7	violet
8	grey
9	white

rainbow (2–7)

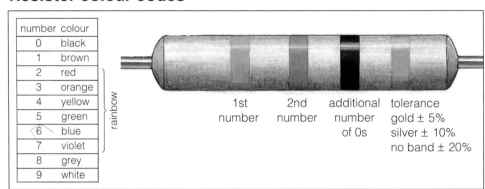

1st number 2nd number additional number of 0s tolerance gold ± 5% silver ± 10% no band ± 20%

Conduction and resistance

A low resistance allows current to flow through it easily and is a good conductor. Higher resistance reduces the current and conducts less well. Insulators are non-conducting

The copper wire in the diagram has a structure with rows of regular atoms bonded very close together. Each atom can free electrons to move along the wire and make the current. The number of electrons (charge carriers) flowing per second is a measure of current

Conventional current flows from a high ⊕ to a low ⊖ voltage. Charge carriers in wires are electrons with a negative charge. They move the opposite way to conventional current. We always use the direction of the conventional current

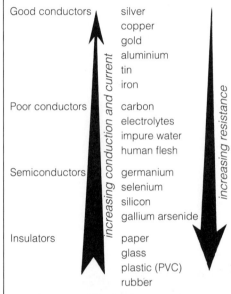

Good conductors	silver, copper, gold, aluminium, tin, iron
Poor conductors	carbon, electrolytes, impure water, human flesh
Semiconductors	germanium, selenium, silicon, gallium arsenide
Insulators	paper, glass, plastic (PVC), rubber

increasing conduction and current ↑ increasing resistance ↓

The light bulb filament has resistance. It is *in series*. It is hard for current to flow through it. It reduces the current in the whole circuit. Not just here

When we charges move we let you know about it. We make the wire get hot, we cause a current and we make a magnetic field.

These two routes are in parallel. Most current goes the easier, low resistance way

low resistance
high resistance
junction

The current recombines after the junction to give the same as it was before the split

Low voltage ⊖

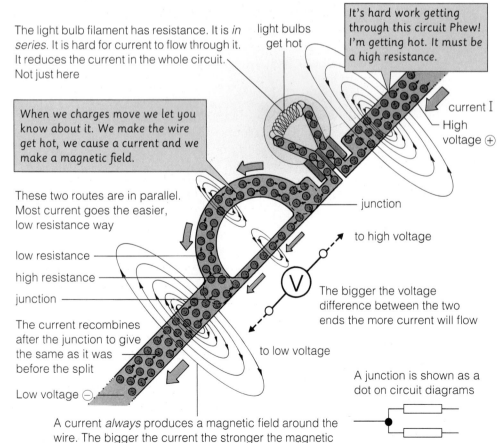

light bulbs get hot

It's hard work getting through this circuit Phew! I'm getting hot. It must be a high resistance.

current I
High voltage ⊕

junction

to high voltage

The bigger the voltage difference between the two ends the more current will flow

to low voltage

A junction is shown as a dot on circuit diagrams

A current *always* produces a magnetic field around the wire. The bigger the current the stronger the magnetic field. The magnetic field is strongest near to the wire

Q1 What materials would be suitable for the following? Give a reason in each case.
a A connecting wire
b The outer insulating sleeve around the wire
c The prong on the plug or terminal?

Q2 You are given three wires, all of the same length and material but they are of different thicknesses. Which will have the least resistance?

Q3 What is the resistor colour code for these resistors?
a 4.7 kΩ **b** 560 Ω **c** 220 kΩ.

Resistances in series

In a series circuit the same *current* flows through all components. Remember *ammeters* are connected in series.

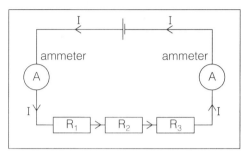

Total resistance: $R = R_1 + R_2 + R_3$

The total resistance is *greater* than any individual one.

Resistance in parallel

In a parallel circuit the same *voltage* or *pd* is present across each component. Remember *voltmeters* are connected in parallel.

Total resistance (R) can be found using:

$$\frac{1}{R} = \frac{1}{R_1} + \frac{1}{R_2} + \frac{1}{R_3}$$

The total resistance is always *less* than any individual one

To understand resistances in parallel think about traffic flowing through a town being like current flowing through a resistor. Adding a bypass makes it easier to get through either.

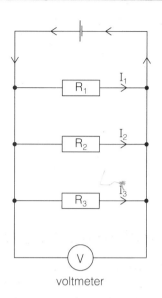

voltmeter

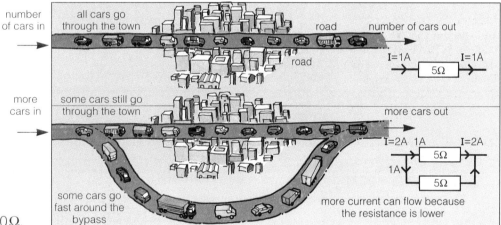

Examples

1 What is the resistance when $5\,\Omega$, $10\,\Omega$, $15\,\Omega$, $20\,\Omega$ are connected in series?

☐ Quote the appropriate formula (there are 4 resistors)	$R = R_1 + R_2 + R_3 + R_4$
☐ Put the numbers in	$R = 5 + 10 + 15 + 20$
☐ Answer and unit (Don't forget to write down all the stages for full marks)	$R = 50\,\Omega$

2 What is the resistance when $10\,\Omega$ and $20\,\Omega$ are connected in parallel?

☐ Quote the appropriate formula (only 2 resistors)	$\frac{1}{R} = \frac{1}{R_1} + \frac{1}{R_2}$
☐ Put the numbers in	$\frac{1}{R} = \frac{1}{10} + \frac{1}{20}$
☐ Find a common denominator	$\frac{1}{R} = \frac{2 + 1}{20} = \frac{3}{20}$
☐ Don't forget to invert	$\frac{R}{1} = \frac{20}{3}$
☐ Answer and unit	$R = 6.67\,\Omega$

Q4 Show that the total resistance of two $100\,\Omega$ resistors connected in parallel is $50\,\Omega$. What would be the colour code on a $50\,\Omega$ and a $100\,\Omega$ resistor?

Q5 What is the total resistance of $3\,\Omega$, $6\,\Omega$ and $9\,\Omega$ connected in series?

Q6 A voltmeter is connected in parallel across a $10\,\Omega$ resistor. The voltmeter itself has a resistance of $1\,k\Omega$. What is the total resistance of the two?

Explain the significance of your answer.

Ohm's law

see science at work

■ **Electricity and magnetism**
p 14 The electrical current
pp 22–24 Electrical induction

Scientists who gave their names to electrical units

André Marie Ampère
(1775–1836)

Ampère was a French physicist and mathematician. The unit of current has been named an **ampere** (amp).

Current (I) is measured in amps (A)

Luigi Galvani
(1737–98)

In 1792 an Italian physiologist called Galvani was dissecting a dead frog. He had two metal tools and when he had them both in contact with the frog's bodily fluids, the frog's legs jerked. The muscle contracted just as it would do if the frog were alive. Galvani had made a small electric current by electrolysis. We use the word 'galvanise' to mean to shock something into action. The process of coating iron with zinc is named after him, as is the instrument which detects small currents – the **galvanometer**.

Michael Faraday
(1791–1867)

This British physicist and chemist discovered how to explain electromagnetic induction. The SI unit of capacitance is called a **farad**.

Capacitance (C) is measured in farads (F)

Alessandro Volta
(1745–1827)

This Italian physicist gave us the name for electrical potential difference – **voltage**. Pd and voltage are the same thing. The SI unit of voltage is the volt.

Voltage or pd(V) is measured in volts (V)

Charles Augustin de Coulomb
(1736–1806)

The SI unit of electric charge is called the **coulomb** after this French physicist.

Charge (Q) is measured in coulombs (C)

Georg Simon Ohm
(1787–1854)

An important law in electricity is **Ohm's law**. This German physicist also gave his name to the SI unit of resistance.

Resistance (R) is measured in Ohms (Ω)

Ohm's law

Georg Ohm found that the bigger the voltage applied to a circuit the more current flowed. His experiments show:

$$V = IR$$

Where V is the voltage, (pd) in volts, I is the current in amps, and R is the resistance in ohms.

> The current flowing through a conductor is directly proportional to the potential difference between its ends, provided that temperature and other physical conditions do not change.

Ohm's law can be applied to whole circuits or to parts of circuits. We can use it to find V or I or R. This triangle helps you to remember how to rearrange the equation, just cover up the one you want and the equation for it is shown. What is the equation for R?

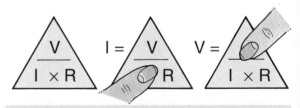

Q1 A 2V cell is connected in series with two 25 Ω resistors. What current flows?

Q2 If a current of 0.5 A flows through a 1 kΩ resistor what is the pd?

Electricity and magnetism

Where will the current go?

Look at this **series circuit**. There is only one way for the current to go. In a series circuit the *same* current flows in all parts

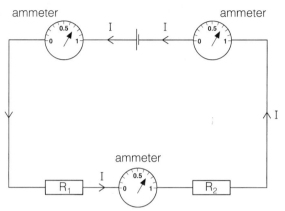

All the ammeters show the same reading

Now look at a **parallel circuit**. At junction X the current can go two ways. In a parallel circuit more current goes the easy or lower resistance way.

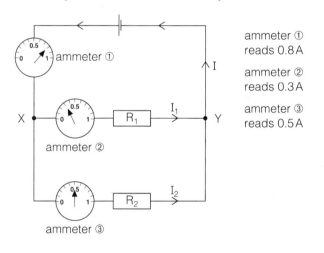

ammeter ① reads 0.8 A

ammeter ② reads 0.3 A

ammeter ③ reads 0.5 A

A current, I, flows from the battery and is measured by Ammeter 1. At X it splits into two parts, I_1 and I_2, measured by ammeter 2 and ammeter 3. At Y the two branches join to give the original current, I, again.

$$I = I_1 + I_2$$

If the resistors (R_1 and R_2) are equal the current will split into two equal halves. If R_1 is a high resistance and R_2 is a lower resistance then more current will go through R_2 because it is easier.

$$\frac{R_1}{R_2} = \frac{I_2}{I_1}$$

Example

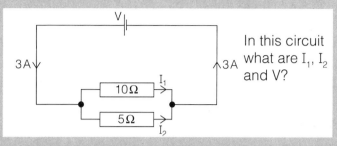

In this circuit what are I_1, I_2 and V?

The 3A current will split into two parts. It is twice as easy to go through the 5Ω resistor so twice as much current goes that way.

3A splits → 1A through the 10Ω → then is a 3A
→ 2A through the 5Ω → current again

Ohm's law can be used in both branches.

$V = I_1R_1$	or	$V = I_2R_2$
$=1 \times 10$		2×5
$=10V$		$10V$

Both branches of a parallel circuit always have the *same* pd (voltage) across them. This is a 10V battery.

Q3 A series circuit contains a 2V cell and two identical filament light bulbs. What will be the pd across one bulb? Draw the circuit diagram.

Q4 **a** What current will flow through the 5Ω resistor in the diagram?
b What current will be measured by the ammeter?

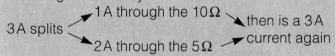

Q5 **a** Find the combined resistance of the two resistors in parallel shown below.
b What is the pd across them?
c Copy the circuit diagram and show which direction currents flow in. Calculate the currents in each part of the circuit.

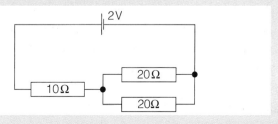

Electrical energy

see science at work

■ **Electricity and magnetism**
pp 30–32 Measuring, paying for and distributing electricity

Like all other forms of energy and work electrical energy is measured in joules (J). The joule is the SI unit of energy named after a Briton, James Prescott Joule (1818–1889). Joule did his experiments at Manchester University.

Definition of electrical energy

This comes from the definition of a volt. The pd between two points is 1 volt if 1 joule of work is done in moving 1 coulomb of charge from one point to the other.

$$\text{Electrical energy} = \text{charge} \times \text{voltage}$$
$$= QV$$

There are several useful versions of this formula. Remembering that:

$$\text{Charge} = \text{Current} \times \text{Time} \ (Q = It)$$
$$\text{and also Ohm's law} \ (V = IR) \text{ then:}$$

$$\text{Electrical energy} = ItV \ or \ VIt$$
$$\text{Joule heating} = I^2Rt$$

Joule heating is another name given to electrical energy or heating because often the electrical energy is converted into heat.

There is a link between power in *watts* and energy in joules

$$\text{Energy} = \text{Power} \times \text{Time}$$
$$\text{Energy} = (VI) \times \text{Time}$$
$$\text{Joules} = \text{Watts} \times \text{Seconds}$$

Home appliances

When you get a new electrical appliance, maybe a hair dryer or a CD player, it will always have information about what fuse to use and what power the appliance uses. Look at the information shown on the back plates of four appliances.

1200W 240V ~ 50Hz Do not insert metal objects to remove toast.

toaster

Capacity 1.5 litres 2.0kW 240V ~ 50Hz Do not immerse in water. Do not overfill.

kettle

Tube 2450MHz 1.1kW 4.8A 240V ~ 50Hz

microwave oven

BEAB approved. Must be fitted by an experienced electrician. 10.5kW 240V ~ 50Hz

cooker

⚡ Danger. Mains electricity can kill.

> *This diagram has a **logarithmic scale**. Each dot represents an energy 10 times bigger than the one before. If 1J was represented by 1mm the Sun's energy would need to be 100 million light years on the same scale*

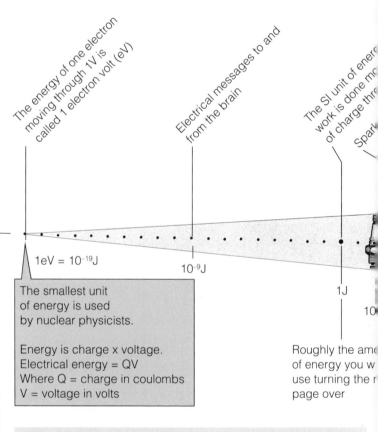

The energy of one electron moving through 1V is called 1 electron volt (eV)

Electrical messages to and from the brain

The SI unit of energy work is done m... of charge thr...

Spark

1eV = 10^{-19}J

10^{-9}J

1J

10

The smallest unit of energy is used by nuclear physicists.

Energy is charge x voltage.
Electrical energy = QV
Where Q = charge in coulombs
V = voltage in volts

Roughly the am... of energy you w... use turning the ... page over

Q1 Which kitchen appliance uses a lot of electrical energy and needs a separate circuit?

Q2 Why do you think a microwave oven uses less energy than a conventional cooker? Give two reasons.

Q3 What unit must *time* be measured in for all the equations on this page?

Kilowatt–hours

The units the electricity meter is read in are kilowatt-hours (kWh).

One joule is a tiny amount of energy, a kilowatt-hour is more than a million (10^6) times bigger.

1000 W (or 1 kW) for one hour = 1 kWh
1000 W for 3600 seconds (60×60) = 1 kWh
3 600 000 W/s = 3 600 000 J = 1 kW

There are 3.6 million (3.6×10^6) Joules in 1 Kilowatt-hour.

One unit (1 kWh) costs a few pence, currently about 7.5.

Measuring mains current and voltage

The ammeters and voltmeters which are used in school laboratories are mainly moving coil meters. They cannot be used with a.c., only with d.c. Special meters are needed to measure mains current and voltage. The mains ammeter shown in the photograph can measure a.c. currents. The appliances which plug in to the ring main can carry a current of up to 13 A. Remember that 10 A is quite a large current and 1 A is a small current.

Mains voltmeters need to be well insulated to protect the user. They must work with a.c. and be capable of measuring 240 V. There are many multimeters but one of the best is called an AVO (this stands for Amps, Volts, Ohms).

Electricians sometimes use a screwdriver with a neon light inside it to test if circuits are live.

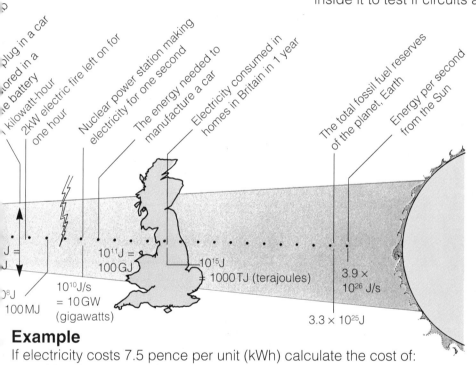

plug in a car
...ored in a ...e battery
...kilowatt-hour
2kW electric fire left on for one hour
Nuclear power station making electricity for one second
The energy needed to manufacture a car
Electricity consumed in homes in Britain in 1 year
The total fossil fuel reserves of the planet, Earth
Energy per second from the Sun

$J = ...J$
$10^{11} J = 100 GJ$
$10^{15} J = 1000 TJ$ (terajoules)
$3.9 \times 10^{26} J/s$
$...^8 J$ 100 MJ
$10^{10} J/s = 10 GW$ (gigawatts)
$3.3 \times 10^{25} J$

Example

If electricity costs 7.5 pence per unit (kWh) calculate the cost of:
a making four slices of toast in a toaster if it take two minutes
b cooking a casserole, jacket potatoes, and pudding in an oven (2.5 kW turbo fan) for one and a half hours.

		a Toaster	**b** Oven
1 Time	Calculate the time in Hours	2 hours / 60	1.5 hours
2 Power	Convert VI to kW (divide by 1000)	1200 kW / 1000	2.5 kW
3 Cost = Power × Time × Cost per unit		1.2 × 2 × 7.5 / 60 = 0.3 p	2.5 × 1.5 × 7.5 = 28 p

Q4 Estimate the number of light bulbs in your school. If each is a 100 W bulb and is on for an average of 4 hours a day, 190 days per year, what is the annual lighting cost? (Cost per unit = 7.5 pence.)

Q5 Explain why an electrical extension cable should always be unrolled from the storage drum before it is plugged in.

Q6 An ordinary light bulb gets quite hot. A fluorescent tube gives out as much light but stays cool. Which one makes the best use of electrical energy and why?

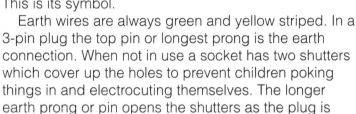

Electrical power

Electrical power is measured in watts (W). The SI unit of power is named after James Watt (1736–1819) who invented the steam engine. The unit of power used in his day was the horsepower (745.7 W = 1 hp).

The relationship between power and energy

Power is the rate of doing work *or* the rate of converting energy.

$$\text{Power} = \frac{\text{Energy}}{\text{Time}} = \frac{VIt}{t}$$

Power = VI

1 watt (1 W) = 1 joule per second (1 J/s)

Fuses

All electrical wiring should be protected by fuses or circuit breakers. This is the symbol for a fuse.

The word fuse means melt. A fuse will melt and break the circuit if too much current flows. It protects the appliance or wiring and it can protect the person. When the circuit is broken heating stops and the possibility of fire or damaged components ceases. The risk of getting an electric shock ends because the current stops flowing.

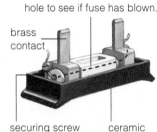

hole to see if fuse has blown.

brass contact

securing screw (one at each end)

ceramic

Protected fuse – The fuse wire passes through the centre of the holder

There are several types of wiring/circuits in your house, for example

- The cooker circuit, thick wires, 30 A fuses
- The ring main circuit, (all the 3-pin plug sockets) 30 A fuses
- The lighting circuit, 5 A fuses.

In addition to the fuses or circuit breakers in the consumer unit near your electricity meter there are also internal fuses in some equipment. All 3-pin plugs have a cartridge fuse fitted in the *live* connection. It is very important to fit a fuse that is not too big or too small for the particular appliance. Cartridge fuses for plugs can be 13 A, 5 A or 3 A. Even smaller fuses may be fitted inside electrical equipment. Some power packs, for example, have a 500 mA fuse.

Example

Which would be the best fuse to fit in the plug of a hair dryer rated 1200 W?

You need to find the 'normal' current using the equation:

Power = VI

Remember V = 240 V

$$\text{Current, } I = \frac{\text{Power}}{V} = \frac{1200}{240} = 5\,\text{A}$$

The correct fuse must be a little higher than the 'normal' current so a 13 A fuse would be the best one. A 5 A fuse may keep blowing and often need replacing.

Earthing

Earth or ground is a potential of 0 V. This is its symbol.

Earth wires are always green and yellow striped. In a 3-pin plug the top pin or longest prong is the earth connection. When not in use a socket has two shutters which cover up the holes to prevent children poking things in and electrocuting themselves. The longer earth prong or pin opens the shutters as the plug is pushed in the socket.

It is very important that an appliance with a metal outer casing, for example, an iron, a cooker, a washing machine or a toaster *never* has current flowing in the metal case. If it did it could give the user a fatal electric shock. The earth wire is fixed to the *outer metal case* and keeps it at 0 V. You are at 0 V so there can be no pd (voltage) between you and the casing. No current can flow through you. The other end of the earth wire is wired into the earth outside your house. Hence the name 'earth' wire. Electricians used to connect the earth wire to the *copper* water pipes knowing that they go down into the ground. This is not possible where *plastic* pipes are used.

Double insulation

Electrical garden tools such as hedge cutters or lawnmowers, electric drills and appliances with a *thick plastic insulating outer casing* often do not have an earth connection. They are double insulated. Each has a *plastic switch* for turning it on and off. This is the symbol for double insulation.

Safety warning. In the garden always work away from the electric wire to avoid cutting it.

Take extra care with electric hedge cutters. Keep hold of them with both hands. Use either an ELCB (wired in or a small plug in one) or an RCD device.

Earth leakage circuit breaker (ELCB)

New houses often have resettable circuit breakers instead of fuses. Many houses have the added protection of an ELCB or as it is sometimes called a residual current device (RCD). This device compares the current in the live and neutral wires. They are supposed to be the same. If they are different some current must be leaking to earth. If more than a pre-set current of 30mA leaks to earth then the button automatically pops out breaking the circuit. If all is well the circuit can be reset by pushing in the button. If the fault is still present the circuit will trip out again protecting the electrical wiring, the appliance and the user.

This type of protection is especially good in the garden where it can be quite dangerous to use electrical appliances. Every year people die because they cut through live cables with hedge cutters or change a light bulb with wet hands when it is still live or do the ironing in the garden, using an extension cable and standing with bare feet on wet grass. If more houses had ELCBs fitted there would be fewer of these tragic avoidable accidents. If you do not have an ELCB it is possible and desirable to buy small circuit breaker plugs.

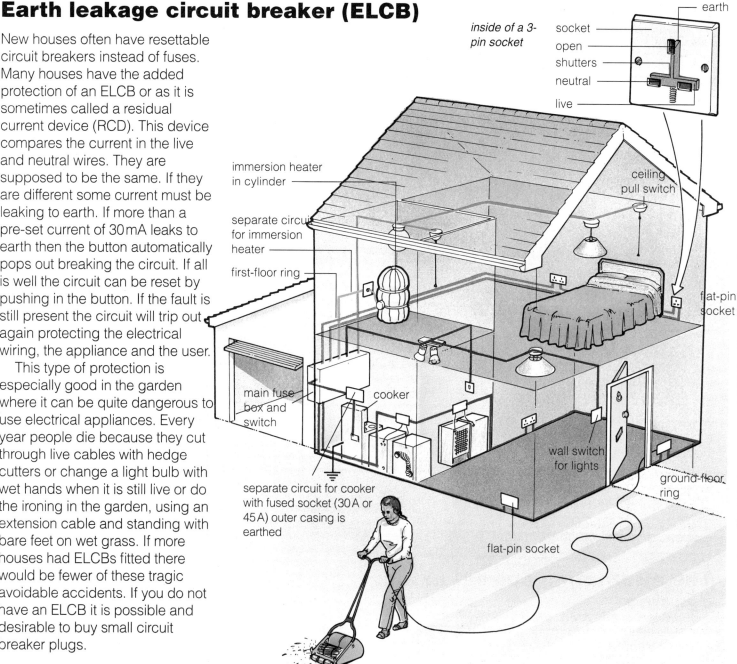

inside of a 3-pin socket — socket, open, shutters, neutral, live, earth

immersion heater in cylinder

separate circuit for immersion heater

first-floor ring

ceiling pull switch

flat-pin socket

main fuse box and switch

cooker

separate circuit for cooker with fused socket (30A or 45A) outer casing is earthed

wall switch for lights

ground-floor ring

flat-pin socket

Q1 What happens if a fuse that is rated too low is used?

Q2 What happens if a fuse that is rated too high is used?

Q3 Why do fuses need to be:

a made of metal
b in the live wire?

Q4 What is the colour of the wire connected to:

a the fuse in a 3 pin plug
b the earth terminal
c the outer casing of an appliance?

Q5 Why is it dangerous to touch electrical appliances with wet hands? Why are bathroom light switches either outside the room or if inside are switched on and off using a pull cord made of insulating material?

Electromagnetic induction

see science at work

■ **Electricity and magnetism**
The effects of an electrical current
p 22–23

In 1831, Michael Faraday discovered that electricity could be made without batteries or cells. He found he could make electricity by
● moving a conductor in a magnetic field
● making the magnetic field around a conductor change.
Faraday had discovered **electromagnetic induction**. Induction means to produce something artificially. Faraday had made electricity artificially by using magnetism, rather than making it 'naturally' by using batteries.

The first law of electromagnetic induction

When a bicycle dynamo is turned, a small magnet rotates inside a coil of copper wire. The picture shows a dynamo connected to a meter. The dynamo makes a current flow in the wire, which moves the needle on the meter. If the dynamo is turned quickly the needle moves further than when the dynamo moves slowly. You may have noticed this effect on bikes: when pedalling faster the lights become brighter.

So the faster a conductor moves in a magnetic field, the higher the induced voltage. Faraday summed this up in his law of electromagnetic induction:

> The size of the induced voltage between the ends of the conductor is proportional to the rate at which the conductor cuts through the magnetic field.

The alternating current or a.c. dynamo

A simple alternating current dynamo or generator can be made by turning a loop of copper wire inside a magnetic field

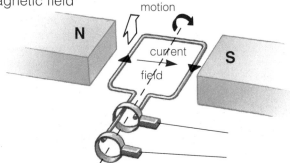

When this half of the loop moves up, the field induces a current which flows into the loop. (Check this using the dynamo rule).

The dynamo rule

You can find the direction in which the induced electric current flows in a wire by using the **dynamo rule**.
● Hold the fingers of your right hand in the position shown in the picture.
● Turn your hand so that:
  your thu**m**b points in the direction the wire is **m**oving
  your **f**irst finger points in the direction of the magnetic **f**ield (from N to S).
● Your se**c**ond finger is now pointing in the direction that the induced **c**urrent flows.

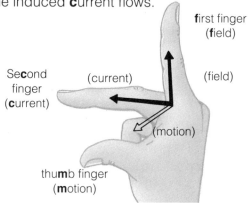

(Remember: thu**m**b for **m**otion, **f**irst finger for **f**ield, and se**c**ond finger for **c**urrent)

When the same half of the loop moves down the current flows out. (Check this using the dynamo rule.)
The flow of current in the loop therefore alternates backwards and forwards.

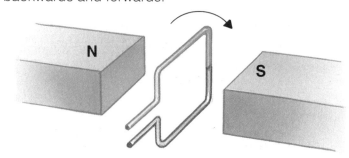

Electricity and magnetism

In an a.c. dynamo:
● each end of the loop is attached to a copper slip ring
● a small spring gently pushes a carbon brush against each ring
● the ring slides against the carbon brush as the loop turns
● the carbon brushes collect the current from the rings
● the current then flows from the brushes into the rest of the circuit.

The graph shows that the current changes direction every half turn.

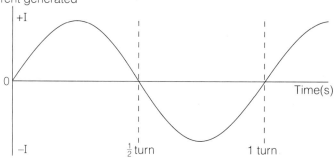

The direct current or d.c.dynamo

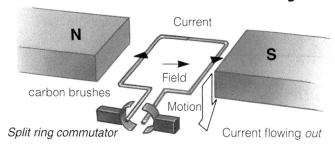

Split ring commutator

A direct current dynamo is identical to an a.c. dynamo in every respect except in the way in which the current is fed into the brushes.

In a d.c. dynamo
● the slip rings are replaced by a single ring split in half, a **split ring commutator**
● each half of the ring is connected to one end of the loop of wire
● as the loop spins the carbon brushes press against each half of the split ring in turn (both halves of the split ring are insulated from each other).

The graph shows that the current flows from the dynamo in one direction only.

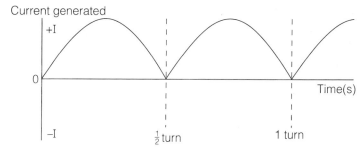

Q1 What is electromagnetic induction?

Q2 Which of the following materials copper, aluminium, nylon, steel, plastic will have electricity induced in it when it is moved in a magnetic field?

Q3 Name two devices which use electromagnetic induction to make electricity.

Q4 What is Faraday's law?

Q5 Look at the diagrams. Use the dynamo rule to show the direction that the induced current will flow in the copper wire.

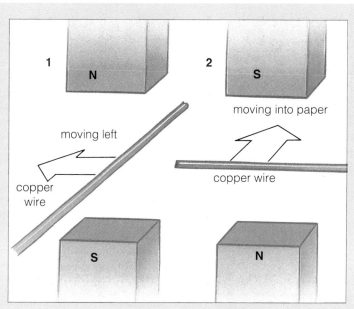

Eddy currents

In the last section you found out that electromagnetic induction can be used to make an electric current flow in copper wires. Electric currents are created in anything made of conducting materials (tin cans, coins and so on) whenever the conductor moves through a magnetic field or the magnetic field around it changes. The currents induced in objects like these form whirlpools of electricity which are called **eddy currents**.

The second law of electromagnetic induction

The effect of eddy currents can be shown using an aluminium disc which spins freely around an axle through its centre. If we spin it between the poles of a very strong magnet it soon slows down and stops. This is because the induced eddy currents swirling inside the metal disc also create their own magnetic fields. These interact with the field of the strong magnet and slow down the movement of the disc. This is one example of **electromagnetic damping**. It is also a good example of the **second important rule of electromagnetic induction**. It is known as Lenz's law:

> The induced current always opposes the change in the magnetic field which caused it.

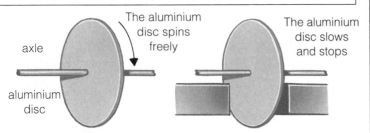

axle

The aluminium disc spins freely

aluminium disc

The aluminium disc slows and stops

Induction brakes

Some heavy vehicles like lorries, buses and trains use electromagnetic induction to help them slow down. A strong electromagnet is switched on around a metal disc on the propeller shaft of the vehicle. Eddy currents are induced in the metal disc; these act to slow down the spinning disc and brake the movement of the lorry.

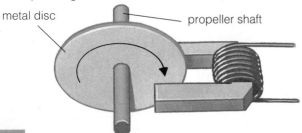

metal disc

propeller shaft

The induction motor

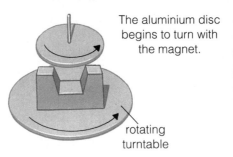

The aluminium disc begins to turn with the magnet.

rotating turntable

An induction motor

The induction motor is the most widely used power motor in the world, and is used in most domestic fridges and freezers. It uses electromagnetic induction and eddy currents. We can show how an induction motor works by placing a strong magnet on a turntable and suspending an aluminium disc above the magnet. As the magnet turns it creates eddy currents in the disc. The eddies generate magnetic fields that make the disc start to spin with the magnet. Actual motors use powerful a.c. electromagnets instead of moving magnets, but they make the disc (called a **rotor**) turn in the same way. as a result, induction motors have fewer working parts to break down than conventional motors and are extremely reliable.

The National Grid

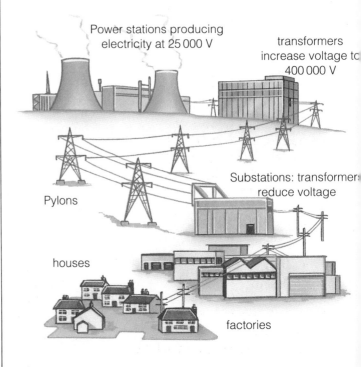

Power stations producing electricity at 25 000 V

transformers increase voltage to 400 000 V

Pylons

Substations: transformers reduce voltage

houses

factories

The transformer

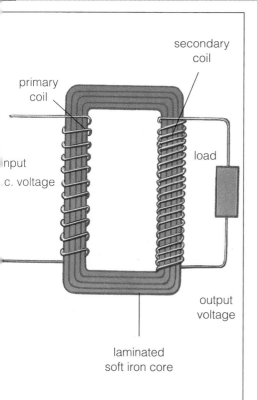

primary coil
secondary coil
input a.c. voltage
load
output voltage
laminated soft iron core

A step-up transformer

A simple transformer has two coils of insulated copper wire called the **primary** and **secondary coils**. Both coils are wrapped around a metal core which is made of soft iron in insulated layers like a wafer biscuit. This layered core prevents large eddy currents which would produce heat in the core. The voltage we wish to change, the **input voltage**, is connected to the primary coil. When the current flows in the primary coil a magnetic field develops. The magnetic field changes as the current alternates backwards and forwards. This in turn induces a changed or **transformed** voltage in the secondary coil: the **output voltage**.

The number of turns of wire on each coil determines how much bigger or smaller the output voltages will be. For example, if the secondary coil has twice as many turns as the primary coil, it will produce twice the voltage.

$$\frac{\text{number of turns on the secondary coil}}{\text{number of turns on the primary coil}} = \frac{\text{output voltage}}{\text{input voltage}}$$

Example

An electronic keyboard needs a transformer to change the mains voltage of 240 V to the keyboard's working voltage of 6 V. The primary coil of the transformer has 4000 turns. How many turns does the secondary coil have?

Answer

$$\frac{\text{number of turns on the secondary coil}}{\text{number of turns on the primary coil}} = \frac{\text{output voltage}}{\text{input voltage}}$$

$$\frac{\text{number of turns on the secondary coil}}{4000} = \frac{6}{240}$$

$$\text{number of turns on the secondary coil} = \frac{6}{240} \times 4000 = 100$$

The secondary coil has 100 turns.

Electricity is carried across the country through a network of underground cables and overhead power lines called the **National Grid**. At the power station a device called a **transformer** is used to increase or 'step up' the voltage (to 400 000 V for example) before it passes through the National Grid. This high voltage is necessary to reduce heat losses in the cables. Smaller transformers are used to reduce or 'step down' voltage to 240 V a.c. in local substations before the electricity reaches our homes. Much smaller transformers are also found in equipment like televisions and computers to change the mains voltage to the correct operating voltage. Transformers can only change a.c. voltages. The electricity generating industry produces and distributes a.c. electricity and not d.c.

Q1
a What is Lenz's law?
b Induction brakes are sometimes called electromagnetic brakes. How do they work?

Q2 What is meant by the terms:
a step-up transformer?
b step-down transformer?
How do their primary and secondary coils differ?

Q3
a Explain how a transformer changes a.c. voltages.
b Why can you not use a transformer to change the voltage from a battery?

Q4 A transformer has 3000 turns of wire on its primary coil and 200 on its secondary coil. What is its output voltage if the input voltage is 240V?

Static electricity

Sometimes you get a small electric shock when you climb out of a car and touch its metal bodywork. This is more likely to happen if the seats are covered in plastic. You may also have noticed crackling and tiny sparks when removing nylon clothing. All these effects are caused by static electricity.

When materials rub against each other, the friction between them rips electrons off the molecules of one material. These static electrons stick to the surface of the other material. If the materials are rubbed together long enough a very high voltage can build up.

This high voltage may be large enough to turn the static electricity into electricity that flows as an electric current. This is what is happening when you get crackles, sparks and shocks.

Electrons are rubbed off the seat onto the driver.

The driver gets an electric shock when the electrons flow off him or her to the car.

What is electricity?

In most cases static electricity is just a nuisance. In other situations it can be extremely dangerous. For instance there are serious risks of fire when fuel tankers make deliveries to petrol stations. As the petrol gushes through the pipes from the tanker, friction produces static electricity. If, as a result, a spark were to jump from the tanker, it could ignite the fuel. To prevent this happening a copper earthing strap is connected from the body of the tanker to a copper stake which is buried in the ground, to 'drain away' any static charge before it can build up to high voltages. Similar precautions must be taken when aeroplanes refuel.

When electricity flows in a wire we think of it as a flow of electrons. When it flows in a fluid it can mean the movement of ions. (An ion is a molecule which has either lost or gained electrons.) The size of charge carried with each electron or ion is measured in **coulombs**. When we measure **current** through an ammeter we are measuring how many coulombs of charge flow through the meter *each second*.

Each coulomb flowing per second is called one **ampere**.

Remember: current = $\dfrac{\text{charge}}{\text{time}}$ *or* amps = $\dfrac{\text{coulombs}}{\text{seconds}}$

Thermionic emission

When water is heated to boiling point, large numbers of molecules gain enough energy to escape the liquid altogether. The water is turned into water vapour.

Steam or water vapour.

Water molecules escaping boiling water.

Metals contain large number of electrons which drift between the atoms of the metal just like water molecules moving randomly around a beaker of water. When tungsten (a metal used as the filament in an electric light bulb) is heated until it is white hot, some of the many electrons in the metal are boiled off. We cannot see the electrons. The next section explains how we know they are there.

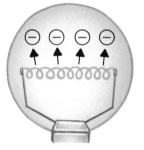

'electron gas' or 'space charge'

electrons are 'boiled off' the filament.

White hot tungsten filament.

The thermionic diode

When electrons flow they make an electric current. In 1904 A. J. Fleming used a heated filament (called a cathode) to make a current of electrons flow through a vacuum. He used a circuit like this one. When this circuit is connected, a current flows. It can be measured on a sensitive ammeter. The electrons are attracted to the positive metal plate, called an **anode**. When the battery is connected with the negative terminal to the plate there is no current. Fleming concluded that:

● electrons must have a negative charge
● electrons can only flow in one direction: from the cathode to the anode.

The device is called a thermionic diode.

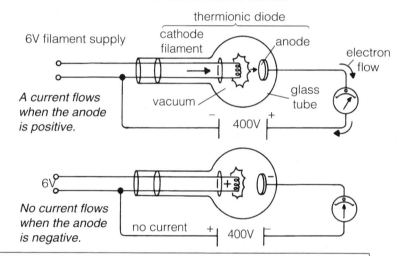

thermionic diode

6V filament supply — cathode filament — anode — electron flow

A current flows when the anode is positive.

vacuum — glass tube

− 400V +

6V

No current flows when the anode is negative.

no current — + 400V −

Colour television

A thermionic diode is one type of thermionic tube. The television tube is another. Its screen is coated with thousands of dots made from three sets of fluorescent chemicals. One set glows red, one green and one blue. Three separate heated filaments called electron guns produce beams of electrons. Each electron beam is swept across the screen by a magnetic deflecting system and focused on to a different set of dots. When the beams hit the screen, one produces a red picture, the second a blue picture and the third a green picture. We see the mixture of the three coloured pictures as a normal colour picture.

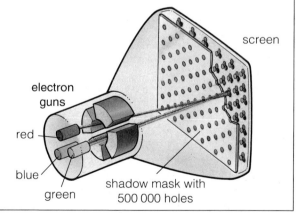

screen

electron guns

red

blue

green

shadow mask with 500 000 holes

Q1 What is an electric current?

Q2 Describe two examples of static electricity turning into current electricity.

Q3 Explain why an oil tanker refuelling a plane must be earthed.

Q4 What is thermionic emission?

Q5 What features do the thermionic diode and television tube have in common?

Q6 Why do you think thermionic diodes were often called valves? (You may find it helpful to look up the word 'valve' in a dictionary.)

Thermionic tubes

The X-Ray tube

X-rays

Electrons travelling across thermionic tubes, like diodes and television tubes, gain a lot of kinetic energy. When they hit anything, such as the anode or the screen of a TV tube, this energy is released. Most of the energy is changed to heat but a very tiny amount is released in the form of X-rays. This is a type of electromagnetic radiation like light, but has a very short wavelength and is invisible to the human eye.

The X-ray tube

A modern X ray tube has a heated cathode which produces large numbers of electrons. The anode is connected to a very high positive voltage. Electrons produced by the cathode accelerate towards the anode at extremely high speeds. When the electrons hit the anode, 99.9% of their kinetic energy changes to heat. The remaining energy changes to X-rays which radiate from the anode. The anode is usually made from tungsten, which has a high melting point (3377°C). An induction motor rotates the anode so that it does not melt. The whole apparatus is surrounded by oil to cool it, and it is enclosed in a lead box.

A window in the lead box releases X-rays for using in medicine and industry.

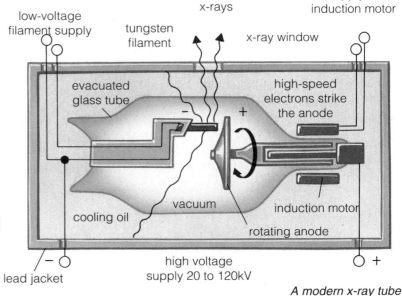

A modern x-ray tube

Uses of X-rays

X-rays and their production are very important in both industry and medicine, particularly for taking X-ray photographs. Although X-rays are very penetrating they cannot pass through dense materials like bone and metal, and so are used to form shadow images on photographic plates. These images can be used to diagnose illnesses and broken bones, and to find fractures in the welds in steel pipes.

Hard X-rays are produced with very high anode voltages, in excess of 100 000 V, and are used to kill cancer cells in deep growths, and for inspecting industrial pipework. X-rays produced by low anode voltages of around 40 000 – 50 000 V are less penetrating and are called **soft X-rays**. They are used to treat skin diseases and for medical X-ray photographs.

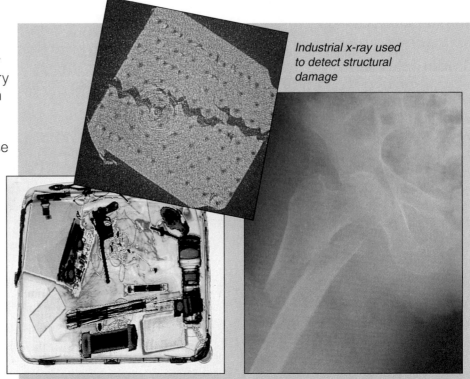

Industrial x-ray used to detect structural damage

Industrial x-ray used in airports.

Medical x-ray showing broken bones.

The CRO is an instrument which is often used in science lessons to measure voltages, and to study the waveforms produced by electrical devices such as microphones and signal generators. It has a tube like a TV tube. In the CRO the main features are:

An electron gun
Electrons are produced by thermionic emission from a heated cathode. The electrons stream towards and through a ring shaped anode. This focuses the electrons into a narrow beam.

X and Y plates
The beam passes between two pairs of parallel metal plates. Connecting a voltage to the X plates makes the spot deflect horizontally across the tube (in the x direction of a graph). A voltage connected to Y plates deflects the spot vertically (in the y direction of a graph).

A screen
At the opposite end to the cathode, the inside of the tube is coated with a special fluorescent chemical. This glows when the electron beam hits it, resulting in a bright spot of light on the screen.

A time base circuit
This controls a voltage to the X plates which pulls the beam across the screen at a steady speed. The voltage varies in a sawtooth pattern so that when the spot reaches the end of the screen, the voltage suddenly changes direction and the beam returns to the left side to start again. If the Y plates are connected to a changing external voltage, the spot will also move up and down to display a wave.

A cathode ray oscilloscope in use

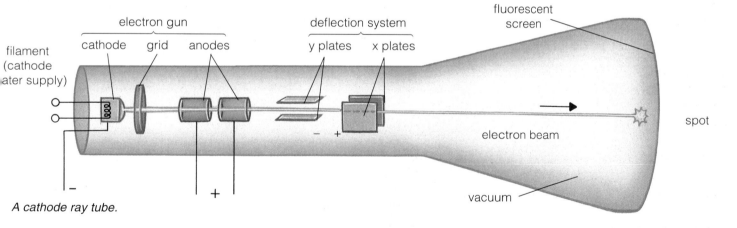

A cathode ray tube.

Q1 a Name three examples of thermionic tubes.
b Which do you think is the most important and why?

Q2 a How is the X-ray tube different to the thermionic diode?
b Why are these differences important in the production of X-rays?

Q3 Why is the X-ray tube enclosed in a lead box?

Q4 Why do you think hospital radiologists use soft-X rays to take X-ray photographs of their patients?

Q5 In a cathode ray oscilloscope, what do the following do?
a the electron gun
b the X plates
c the Y plates
d the time base circuit

Feedback

When your teacher asks you a question often it is to get **feedback** – to see how many people in the class understand the lesson or if there is a need to make some points clearer.

Feedback occurs when information about an end result or outcome is 'fedback' to the beginning so that it can affect the later outcome.

Negative feedback

Eat too much → feel sick → stop eating

Work out at gym → get too hot → start to sweat → evaporation causes cooling → **cool down**.

Oven temperature gets too hot ➡ thermostat switches off current

oven temperature increases

joule heating stops

joule heating starts again

oven cools down

thermostat switches on current ⬅ oven temperature gets too cold

All of these are **negative feedback**. Negative feedback is a very good thing. It leads to stability and predictability.

Positive feedback

Some feedback is not so useful. **Positive feedback** happens when the feedback exaggerates the change and it leads to instability and unpredictability.

Person is sober → has a pint of beer → person gets 'merry' → fancies another pint of beer → more beer drunk → person gets drunk and loses judgement and willpower → drinks another pint of beer → outcome is definitely **unstable**

A stock market crash happened in America in the 1920s. In Britain we had a similar economic disaster in 1987. In the Stock Market people buy and sell stocks and shares.

Selling stocks and shares → they sell → so I must sell → prices fall → more people sell → **economic disaster**.

Loudspeaker and microphone close together → sound from microphone is amplified and fed to loudspeaker → microphone picks it up and amplifies it again → outcome is a **loud screech** or **howl**.

Personal feedback

Give yourself a little bit of feedback. Do you remember enough about earlier work to understand how the pointer on an ammeter stops at the correct reading without swinging about? When an electrical meter has a pointer that stops dead on the right reading it is called a **dead beat** instrument.

Current flows into the ammeter and the moving coil starts to move. The bigger the current, the bigger the movement. The coil is in a magnetic field and so electromagnetic induction takes place. Eddy currents are produced in the moving coil. The pointer is like a pendulum swinging, you might expect it to swing too and fro around the correct reading. It uses the negative feedback of the eddy current to stop itself dead. This is also called **electromagnetic damping**.

Another bit of negative feedback is taking place when you look at the pointer and its image in the plane mirror which is behind the scale. If you see both the real pointer and its image you think:

Move my head as I am not in line → now I have gone too far the other way → move back until I can only see one pointer → **I am in the correct place to take a reading**.

You have used **parallax** to give the feedback.

Think of each question in terms of either positive or negative feedback and state which you think it is.

Q1 Explain how unemployment can cause more unemployment.

Q2 Explain how a car's shock absorbers make the ride better.

Q3 Why might a parent punish a small child? What is the punishment supposed to do?

Q4 How does a record get to number 1 at the top of the charts?

Q5 Would you join a long queue? What would you do and why?

Q6 The world population is growing. Will it keep on growing forever? Explain carefully three different things that might eventually stop population growth.

Start

(Follow the alphabet)

A — Artificial intelligence is being researched. This type of computer system, which is also called a 'knowledge based system' (KBS) feeds lots of rules and/or knowledge into the computer and then it attempts to predict or diagnose the likely answer. For example a medical diagnostic programme may give an answer that it is 95% likely that the patient has liver cancer. Another similar area which is developing is 'neural networks' which copy the action of the neurones in the human brain. Computers are still not as sophisticated as the human brain.

B — Bugging devices can be used by spies. Many of these devices use electromagnetic induction.

H — Holiday tour operators give information to travel agents via computers. You can check the availability of holidays on the spot.

G — Girls can do it! An important change in lifestyle over the last 25 years is that there are many more women working in good jobs.

F — Fax is short for facsimile copy. A fax machine can send an exact copy of a document to another machine anywhere in the world.

E — Electronic banking and electronic mail are now qu... common. Computers send money from one to anothe... electronically.

I — Infra-red sensors are used as remote controls for TV and video players. Security systems use infra-red detectors.

J — Jobs are lost when a process is automated. People need to learn different skills as the job market changes.

K — Keyhole surgery uses fibre optic technology to avoid major operations on some patients. Many new non-invasive procedures are being used by doctors.

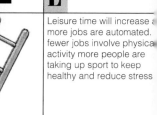

L — Leisure time will increase a... more jobs are automated. ... fewer jobs involve physica... activity more people are taking up sport to keep healthy and reduce stress...

R — Robots do many repetitive, simple or dangerous tasks such as stripping uranium fuel rods for reprocessing. Many production lines use robots to do part of the work.

Q — The queue at the supermarket checkout moves faster when the assistant has a bar code reader. The stock control record is automatically updated at the same time.

P — Plastic money. Visa, Access, American Express and many other cards are used every day to pay for things. The magnetic stripe contains digital information about the account and can be used to get information about the account.

O — Oracle is an information se... available on many TV sets... Information about share pr... the weather etc. are updat... frequently by computer.

S — Security is improving. Many homes have an alarm system with different detectors and sensors. Alarms may be connected to pressure sensors (strain gauges) or heat sensors (thermistors) or light sensors (light dependent resistors, LDRs). Many alarms have a digital code number, chosen by the owner, to arm the system.

T — TV is changing – satellite and cable TV have arrived. Special interest programmes can be broadcast in an encripted form. Customers pay to have a decrypter to receive the programmes.

U — Unemployment is rising.

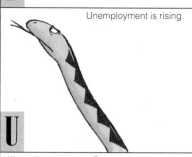

V — Virtual reality games take co... games into a new dimension... play, a headset is worn whic... shows the wearer pictures. The player operates hand controls and takes part in th... scene he sees. Although a v... reality game contains quite... sophisticated programmes... resolution of the picture... A person who had eyes... similar to the machine v... be 'registered blind'.

Finish

Z — What will be the outcome of new technology–up or down?

Y — You and your life! How ma... changes in IT and control technology have you seen... What others do you expec...

CAD and CAM, (computer aided design and computer aided manufacture) are used by engineers, designers and manufacturers. Aeroplanes and cars can be designed and tested on the computer screen. Architects and graphic designers use CAD too.

The Data Protection Act gives you the right to know of information about you held in computers. Banks and financial organisations and some government departments may have such information and you can check that it is correct.

A modem is a device used to send information from one computer to another down a telephone line.

Newspapers are planned and printed using computers. They can print the papers in different parts of the country and save money on distribution costs. Journalists can write their articles on a small personal computer and send their work in to the main editorial office using telephone lines.

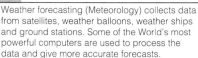

Weather forecasting (Meteorology) collects data from satellites, weather balloons, weather ships and ground stations. Some of the World's most powerful computers are used to process the data and give more accurate forecasts.

X-rays can be used to examine things without damaging them. Archaeologists look inside Egyptian mummies. Engineers check welds.

A short history of passing messages

490BC A Greek runner ran just over 26 miles to Marathon to pass on a message. We still have marathons today.

1837 Wheatstone and Cooke, two British scientists, invented the telegraph. Messages could be sent along wires.

1864 James Clerk Maxwell, a Scottish scientist, proved that radio waves existed, but no one believed him!

1872 Samuel Morse invented Morse Code.

1887 Heinrich Hertz, a German scientist, was the first person to make radio waves.

1901 Guglielmo Marconi, an Italian scientist, sent a radio message across the Atlantic Ocean.

1920 Karel Copek, A Czechoslovakian, wrote a play about slave-like machines. *Robota* is the Czech word for this.

1932 Karl Jansky, an American engineer, was the first person to listen to the radio waves from the stars. Oliver Lodge, a British scientist had tried to find radio waves from the Sun but had failed because the trams in Liverpool made so much radio noise the Sun's signal was drowned.

1940s British scientists in World War II developed radar which helped the UK detect enemy shipping and aircraft. ENIAC, the first all-electric computer, was built using valves.

1947 The transistor was invented.

1958 The integrated circuit or silicon 'chip' was invented.

1960s Small, powerful transistor radios and very large mainframe computers were built.

1990s Small, powerful desktop and laptop computers and large 'ghettoblaster' radios are common.

Q1 The snakes and ladders game suggests that some of the developments in IT and control technology are bad and some are good. Discuss which developments you feel merit a 'snake' and which a 'ladder'. Discuss also which developments have good and bad points.

Q2 Discuss which sort of job robots can do well and which sort of job still must be done by human beings.

Q3 Discuss whether teachers will eventually be replaced by computers.

Q4 Give reasons why you will probably start your working life later and end it earlier than your grandparents.

Q5 Optical fibres are a 'new technology'. Find out what they can be used for. Look for their applications in medicine and telecommunications.

Q6 'Privacy is no longer possible.' Do you agree or disagree? Give reasons to support your answer.

Waves

A wavy world

There are many types of wave. Each comes from some kind of regular to-and-fro change. Each wave transfers energy away from its source by some kind of regular to-and-fro change.

Imagine you are at the top of a cliff looking at the seaside scene in the top picture.

Q1 Where have the waves come from?

Q2 What evidence have you that the waves transfer energy?

Q3 Where do you think the waves got their energy from?

Q4 Invent and describe a way to take useful energy from sea waves.

Q5 Identify a source of radio waves in the bottom picture. Identify a detector of radio waves. How do you know the radio waves transfer energy?

Q6 Repeat Q5 for

a light waves
b sound waves
c 'heat' waves (called infra-red)
d ultra-violet waves
e water surface waves
f radar waves.

Q7 Which of those waves in Q6 can we actually see?

Q8 One type is particularly dangerous to people. Which one? Why?

We can see the waves on the surface of a liquid like the sea. Most waves, however, are invisible. Some invisible waves appear as dotted lines in the picture.

124

Waves in a slinky spring

Think about stretching a 'slinky' spring along the floor and making waves, by some kind of regular to-and-fro motion. How can you prove that slinky spring waves transfer energy? Does as much energy reach the other end of the spring as you put in?

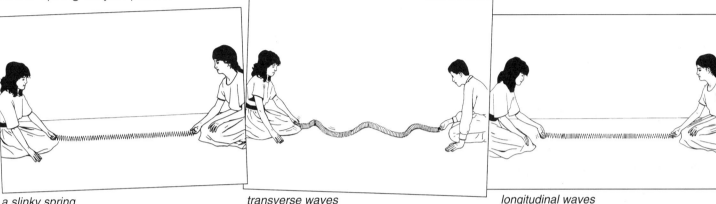

a slinky spring

transverse waves

longitudinal waves

The regular to-and-fro motion of a **transverse** wave is across the direction of energy transfer (*trans* = across). In a **longitudinal** wave, the regular to-and-fro motion is *along* the direction of energy transfer. Radio, radar, infra-red, light, ultra-violet, and some earthquake waves are all **transverse waves**.

Sound waves and some earthquake waves are **longitudinal waves**:

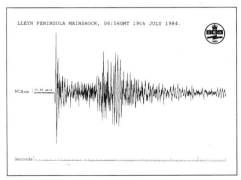

Liquid surface waves

Liquid surface waves, like those on the sea and in a ripple tank, transfer energy as we have seen. People have tried various ways to remove useful energy from sea waves, such as 'Salter's ducks'.

Water surface waves transfer energy by the regular to-and-fro *and* up-and-down motion of water particles, like the dots in the picture.

Liquid surface waves are therefore both longitudinal *and* transverse. Try to create a wave like this in a slinky spring.

Sound waves also travel by the regular 'wavy' motion of particles of matter. In this case, the regular motion is purely longitudinal.

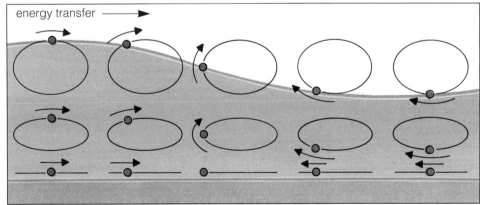

energy transfer ➝

Q9 Where have the sound waves come from that you hear now? What different substances have they passed through? How do you know they carry energy?

Q10 Where have the light waves come from that let you read these words? How do you know they carry energy?

Waves

Light

A laser, like the one in the picture, produces a very intense light **beam**. A beam is a set of light waves. You know that light waves transfer energy because something happens when they enter your eye, but the actual light waves themselves are invisible. **Chemical changes** happen when the eye absorbs the light energy.

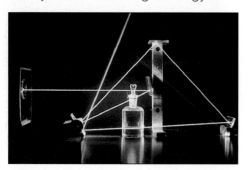

The leaves of a plant also absorb light energy, but in this case the chemical changes make food. When a photographic film absorbs light energy, the chemical changes make up the picture.

The wave equation

For any wave (either longitudinal or transverse), the wave equation relates speed (v), frequency (f) and wavelength (λ):

$$v = f\lambda$$

Another wave measure: amplitude

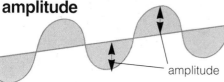

amplitude

The amplitude of a wave is the greatest variation in a cycle from the centre. What range of longitudinal wave amplitudes are possible with a slinky? Amplitude relates to the energy content of the wave: to loudness in the case of sound waves. (Think of the word 'amplify'.)

Measuring waves

Light waves are **electromagnetic**. This is because they involve the regular transverse change of electric and magnetic **fields**. In this picture the electric field is blue and the magnetic field is yellow.

a light wave from a laser

direction of energy transfer (speed v)

wavelength λ

Unlike water waves, light waves involve very fast changes at a **high frequency**. The frequency of yellow light is 500 million million cycles of change per second: 5×10^{14} hertz (Hz). As well as frequency, there are other important measures of waves. The speed of light in air is almost 300 000 km/s.

Q1 Roughly, what is the range of frequency of water waves?

Q2 Estimate values for the length and speed of water waves on the surface of a pond.

The hertz (symbol Hz) is the unit of wave **frequency** (symbol f): one cycle per second.

The metre (symbol m) is the unit of **wavelength** (symbol λ): the distance covered by one wave cycle.

The metre per second (symbol m/s) is the unit of wave **speed** (symbol v): the rate of energy transfer through a distance.

Q3 What is the speed of a sound wave of frequency 256 Hz ('middle C') and length 1.25 m?

Q4 Copy and complete the table.

wave	speed (m/s)	frequency (Hz)	wave length (m)
yellow light	3×10^8	5×10^{14}	–
earthquake 'S' waves (transverse waves)	4000	–	10 000
BBC Radio 1 (MW)	–	1053×10^3	285

Q5 What do you notice about light and radio waves?

Compare this diagram to the laser picture opposite.

When a wave, in this case of light, passing through one **medium** (substance) hits the surface of a second medium, one or more of three things can happen:
Reflection: the wave bounces off the surface, to stay in the first medium.
Refraction: the wave passes on through the second medium, often changing direction at the surface.
Absorption: the wave disappears; its energy appears in some other form.

The photo on page 126 shows **reflection** *of a laser beam*

Young's experiment
In 1801 Thomas Young showed the reinforcement and cancellation effects of interference between light waves. They looked like this.

Young's experiment – interference of light waves, showing light and dark bands.

Only waves show interference effects. Young's experiment therefore proved that light energy travels as a wave form.

Diffraction and interference

Diffraction and interference are two more features of any type of wave.
Diffraction: the wave bends round the edge of a second medium.
Interference: when two waves of the same type, the same amplitude, and the same wavelength pass through the same space at the same time, they **interfere** with each other. In some places they reinforce each other and have a strong effect; in others, they cancel each other and have no effect.
    The photos show these for ripple tank waves.
Try the experiments yourself.

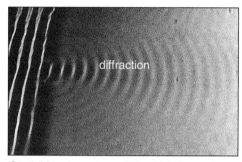
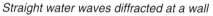

Straight water waves diffracted at a wall

Interference of two circular waves

Q6 Copy the diagram at the top of the page of the light beam and label the reflected wave.

Q7 Label the refracted wave and the region which absorbs input wave energy.

Q8 The amplitude of a sound wave relates to its loudness. What does the amplitude of a light wave relate to? With that in mind, comment on the light waves in the laser photo and the diagram.

Q9 The diagram below models reflection, refraction and absorption in the case of a school 'crocodile'. Which is which? Describe the model in each case.

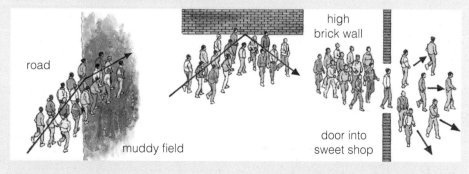

Q10 What happens to a wave's length during refraction? And it speed? Relate your answers to the wave equation.

Q11 Describe reflection, refraction and absorption as appropriate for waves in **a** a slinky spring, **b** a ripple tank.

Sound waves

see science at work

■ **Sound**
p 4 How do we hear?
p 11 Sound waves through air
p 24 How the moving coil microphone works

Hearing with waves

If you stand near a large speaker playing bass notes in a disco, you can feel the **vibrations** caused by the sound waves from the speaker. (Holding a balloon lets you feel this vibration even more strongly.)

All sound sources produce the sound waves by vibration and the waves travel through matter by vibration. Sound waves that enter your ear vibrate the ear drum to produce signals in a big nerve (the auditory nerve) that leads to your brain.

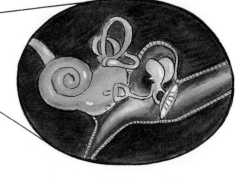

Sounds that are so loud you can feel them can cause major damage to your hearing!

A vibrating object pushes the air molecules next to it to and fro. They push their neighbours to and fro, and so on, so energy radiates from the source by the to-and-fro motion of the particles of air. In fact, sound travels this way through all matter.

● If the molecules are close together, the air pressure is high.
● If the molecules are far apart, the air pressure is low.
● In between these positions, the pressure is in between.
● A graph of the pressure in the air is wavy: that's what a sound wave looks like.

Q1 Why can't sound waves travel through a vacuum?

Q2 What is the central straight line (x-axis) in the sound wave graph?

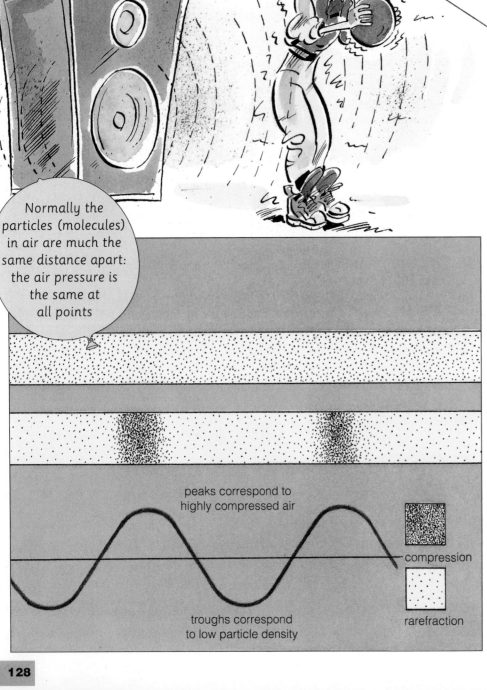

Normally the particles (molecules) in air are much the same distance apart: the air pressure is the same at all points

peaks correspond to highly compressed air

compression

troughs correspond to low particle density

rarefraction

Q3 On a clear copy of the sound wave graph, mark
a the amplitude
b the wavelength.

Q4 Sound travels faster in liquids than in gases (such as air), and faster in solids than in liquids. For a sound of 500 Hz, find how fast it travels in
a helium, wavelength 1.96 m
b sea water, wavelength 3 m
c steel, wavelength 12 m.

Q5 Why do sound waves travel
a faster in solids than in liquids
b faster in liquids than in gases?

Q6 Do sound waves travel faster in a hot liquid than a cold one?

Q7 The sound sensor in a level meter is a microphone. How does the sound level meter work?

Q8 Discuss how loud the sound output would be of each of the scenes in the photos.

Loud and soft

The loudness of a sound wave relates to its amplitude (its energy content). The best way to measure loudness would be to measure the amplitude, in other words how much the pressure varies from the standard, central value.

In practice, this is not at all easy, so we don't measure loudness by pressure (unit **pascal**). Instead we use sound level meters, and the unit of loudness is the **decibel**, symbol dB.

Difficult decibels
How loud a sound is depends on many factors, in particular distance and frequency (as the sensitivity of our ears depends on frequency).

Level	loudness
threshold of hearing	0 dB
a whisper	40 dB
traffic	60 dB
road drill	80 dB
disco	100 dB
threshold of pain	120 dB

Sound waves in air **diverge** (spread out) from any source. This is a major reason why a distant sound is soft. (In just the same way, a distant star is fainter than our Sun.)

If you double the distance from a sound source, the energy spreads over four times the area, so the loudness falls to a quarter.

If you treble the distance, the loudness falls to a ninth.

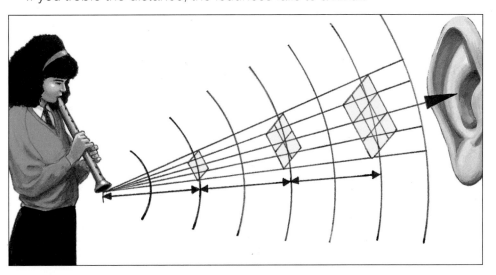

Sound and music

see science at work

■ **Sound**
p 3 What is a wave?
p 17 Musical instruments
pp 20–21 Resonance

Making music

It is easy to understand how a guitar string makes a sound – its vibration (to-and-fro motion) pushes the air molecules to and fro to make a pressure wave.

In a wind instrument, like the organ, the whole set of vibrating air particles in a tube acts as the source of sound.

An organ is one of the biggest musical instruments. Pressing a key makes air blow over the end of one of the many 'pipes'. A large organ has hundreds of pipes.

Organ pipes can be as much as 10 m long and as short as a few cm.

Sounds different

The loudness (energy content) of a sound depends on its amplitude.

The pitch of a sound (high note or low note) depends on its frequency (or wavelength) – the higher the frequency (or the smaller the wavelength), the higher the pitch.

blow

Q1 "A noisy noise annoys an oyster." Noise and music are both sounds. How do they differ?

Q2 Waves from a guitar string can differ in frequency (wavelength). In what way do these waves sound different?

Sound and vibration

Imagine linking a signal generator to a TV speaker, fitted as shown with an acetate or paper tube. If you increase the signal frequency from the very lowest setting, how do you think the spheres will behave? Try it!

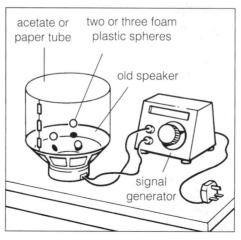

acetate or paper tube

two or three foam plastic spheres

old speaker

signal generator

Q3 How do you get sounds that differ in frequency from a bottle mouth organ?

Q4 How do you get sounds that differ in frequency from a bottle xylophone?

Q5 How do you get sounds that differ in frequency from a wooden model organ pipe?

Resonance

There are many types of wind instrument. Each is a tube of air with an open end for you to blow over or through. The other end may be open or closed. Here's how they make waves, by a process called **resonance**.

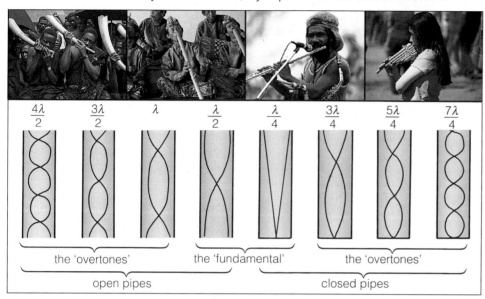

| $\frac{4\lambda}{2}$ | $\frac{3\lambda}{2}$ | λ | $\frac{\lambda}{2}$ | $\frac{\lambda}{4}$ | $\frac{3\lambda}{4}$ | $\frac{5\lambda}{4}$ | $\frac{7\lambda}{4}$ |

the 'overtones' the 'fundamental' the 'overtones'

open pipes closed pipes

In these diagrams, the dotted lines represent how much the air particles vibrate (their amplitude) by how far apart they are at each level in the tube. Each diagram shows how the wavelength of the sound produced relates to the length of the tube.

Any time you gently blow over the top of an empty bottle to produce a sound, it's the same sound. The air inside 'resonates' to produce the fundamental note. Blowing much harder can produce one or more **overtones**.

Resonance is the way something vibrates at its natural (fundamental) frequency when treated suitably. It doesn't need much energy. Gently tapping a bell or a gong makes it resonate.

Resonance can be a good thing: without it we would have no voices and no musical instruments. Resonance is the process involved in tuning a radio or TV set, and in swinging a swing.

Resonance can be a nuisance. Strong gusts of wind along a New York valley made a suspension bridge resonate and collapse. If buildings resonate during an earthquake, they sometimes collapse too.

Q6 There is a pattern in the tube length/wavelength relationship for an open tube. What is it? What is the pattern for a closed tube?

Q7 Name the wind instruments shown in the pictures at the top of the page, and as many others as you can.

Q8 Design a table top model to show the earthquake effect.

Q9 List some other examples of resonance.

Stringing along

In any stringed instrument each string has two fixed ends. Here is the fundamental sound.

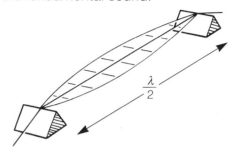

$\frac{\lambda}{2}$

Q10 Sketch the string's first two overtones.

Q11 Write down the pattern in the string length/wavelength relationship.

Q12 Name the stringed instruments shown in the pictures, and as many more as you can.

Using sound waves

Using sound waves

We have seen that sound energy, produced by vibration travels in the form of pressure waves through matter, Also:

● the more closely packed the matter molecules are, the faster the sound travels
● given the right input, an object can resonate to produce sound
● a surface between two media can reflect, refract, absorb and/or diffract the sound energy
● like all waves, in a constant medium, sound travels in straight lines.

Working on sound waves

The drawings describe some experiments on sound. (Maybe you can try them.)

Q1 Sound travels in straight lines. How then can we hear what happens round the corner of a building? Discuss and describe the various ways the robber in the picture can hear the alarm, the police officer's feet, and the whistle.

Q2 Work out ways to insulate the robber from these sounds.

Q3 How are the people in a car insulated from the noises of driving?

Q4 Discuss the related problems of hi-fi speakers and speaker cases, and how to overcome them.

Q5 Group A are banging a long ruler on a table and measuring the time between bang and echo. What else should they measure to find the speed of sound in air? How would they do the calculation?

Q6 Without diffraction, Group B wouldn't hear much traffic noise in the shaded area. In fact they find that high frequencies (such as sirens sounds) diffract less than low ones (such as lorries). Why is this?

Q7 In the lab, Group C have set up an experiment: two speakers radiate the same high-pitched note through the same part of the room; the group members walk to and fro through that area. What are they trying to explore?

Group B

Group C

Group A

Working with sound waves

Antisound

Car engines make a lot of noise. Sound insulation can help, but is far from perfect. The situation is far worse with larger engines, such as in lorries. Feeding anti-sound into the cab can cancel out almost all the noise.

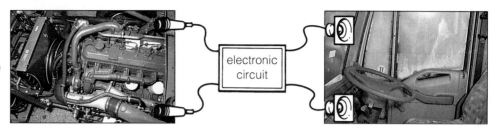

electronic circuit

Q8 Explain with care how this system works and why. What aspect of how waves behave does it depend on?

1 Engine noise picked up by microphones
2 and fed to electronic circuit
3 which produces the opposite signals
4 to feed to speakers in the cab

All at sea

Sonar: so(und) **na**(vigation) **r**(anging)
Asdic: a(nti) **s**(ubmarine) **d**(etection) **i**(nvestigation) **c**(ommittee)
Sonar and asdic are rather like radar but for use underwater (water absorbs radio waves). The users study the echoes of sound pulses sent out through the water. Some whales and dolphins do this too.

In much the same way, people in ships use echo-sounders to
● find the depth of objects underwater
● study the sea bed
● find shoals of fish.

Q9 Why do blind people have sticks?

Q10 What aspect of how waves behave do all these examples of working with sound waves depend on?

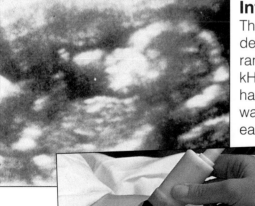

Infra-sound and ultra-sound

The human sense of hearing can detect sound waves in the frequency range of (approximately) 20 Hz to 20 kHz. However, sound waves can have any frequency. We call sound waves below 20 Hz **infra-sound**. Like earthquake waves (some of which *are* infra-sound), these can be very destructive. Indeed, some people have tried to develop infra-sound 'death rays'. Ultra-sound waves, on the other hand, have frequencies above 20 kHz.

Q11 What evidence do you have that animals smaller than us can hear ultrasonics?

Q12 Why do you think this is? (*Hint.* Think about musical instruments that make high sounds.)

Q13 Many forms of sonar and echo-sounder use ultra-sonic rather than sound waves. This is because we can pick up more detail at high frequencies. Why do you think this is?

Q14 People also use ultrasonics for cleaning clothes and getting sonar-like pictures of babies in the womb. Why not use X-rays for scanning babies in the womb?

see science at work

Light
p 18 Making a spectrum

Seeing by frequency

Why is there colour in our lives?
● Light waves have a range of frequencies.
● Each frequency affects our sense of vision in its own way: we see colour.

Exploring colour

raybox
glass prism
lens
card
slits for light box

What is a spectrum?

Wavelength $\lambda \times 10^{-7}$ m

7	6	5	4

Frequency $f \times 10^{14}$ Hz

?	5	6	?

Q1 What is the best way to use this equipment to make a colour spectrum? Try it!

Q2 What would the spectrum look like if you viewed it through different colour filters? Try it!

Q3 What would the spectrum look like if it fell on pieces of differently coloured card? Try it!

Q4 Explain the effects of coloured filters on coloured lights, and of coloured lights on coloured cards.

Q5 Write down and explain the wave equation and the symbols, units and unit symbols.

Q6 Use the wave equation and the data shown in the spectrum photograph to find the speed of light.

Q7 Now use the speed of light to find the two missing frequency values marked.

Q8 Important theories of Max Planck and Albert Einstein early this century showed that the energy of a light wave is directly proportional to the frequency. Which has more energy – red light or blue light? What other evidence do you have to support that?

White light and white noise

The colour spectrum we have just looked at is the 'white light' spectrum. True white light, produced by very hot objects like a lamp filament or the Sun, contains light waves of all the frequencies we can detect with out eyes.

Not all light sources give out 'white light'.

Q6 Why does a candle flame look yellow?

Q7 Why does a torch lamp shine red if the battery is run down?

Some sources of light may look white, but don't produce 'white light' in the sense used here.

Q8 Why does a discharge (tube) light appear white if it doesn't produce 'white light'?

Q9 Explain this graph to a friend.

Q10 How do you think spectral graphs of the Sun and a candle flame would differ?

Q11 Use the data in the diagrams on page 131 to produce spectral graphs of the sound output of
a an open pipe
b a closed pipe
c a stretched string.(Two of these are much the same.)

Check your answers to 6–8 if you can by looking at the spectra of the sources in the photographs. (A hand spectroscope is the best way.)

When we studied musical instruments, we found that the sound they produce consists of a fundamental (basic) note and a number of fainter overtones. However, there are some sources of 'white noise' (all frequencies). The best known is the hiss of a TV speaker when it is not tuned into a station.

The spectrum of 'white noise' looks something like this.

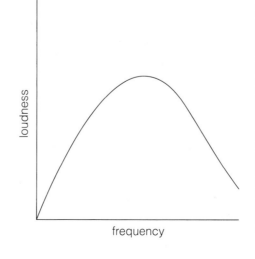

Light and its family

Visible light has a range of frequencies (of wavelengths), but is just a small part of a very large spectrum of wave radiations. We call the whole family **electromagnetic** radiation, as the energy travels by electric and magnetic fields. See the diagram on page 126.

wavelength (λ)m		10^{-15}	10^{-14}	10^{-13}	10^{-12}	10^{-11}	10^{-10}	10^{-9}	10^{-8}
			gamma radiation				X-rays		ultra
frequency (f)Hz		10^{24}	10^{23}	10^{22}	10^{21}	10^{20}	10^{19}	10^{18}	10^{17}	10^{1}

Q1 List the properties of any wave.

Q2 What is the speed of light (and of the other waves in the family) in space or air?

All these radiations are waves, so they show the usual wave properties. They also travel very fast.

Study the electromagnetic spectrum that crosses this double page. You don't need to know the numbers on the two scales (though you probably know some in the radio region, and perhaps those for light). You *do* need to be able to list the members of the spectrum in order.

Q4 Try doing that now, without looking. List the types of electromagnetic wave in order of *decreasing* wavelength.

Gamma radiation

Gamma (γ) rays are very high frequency small wavelength electromagnetic waves. They come from to-and-fro electric field changes inside the nuclei of atoms, from a type of radioactivity.

There are three main types of radiation from radio-active nuclei: alpha (α), beta (β) and gamma (γ).

Q3 The photo shows one source of gamma rays; name it and one other.

More infra-red

An infra-red camera can detect infra-red waves from warm surfaces, even in the dark, and display a visible image on a screen for the user to look at or photograph.

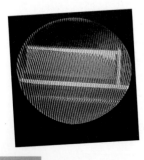

The pictures show an infra-red headset which works like this, and a fire officer's view of a smoke-filled room.

Q5 People use gamma rays like X-rays for 'looking' deep inside solid objects: for example for finding air bubbles or cracks inside solid steel structures. How does this technique work?

Q6 Why are γ-rays better for this purpose than X-rays?

Q7 Why these names?

Q8 Which surface reflects infra-red? Which absorbs it?

Q9 How much
a light
b infra-red leaves a 60 W lamp?

Infra-red waves

People often call infra-red **thermal radiation** (or **heat radiation**). That's because most of the wave energy from a hot surface is in the infra-red region of the spectrum. You know that a filament lamp is hot to touch when it's 'burning'. In fact only about 5% of the input energy comes out as light.

Think about this experiment with an infra-red radiator (or try it!). Use a drop of water to stick the following to the back of your hand;
a a 40 mm × 40 mm square of white paper
b a 40 mm × 40 mm square of black paper.
Then switch on the radiator and hold your hand near it.

 Be careful not to burn your hand on heat from the radiator.

Q10 Why do some objects look brighter than others?

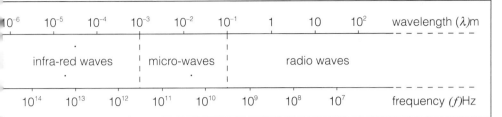

10^{-6}	10^{-5}	10^{-4}	10^{-3}	10^{-2}	10^{-1}	1	10	10^2		wavelength (λ)m

infra-red waves   micro-waves   radio waves

10^{14}	10^{13}	10^{12}	10^{11}	10^{10}	10^9	10^8	10^7	frequency (*f*)Hz

The wave equation again

Q11 Write down and explain the meaning of the wave equation.

Q12 Find the speed of blue light in sapphire: wavelength 400×10^{-9} m, frequency 4.25×10^{14} Hz.

Q13 Why don't the wavelength and frequency values fit together on the spectrum.,

Microwaves

Microwaves are very short radio waves, mostly used for radar.

Q14 Explain how radar works. Compare it to sonar (page 133), to the echo-location system of bats, and to the use of γ-rays to 'look inside' metal objects.

Q15 Find out what you can about, and write illustrated essays on
a cooking with microwaves
b microwave link communications.

Read and discuss this item from *New Scientist* (September 1992), then answer these questions.

Q16 Is the device described really a 'heat camera'?

Q17 What do pilots do now if the runway they want to land on is fogbound?

Q18 What is an acousto-optical crystal? Describe how it does what it does.

Q19 At higher temperatures, are the microwaves produced longer or shorter in wavelength?

Q20 Explain what 'infra-red imaging' is, when it is of use, and how it works.

Heat camera helps pilots see through fog

Jonathan Beard, New York

Pilots landing in darkness or fog may soon find their way by viewing the runway with a microwave camera.

The camera uses an optical system, developed by electronics company ThermoTrex of San Diego in California, that avoids the large amounts of computer power normally needed to convert microwave signals into a video image. First, the microwave signal is converted into sound waves and then, using an acousto-optical crystal, the sound is converted into a pattern of light which is picked up by a video camera and displayed on a screen.

John Lovberg, the engineer in charge of developing the camera, explains that all materials, unless they are at absolute zero (-273°C), emit microwaves with wave-lengths as long as several centimetres. "At these wavelengths, clouds, smoke, fog – and even plywood – are transparent."

The system is entirely passive: it does not emit any radiation. Radar, which emits microwave signals and picks up the reflections, is used in airliners but only to spot clouds and other aircraft at high altitude. At low levels, the amount of reflection from objects on the ground is too great to process quickly.

Infrared imaging is used by military aircraft for night vision but rain and fog tend to scatter infrared wavelengths.

The problem with passively picking up microwaves is that their faintness and long wavelength requires a lot of

antenna. But, explains Lovberg, "We needed an antenna that could fit on a helicoper or in the nose of a 757". It is possible to produce an image using a small antenna if the system is capable of processing large amounts of information. But doing this fast enough so that the pilot sees an instant image of the view ahead is very difficult.

ThermoTrex's camera uses an acousto-optical technique to avoid complex processing. The antenna is small and is made up of a grid of small antennas known as a phased array. Each element of the array detects incoming microwaves, sensing their power, wavelength and angle of incidence.

Instead of then electronically processing the signals, they are converted by transducers into sound waves travelling through an acousto-optical crystal. Such crystals change their refractive index, the ability to bend light, under pressure. The pressure of the sound waves creates a pattern of refractive index inside the crystal which represents the signals received by the antenna.

The camera then shines a laser beam through the crystal which is deflected by the refractive index pattern. "The deflected light precisely duplicates the original source pattern seen by the antenna. We then use an ordinary CCD image sensor to detect this light pattern and display it to the pilot," Lovberg says.

ThermoTrex expects its camera to be small enough to be mounted with the radar antenna in the nose of an airliner. Lovberg says the system could be ready for use in army helicopters by next year with a version for airliners by 1995.

Q1 Copy the spectrum from these two pages. In pencil, add the names of the seven main regions and one or two of the wavelength and frequency values. Check with pages 136 and 137 before you ink the information in.

Q2 For each region, write down two or three things you know about it (such as sources and uses).

wavelength (λ)m

frequency (*f*) Hz

Electromagnetic astronomy

Every star, including the Sun, and galaxy produces a range of electromagnetic radiations. (A galaxy is a group of millions of stars).

● We can see the Sun and stars: **visible light.**
● We can feel thermal energy from the Sun: **infra-red.**
● **Ultra-violet** from the Sun (partly filtered by the ozone layer) darkens and burns fair skin.
● **Radio** waves from the Sun and our galaxy produce the hissing noise in a TV or radio set not tuned to a station.
● **Gamma** waves from the Sun form part of the 'background radiation' everywhere on Earth (which people believe causes the genetic mutations behind evolution).

X-rays

X-rays can be dangerous in excess!

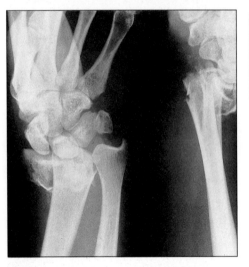

You have probably seen an X-ray photo of some part of your body (perhaps of your teeth, or if you broke your wrist). The hard and soft parts under the skin absorb X-rays differently, so we obtain a sort of shadow picture.

Q3 People use the same technique to study faults in steel objects. Explain how this works.

Never look directly at the Sun through telescope or binoculars.

For hundreds of years scientists have studied light from the Sun, stars and galaxies to learn about the Universe. However, light is just a tiny part of the electromagnetic spectrum – other kinds of telescope produce much more information too.

Satellites also carry infra-red, ultra-violet and γ-ray telescopes. Views from above the atmosphere give better pictures. Why?

radio telescope

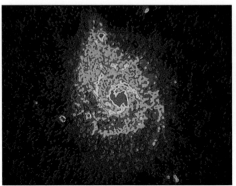
radio telescope view of a galaxy

X-ray telescope

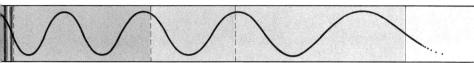

wavelength (λ)m

frequency (*f*) Hz

How can cleaned clothes be whiter than white?

Washing powders contain substances that **fluoresce**.

Fluorescence is the absorption of ultra-violet waves and the release of the energy in the form of visible light.

Ultra-violet radiation

Some disco lights produce a lot of ultra-violet. Clothes washed with powders that include fluorescers therefore glow brightly.

Tube (discharge) lamps involve a current in a low pressure gas. This produces ultra-violet inside the tube.

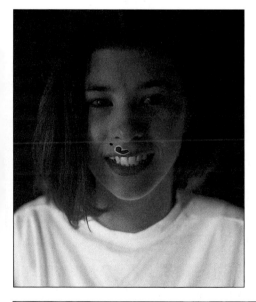

Q4 How can cleaned clothes be whiter than white?

Q5 What else glows brightly in ultra-violet light?

Q6 How can your teeth appear whiter than white?

 The fluorescent powder inside these tubes is harmful!

fluorescent powder inside glass

Radio waves

Q7 What is the speed of light in air and space?

Q8 What is the speed of radio waves in air and space?

Q9 A communication satellite is 30 000 km from London. What delay would there be in a phone call using it between two people in London?

Q10 Explain what ozone holes are, and what they have to do with the warning below!

Many minerals (substances inside rock) fluoresce like this. One of the first to be discovered is called **fluorspar**.

 Ultra violet radiation can cause eye damage and skin cancer

Converting waves

Waves to waves
How does a TV programme get from the studio to your home?

Q1 Write down what you know about the process. It involves the transfer of energy by various kinds of wave, including a number of those we have met in the last few pages.

1 The studio lamps produce *light waves* which reflect from the objects in the scene. Some of the reflected light waves enter the camera lens. This focusses (by refraction) an image onto a special plate (like a large **photocell**).

2 The people talking produce *sound waves*. Some of the sound waves enter the microphone by the camera.

Q2 Your voice box (larynx), throat and mouth form a kind of musical instrument. What kind? How does it produce sound waves?

3 The camera output consists of *electric waves* (a 'signal') matching the input light and sound.

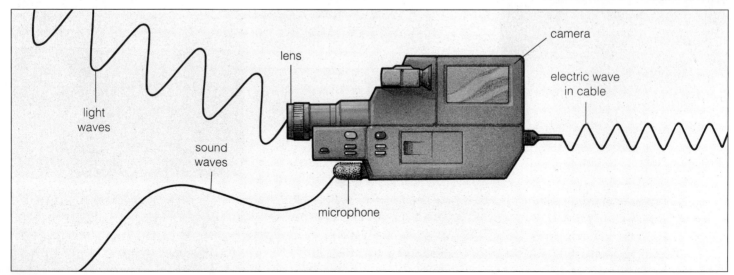

light waves

sound waves

lens

microphone

camera

electric wave in cable

Sarah and Chris use an oscilloscope to study the electric waves produced by making sounds into a microphone. Perhaps your teacher will guide you on how to do this yourself.

Q3 Sketch typical patterns obtained.

Q4 How do the patterns depend on whether a note is loud or soft?

Q5 How do they depend on whether it is high or low?

Q6 How do they differ for two people humming the same note?

4 The electric waves go to a video tape recorder. This stores them in the form of 'frozen *magnetic waves*' on the tape surface.

5 After being processed and amplified, the electric waves pass to the transmitter which **broadcasts** them (sends them out in all directions) as radio waves. Of course, the waves become very weak after a few kilometres. (See page 129.)

6 Your aerial converts the radio waves back into *electric waves*. These pass along the cable to the TV set, which selects the right ones and amplifies them. The set then separates the audio and video signals.

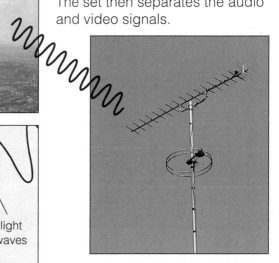

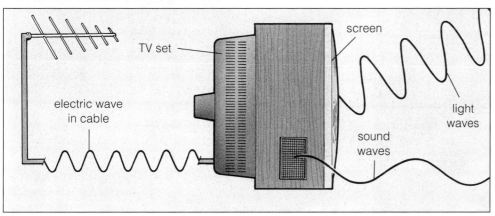

electric wave in cable — TV set — screen — light waves — sound waves

7 The video signal (still an electric wave) goes onto the electron beam inside the TV set tube. *Light waves* leave the screen at the front.

8 The audio electric signal goes to a speaker which converts them to sound waves again.

Q7 What does 'amplify' mean? Explain, with examples.

Q8 Compare with care the structures of a simple microphone and speaker, what they do, and how they work.

Sometimes our perceptions about force and motion are not quite the same as scientists' ideas.

Newton's first law tells us what an object will do when there is no **resultant force** acting on it. An object will either be **stationary** (at rest) or **travelling in a straight line at constant speed**.

The object will stay in one of these two states for ever, until someone or something pushes or pulls it.

All the forces on an object are balanced when there is no resultant force on it. If it starts to speed up, slow down or change direction a resultant force is pulling or pushing it.

Understanding the **stationary state** is fairly easy – we see it around us all the time. Your bag will remain on the floor until you pick it up. Your book will remain on the table until you decide to change its position. Many people would say that there are no forces acting on a book lying on a table, but in fact there are two pairs of forces acting on all stationary objects. We do not notice them because they are balanced.

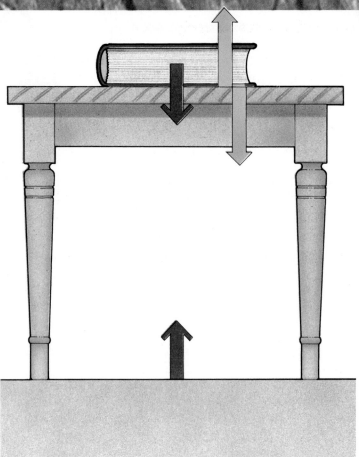

Force of book on table	=	force of table on book
Force of gravity of the Earth pulling down on book	=	force of gravity of book pulling up on Earth

It is much more difficult to understand how something can travel in a straight line and not slow down when there is no observable force pushing. The reason is the force of friction, which acts when two surfaces come into contact or move across each other. Friction always acts in the opposite direction to motion.

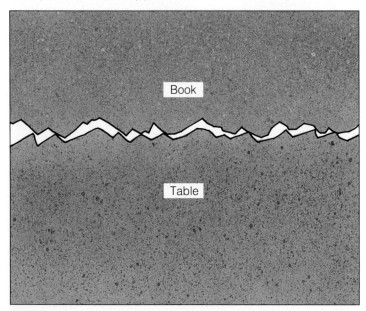

There are no surfaces in real life which are completely frictionless and this is why we never see Newton's first law in action when we push things – the lumps on one surface catch and stick to the lumps on the other surface. We can however, reduce friction in a number of different ways:

1 by rubbing off the 'lumps' by sanding and polishing (for example a wooden floor)
2 by filling in the little 'hollows' in the surface with varnish or paint (for example on a child's garden slide)
3 by lubricating surfaces so that liquid fills the space between them and separates them (for example moving metal parts in an engine)
4 by separating the surfaces with air (for example, a hovercraft moves along on a cushion of air above the sea in a similar way to the rider on an air track)

On a linear air track, friction due to surface contact is zero because air is forced out of little holes along the track which separate the surface of the rider from the surface of the track. The rider and the track are no longer in contact. We can use this apparatus to see Newton's first law in action.

Friction at work

A car can travel at constant speed in a straight line because it has its own source of energy on board (a petrol or diesel engine). As the fuel is burned, energy is transferred from the engine to the axle which turns the wheels. Two forces act on the car as it starts to move:

- the forward force of the engine

- the backward force of friction between the car and the air it pushes as it moves. This force is called **air resistance** – it is a force of friction. It opposes the car's motion. This force increases as the speed of the car increases.

When the car travels at constant speed, the forward and backward forces are equal. Here Newton's first law is obeyed – there is no resultant force on the car, yet it is moving at constant speed.

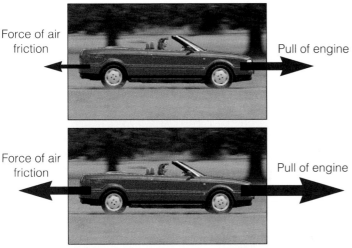

Force of air friction — Pull of engine

When the accelerator pedal is pushed down further, energy is transferred at a faster rate to the wheels. The forward force on the car increases, and the car accelerates. However, the car does not keep on accelerating for this same position of the accelerator pedal, because as the car's speed increases the air resistance increases too. Eventually the forward and backward forces will balance, and the car will travel at a constant speed again. To accelerate more, the pedal must be pushed down even further.

Although forces of friction oppose the car's motion this does not mean that they are always inconvenient. The car wheels could not turn at all if there was no friction between the tyres and the road. If you have ever cycled on an icy surface you may have noticed the wheels of your bike skidding.

Answer these questions by yourself. Then work in a small group to discuss your answers. Put your ideas on a large sheet of paper and present them to your class.

Q1 The student has just pushed this trolley. Copy this diagram and draw the forces on the trolley and describe what will happen to it.

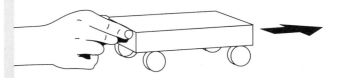

Q2 Copy this diagram and draw the forces here.

Q3 A student cycles along a level road and then stops pedalling. Draw a diagram and show the forces acting at this point. Describe what will happen.

Q4 A car goes round a corner at constant speed. Is there a resultant force acting on it?

Q5 The buggies and road surfaces are identical. One buggy is on the Moon and the other is on Earth. Both drivers are accelerating and have the accelerator pedal in the same position. Describe how the motion of both vehicles would differ.

Q6 Why is it that rockets are streamlined but satellites are not?

Exploring force & motion 2

Two types of force

1 Contact force

This is exactly what is says it is. A contact force exists when two surfaces push against each other.

For example, when you push a shopping trolley you apply a continuous contact force.

When you kick a ball you apply a contact force for a short time (an **impulse**). The force stops when the contact stops.

Lots of people think that the contact force 'stays with' the ball after it has been kicked and this is why the ball moves. This is *not* true. If you think like this, you will have to change the way you think about contact force! The force stops when the contact stops.

2 Non-contact force

This acts across a distance without touching. Examples include gravity, magnetism or static electricity. Gravity cannot be switched off – it is always acting. When you throw a ball in the air, it starts its motion with a resultant contact force from the hand. Once it has left the hand the resultant force on it is due to gravity – it is the ball's weight. Gravity always acts downwards. By 'downwards' we really mean towards the centre of the Earth.

Resultant force

Newton's second law tells us what happens to an object when it is pushed by a continuously acting **resultant force**. The force can be either contact or non-contact.

It tells us that:
a) the acceleration of an object is directly proportional to the size of the resultant force acting on it, so if the force doubles the acceleration doubles
b) the acceleration (**not** the velocity) always takes place in the direction of the resultant force.

A resultant force is an unbalanced force – it can speed things up (accelerate), slow things down (decelerate) or change the direction or shape of things.

For example, in the case of a model car with a pulling force of 60 N and a frictional force of 40 N, the 60 N acts to the right and the 40 N acts to the left.

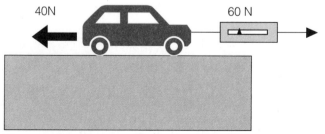

40N   60 N

The resultant force = 60 – 40 = 20N (to the right)
The resultant 20 N would *accelerate* the toy car to the right.

If a continually acting resultant force is in the same direction as the motion the speed will increase. The object will accelerate.

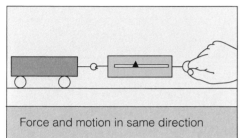

Force and motion in same direction

If a continually acting resultant force is in the opposite direction to the motion the speed will decrease. The object will decelerate.

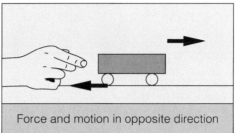

Force and motion in opposite direction

If a continually acting resultant force is at an angle to the motion, it will change the object's direction.

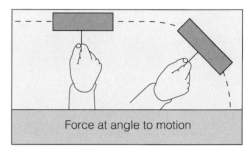

Force at angle to motion

Lots of people think that the velocity of a body is always in the same direction as the resultant force acting on it. This is *not* always true. Let us examine what happens when a ball is thrown straight up in the air.

This student has thrown a ball straight up in the air. The picture shows the ball in three positions: on its way up, stationary at the top, and on its way down.

Many people think that:

1 because the ball is moving upwards the resultant force must be an upward one. This is *not* true. The contact force no longer exists, as the ball has left the hand and gravity does not act upwards, it always acts downwards.

2 when it is at rest the force on the ball is zero. This is *not* true. Gravity is not suddenly switched off at the maximum height.

3 on the way down the resultant force is a downward one. This *is* true.

Ball positions

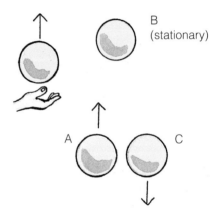

B (stationary)

A   C

If you think as in points **1**, **2** and **3** you need to change the way you think about force and motion.

At the start the ball is at rest in the hand. The resultant contact force from the hand has to be bigger than the weight to accelerate the ball upwards.

Force of gravity of Earth pulling down on ball

Ball decelerating upwards

At the instant when the ball leaves the hand the contact force no longer exists – it stops when the contact stops. The resultant force on the ball is the weight of the ball, so it is entirely due to the pull of gravity. On the way up, the resultant force on the ball slows it down (decelerates it) because it is acting in the opposite direction to its velocity.

When the ball is stationary at the top, it is the ball's weight that changes the ball's direction and speeds it up. On the way down the ball accelerates because this time the weight is acting in the same direction as its velocity.

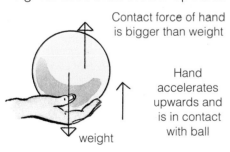

Contact force of hand is bigger than weight

Hand accelerates upwards and is in contact with ball

weight

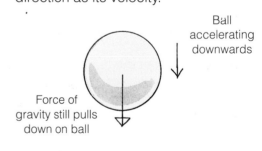

Ball accelerating downwards

Force of gravity still pulls down on ball

Q1 If the resultant force is an upward one when the ball is moving upwards, write down what it should be doing according to Newton's second law.

Q2 If the resultant force is zero when the ball is at maximum height, write down what it should be doing according to Newton's first law.

Q3 Let us assume that friction is zero everywhere in the picture – on the slope and on the flat.
a Describe the motion on the slope.
b Describe the motion on the flat.

Speeding up & slowing down

see science at work

■ **Structures and Machines**
p 10 and Extension exercise 4 Forces and movement

Forces can speed things up, slow things down, or change their direction of movement. A scientist would say that forces can change the velocity of things, as velocity has direction as well as magnitude. Changing the direction of something is changing its velocity, even if its speed remains the same.

If something slows down its velocity decreases – this is still an acceleration, but we write it with a minus sign in front.

The acceleration depends on the force applied and on the mass of the object. The acceleration is equal to the force applied multiplied by the mass of the object.

The cyclist has the same speed all the way along the road. Her velocity changes each time her direction changes.

A small mass will accelerate more rapidly than a large mass if the same force is applied to both.

However, it is more usual to write it down as:

Force = mass × acceleration

To get the same acceleration a large mass needs a larger force than a small mass.

Racing cars are built with as small a mass as possible. The lighter the car, the faster it will accelerate. The same rule applies to racing cycles as well. Olympic champion Chris Boardman used a special, lightweight bike made from carbon fibre, because carbon fibre materials are light and strong.

It is difficult to get massive things moving, but it is also difficult to stop them. The same rules apply to slowing things down – the more mass something has, the harder it is to slow down. Large ships can have masses of 200 000 tonnes or more, so even though they have powerful engines it takes them a long time to get going and a long time to slow down again. Captains of large ships have to start slowing down several kilometres before they reach a port to give themselves enough space to stop.

Q1 A motorcycle can accelerate much faster than a car even though it has a smaller engine. Why?

Q2 The following results were obtained from a test-car with a specially calibrated speedometer. Draw a speed/time graph of these results (time should be on the x-axis).

Time (sec)	0	5	10	15	20	25
Speed (m/s)	0	5	10	10	15	0

a Describe in words what happened to the car.
b Calculate the acceleration from 0 to 10 seconds, from 15 to 20 seconds, and from 20 to 25 seconds.
c If the mass of the car was 850 kg, calculate the force on the car during each period of acceleration.

Q3 The driver of a car travelling along the motorway at 90 km/h takes her foot off the accelerator. The car slows down by 15 km/h during the next 10 seconds. The mass of the car is 900 kg.
a Calculate the size of the force that is making the car slow down.
b What causes this force?

Moving in circles

Uzma is whirling a conker around her head on a string. The speed of the conker stays the same, but its velocity is changing all the time because its direction is changing.

The force that is causing the changing velocity is the pull in the string. The direction of the pull is always at right-angles to the velocity of the conker. This force is called **centripetal force**. The formula for calculating the size of a centripetal force is

$$F = \frac{mv^2}{r}$$

where F is the centripetal force (in newtons)
  m is the mass of the object (in kilograms)
  v is the speed of the object (in m/s)
 and r is the radius of the circle (in metres)

This means that:
- bigger masses need bigger centripetal forces to keep them moving in a circle
- faster moving objects also need bigger forces (in fact, if the speed is doubled, the centripetal force needed goes up four times)
- objects moving around small circles need bigger centripetal forces than objects moving around large circles.

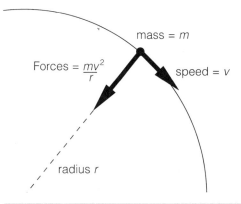

mass = m

Forces = $\frac{mv^2}{r}$ speed = v

radius r

There is a centripetal force on a vehicle going around a bend. The force comes from the friction between the tyres and the road. If the tyres cannot provide enough friction then the car will skid.

When roads are wet or icy, tyres do not provide much friction, so vehicles must travel very slowly around bends.

Vehicles can travel quite fast around shallow bends (where the radius of the bend is large), but must slow down to go around sharp bends (where the radius is small).

Q1 A loaded truck can travel around a bend at 50 Kmph. If it travelled any faster it would skid. Would the truck be able to go around the bend faster, or would it have to slow down if
a it was unloaded
b it came to a sharper bend
c the road was muddy?

Q2 Explain how an object can accelerate without changing its speed.
(*Hint:* acceleration is a change in velocity.)

Q3 The diagram shows a stone attached to a string going around a circle.
a Copy the diagram and mark the direction of the force at X.
b The mass of the ball is 200 g, its speed is 4 m/s, and the length of the string is 60 cm. Calculate the force in the string.
c The string breaks at Y. Mark on your diagram the direction the ball will travel after the string breaks.

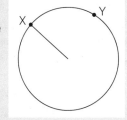

An engineer building a structure has to choose the right material for the job. Most things have to be designed to withstand forces, so engineers have to know how different materials behave when forces are applied to them.

Forces on structures or materials are described according to the effects they produce.

A compression force   A tension force   A bending force
Compression, tension and bending forces

When something is bent part of it is being stretched and part is being squashed. Look at the diagram below. Bending forces are really just a combination of compression and tension forces.

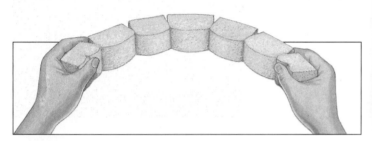

Every material changes shape a little when a force is applied to it. If the material returns to its original shape when the force is removed it is an **elastic** material. If the material stays permanently bent or stretched the material is **plastic**. Plasticine and clay are plastic materials. Some materials, like steel or wood, are elastic but become plastic if very large forces are applied. If the force is large enough the material will crack or shatter. Different materials behave in different ways.

Bricks, concrete and stone are good at resisting compression forces. You can support heavy weights on top of piles of bricks or concrete blocks. They are not very good at resisting tension forces, so they are not very good at resisting bending forces either. If tension forces are applied to bricks or concrete they tend to crack and break.

Wire, chain and string are good at resisting tension forces. You can hang heavy weights from wires or chains,

but they just crumple up if you squash them or bend them. **Glass fibres** (thin strands of glass) or **carbon fibres** are also good at resisting tension forces. They can be bent, but they will break if you try to bend them too far.

Wood and metal are good at resisting both tension and compression forces. Because bending forces are a combination of tension and compression forces, wood and metal are also good at resisting these too.

What about 'plastics' like polythene? These materials are called plastics because when they were being made their shape could easily be changed. When the material had been moulded into the right shape it was treated with chemicals or heat to make it set. Some plastics get soft when they are heated up (like plastic teaspoons) – they are called **thermoplastic** materials. Some plastics do not get soft (like the plastic in electric plugs) – they are called **thermosetting** materials. So not all 'plastics' are really plastic.

Making materials stronger

Concrete normally cracks if it is under tension, but it can be reinforced with steel to make it resist tension and bending forces. Steel wires are stretched using large forces, and the concrete mix is poured over them. When the concrete has set hard the wires are released, and compress the concrete. This is called **pre-stressed concrete** because, even when no forces are applied to it the concrete is already being compressed. Look at the diagram to see how pre-stressed concrete resists bending forces.

The concrete beam is being compressed by the steel rod.

The bending force increases the compression in the bottom of the concrete, and decreases the compression in the top, but the top is *still in compression.*

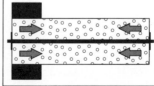

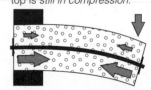

Choosing the right materials

The walls of buildings have to support the weight of the roof and the upstairs floors, so they are made of bricks or concrete which are good at resisting compression forces. Roofs and ceilings have to be made of things that are good at resisting bending forces, so they are made of wood or pre-stressed concrete.

Centuries ago, bridges were made of wood or stone. Stone slabs and wooden planks can be used for bridges as long as the supports are close together. Arched structures were built if wider gaps had to be crossed. In an arch all the stones are under compression (the forces are trying to squash them) and so stone is a good material to use. Modern suspension bridges use wires or chains under tension to support the bridge and the vehicles on it, and can span even wider rivers.

All the stones in the arch are being compressed

Q1 This picture shows part of a TV mast on a windy day. What do the wires do? Which wires are in tension? Why are the other wires there?

Q2 This picture shows part of an adventure playground. Which parts of the beam are in tension and which parts are in compression? If the girl moves along to the end of the beam, which parts are now in tension and which parts are in compression?

Q3 These graphs show deflection against load for two different materials. Which material would you use to make
a a diving board
b a footbridge across a stream?
Explain your answers.

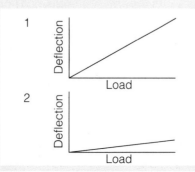

Q4 Concrete can withstand crushing pressures up to 70MN/m², and steel can withstand crushing pressures up to 400MN/n². A bridge (and any vehicles on it) weighs 150MN, and it has two supports. What area should each support have if they are made from **a** concrete **b** steel?
(*Hint:* force/area = 70MN/m² for concrete, and 1 MN= 1 000 000N)

Q5 The tension force that a wire can resist without breaking depends on its cross sectional area. A thick wire is stronger than a thin wire. If a steel wire with a 1m² cross section breaks under a force of 200MN, what cross sectional area would the wire need to have to support the following items? What diameter would the wire have?
a a bag of sugar weighing 10N
b a box weighing 300N
c a crate weighing 1000N
d a car weighing 9000N

Momentum

The momentum of a moving object is the product of its mass and velocity. That is:

Momentum = mass × velocity

Momentum is an idea that is useful when we think about things stopping, starting, or colliding.

Acceleration and momentum

The effect of a force is to accelerate an object, and the acceleration can be found using the formula $F = ma$. Acceleration is the rate of change of velocity, or $\dfrac{v - u}{t}$

where u is the initial velocity, v is the final velocity, and t is the time taken for the change in velocity. So the formula for acceleration can be re written as

$$F = m\frac{(v - u)}{t} \text{ or } Ft = mv - mu$$

Now mu is the initial momentum and mv is the final momentum of the object. So we can say

force × time = change of momentum

A large force acting for a short time can produce the same change in momentum as a small force acting for a long time.

Both trolleys have the same momentum.
Mrs Smith pushed her trolley hard for a short time.
Julie could not push as hard, so she had to push for longer.

Q1 Why are seat belts necessary in cars?

Q2 A 1 tonne railway truck moving at 5 m/s hits a stationary truck with the same mass. If the two trucks stay together after the collision, how fast will they be moving?

Conservation of momentum

The idea that the total momentum before a collision is equal to the total momentum after a collision is the principle of conservation of momentum.

Imagine that you and a friend are wearing roller skates. You stand still facing each other, then you push each other. You will both move backwards.

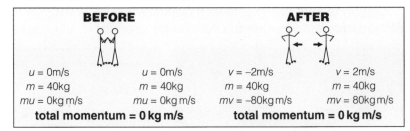

BEFORE		AFTER	
$u = 0$ m/s	$u = 0$ m/s	$v = -2$ m/s	$v = 2$ m/s
$m = 40$ kg	$m = 40$ kg	$m = 40$ kg	$m = 40$ kg
$mu = 0$ kg m/s	$mu = 0$ kg m/s	$mv = -80$ kg m/s	$mv = 80$ kg m/s
total momentum = 0 kg m/s		**total momentum = 0 kg m/s**	

If you and your friend have different masses, you will move backwards at different speeds.

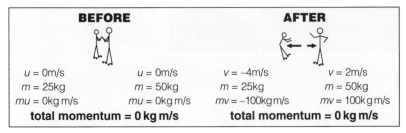

BEFORE		AFTER	
$u = 0$ m/s	$u = 0$ m/s	$v = -4$ m/s	$v = 2$ m/s
$m = 25$ kg	$m = 50$ kg	$m = 25$ kg	$m = 50$ kg
$mu = 0$ kg m/s	$mu = 0$ kg m/s	$mv = -100$ kg m/s	$mv = 100$ kg m/s
total momentum = 0 kg m/s		**total momentum = 0 kg m/s**	

If you were moving on your roller skates and you grabbed hold of your friend as you went past her, you would both end up moving (if you did not fall over!). The final momentum of you and your friend would be the same as your initial momentum (your friend had no momentum to start with, because she was not moving).

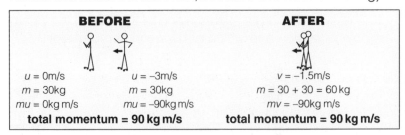

BEFORE		AFTER
$u = 0$ m/s	$u = -3$ m/s	$v = -1.5$ m/s
$m = 30$ kg	$m = 30$ kg	$m = 30 + 30 = 60$ kg
$mu = 0$ kg m/s	$mu = -90$ kg m/s	$mv = -90$ kg m/s
total momentum = 90 kg m/s		**total momentum = 90 kg m/s**

If you tried the roller skate experiment again, but you took your skates off before you pushed your friend, she would move away but you would not. This is because there is friction between your shoes and the floor which stops you moving. Momentum is only conserved if there are no external forces.

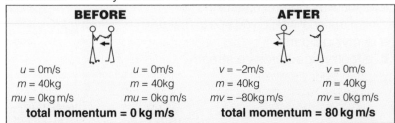

BEFORE		AFTER	
$u = 0$ m/s	$u = 0$ m/s	$v = -2$ m/s	$v = 0$ m/s
$m = 40$ kg	$m = 40$ kg	$m = 40$ kg	$m = 40$ kg
$mu = 0$ kg m/s	$mu = 0$ kg m/s	$mv = -80$ kg m/s	$mv = 0$ kg m/s
total momentum = 0 kg m/s		**total momentum = 80 kg m/s**	

Car crashes and crumple zones

The diagram shows two cars colliding. The total momentum of the cars before and after the event is the same.

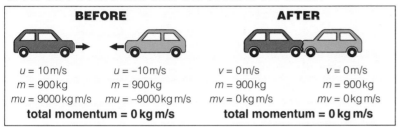

BEFORE		AFTER	
$u = 10\,\text{m/s}$	$u = -10\,\text{m/s}$	$v = 0\,\text{m/s}$	$v = 0\,\text{m/s}$
$m = 900\,\text{kg}$	$m = 900\,\text{kg}$	$m = 900\,\text{kg}$	$m = 900\,\text{kg}$
$mu = 9000\,\text{kg m/s}$	$mu = -9000\,\text{kg m/s}$	$mv = 0\,\text{kg m/s}$	$mv = 0\,\text{kg m/s}$
total momentum = 0 kg m/s		**total momentum = 0 kg m/s**	

In this diagram a car has collided with a wall. The momentum before and after the crash is different because the wall provides a force which stops the car.

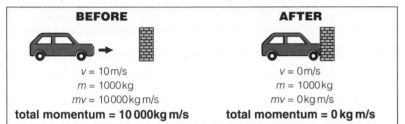

BEFORE	AFTER
$v = 10\,\text{m/s}$	$v = 0\,\text{m/s}$
$m = 1000\,\text{kg}$	$m = 1000\,\text{kg}$
$mv = 10\,000\,\text{kg m/s}$	$mv = 0\,\text{kg m/s}$
total momentum = 10 000 kg m/s	**total momentum = 0 kg m/s**

Cars are designed with crumple zones at the front and rear. If the car hits another vehicle or a wall the front of the car crumples. This means that it takes longer for the car to come to a complete stop, so the stopping force is less. This means that there is less force on the driver and passengers, so they are less likely to be injured.

Playing snooker

In the activity you found out that momentum is conserved if two moving balls hit each other and travel off in different directions. If you have ever watched a snooker match on the TV you will know that a good player can make the white ball do all sorts of things after it has hit a coloured ball. Snooker balls do not always seem to conserve momentum!

The secret is spin. If the player hits the ball near the top instead of in the middle, it will be spinning slightly as it travels. When the ball is travelling fast the spin does not have much effect on it. When it hits another ball the spin makes it carry on moving in the original direction.

The friction between the spinning ball and the table is an external force, and momentum is not conserved if there are external forces acting on the balls.

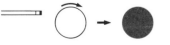
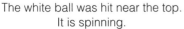
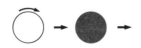

The white ball was hit near the top. It is spinning.

Because the white ball is spinning, it carries on moving in the same direction after it has hit the red ball.

Q3 The diagram shows two sets of ice skaters running into each other. Calculate the velocities of each pair after the collisions if they hold onto each other.

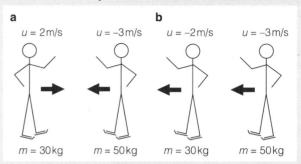

a		b	
$u = 2\,\text{m/s}$	$u = -3\,\text{m/s}$	$u = -2\,\text{m/s}$	$u = -3\,\text{m/s}$
$m = 30\,\text{kg}$	$m = 50\,\text{kg}$	$m = 30\,\text{kg}$	$m = 50\,\text{kg}$

Q4 Why does a 30 tonne truck need more powerful brakes than a 1 tonne passenger car? If the truck and the car are both travelling at 100 km/h, and their brakes exert a force of 10 kN, how long will each vehicle take to stop?

Q5 This picture shows an astronaut who is stranded in space near her spaceship. She is trying to get back by throwing rocks. The mass of the astronaut, her equipment and the rocks is 150 kg. The rocks each have a mass of 5 kg, and she gives them a velocity of 5 m/s away from her when she throws them. She throws three rocks altogether. How fast will she be moving

a after she has thrown the first rock
b after she has thrown the second rock
c after she has thrown the third rock?

Q6 What will happen if a cyclist travelling at 35 km/h down a hill puts on his front brake? Explain your answer, using a diagram if necessary. (*Hint:* you may need to think about centre of mass as well as momentum.)

Propellers, jets and rockets

see science at work

■ **Structures and machines**
pp 37 and 38 Momentum

■ **Earth in space**
pp 11, 12 and 13 Spacecraft

The movement produced by propellers, jet engines and rockets can be explained using the principle of conservation of momentum.

When a propeller is spinning it pushes air backwards. The air has been accelerated, so its momentum has changed. Conservation of momentum means that the momentum of the propeller and aeroplane has been increased by the same amount, but in the opposite direction. The effect of the spinning propeller is to produce a force on the aeroplane. This kind of forwards force is called **thrust**.

Jet engines also accelerate air backwards. The diagram shows a simplified jet engine. The compressor at the front sucks in air and compresses it, then fuel is sprayed into the compressed air. The fuel burns, and this causes a large increase in the pressure of the gases. These hot gases escape at high speed through the exhaust nozzle. Some of the energy in the gases is used to turn a turbine. The turbine is on the same shaft as the compressor, and turns the compressor to suck more air into the engine.

The air going through the engine has accelerated, so its momentum has increased. The momentum of the engine (and the aeroplane that it is attached to) increases by the same amount, but in the opposite direction.

Rockets also force out gases at high speeds. A simple rocket has a tank for fuel and a tank for liquid oxygen (or LOX). The fuel and oxygen are mixed and burned in the combustion chamber. The increase in temperature raises the pressure of the gases, and they escape from the nozzle at high speeds.

This rocket uses 1000 kg of fuel and 1000 kg of oxygen every second, and the exhaust gases escape at a speed of 2000 m/s. The thrust produced by the rocket can be calculated by calculating the change in momentum of the exhaust gases.

The fuel and oxygen were originally stationary inside the rocket. The fuel and oxygen used in one second has a momentum of

$$(1000 + 1000) \times 2000 \, \text{kg m/s} = 4 \times 10^6 \, \text{kg m/s}$$

The equation $F = \dfrac{mv - mu}{t}$

shows that the change in momentum per second is equal to the force. So the thrust produced by this rocket is 4×10^6 N.

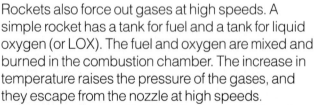

How a propeller works

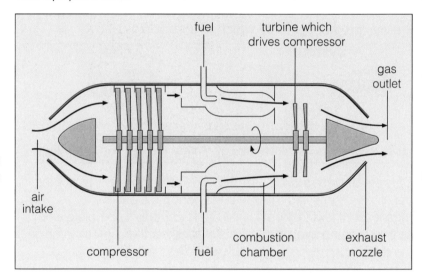

A jet engine

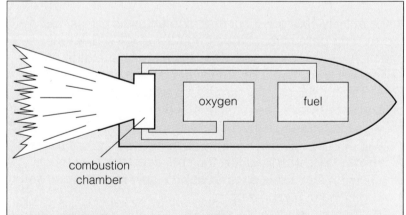

A simple rocket engine

Q1 Why are rocket engines used for space travel?

Q2 Why do large aeroplanes have bigger propellers than small aeroplanes, and why do they usually have more engines and propellers?

Launching satellites

The American Space Shuttle is the most recent design of launch vehicle. It can be used to put satellites into orbit around the Earth. Unlike other types of space vehicle it can also collect satellites for repair on board, or bring them back to Earth for repair.

When the shuttle is launched it is attached to a large external fuel tank, and two solid fuelled rocket boosters. When the fuel in the boosters has been used up they fall off. The external fuel tank also drops off when it is empty, so that the shuttle does not have to accelerate the extra mass of the empty tanks into space. The shuttle can only carry enough fuel in its tanks to put satellites into a low Earth orbit. Satellites that need to go into a higher orbit must use their own rocket engine once they have left the shuttle.

The first rocket to carry a man into space was the Vostok launch vehicle. It had four booster rockets attached to it; these dropped off when their fuel was used up. The central part of the rocket was in two stages. The engine in the first stage (the bottom part of the rocket) was used until its fuel

A Vostok rocket

A Saturn V rocket

The Space Shuttle being launched

central part of the rocket was in two stages. The engine in the first stage (the bottom part of the rocket) was used until its fuel was used up, then it dropped off as well. The second stage included the cabin for the cosmonaut. It was only in this final stage that enough height was gained to go into Earth orbit.

The first men to go to the moon were put into space using a Saturn V (Saturn Five) rocket. This rocket had three stages. The first stage carried five rocket engines and fuel and LOX for them. When the fuel was used up the first stage dropped off and the five engines in the second stage were turned on. When the fuel and LOX in the second stage was used up it dropped off. The third stage was used to send the Apollo spacecraft towards the moon and then it, too, fell away. The small section above the third stage was the only part of the rocket to go to the moon and back.

Q3 Use the information below to sketch the three launch vehicles to scale, then describe what each rocket was used for. You may need to look up information in a library. (Key words to look up are Gagarin, Vostok, Apollo, moon landings, space shuttle.)

Vehicle	Vostok	Saturn V	Shuttle
Height of vehicle	38 m	108m	56.1m

Q4 The following information refers to an Airbus 320 engine at take-off. An Airbus 320 has two engines.
Air flow through each engine = 358 kg/s
Fuel flow rate = 1.75 kg/s
Exit velocity (speed of gases coming out of the rear of the engine) = 300 m/s
a Calculate the thrust of each engine at take-off.
b Calculate the total forward thrust on the Airbus at take-off.

Q5 A rocket has a mass of 4×10^5kg when it is full of fuel. When it is working it uses 2400 kg of fuel per second, and the exhaust gases are ejected at a speed of 1800 m/s.
a What thrust (force) does it produce?
b If the rocket is in space (so you can ignore air resistance and gravity), what is its initial acceleration?
c What is its acceleration 60 seconds later?
d If the same rocket is being launched vertically from the surface of the Earth what will its original acceleration be?
e What factors will affect its acceleration 60 seconds later?

Q6 Describe four different uses for satellites, and explain why satellites are needed for each use.

Energy and temperature

When you heat an object the resulting change in temperature depends on three things:
- the mass of the object
- the amount of energy given to the object
- what the object is made of.

Material	Specific heat capacity (J/kg °C)
Water	4200
Methylated spirits	2500
Alcohol	2400
Paraffin	2200
Ice	2100
Aluminium	880
Sand	800
Steel	450
Copper	380
Lead	130

If you did a very accurate experiment to measure the temperature rise when you heated water, you would find that 1 kg of water needs 4200 J of energy to become 1°C hotter. This number is called the **specific heat capacity** of water. The units for specific heat capacity are J/kg°C.

Different substances have different specific heat capacities. The table gives you some examples.

All these numbers are for 1 kg and 1°C. To calculate the energy needed, you need to used this formula:

Energy needed = specific heat capacity × mass × temperature change

For instance, if you wanted to make a cup of tea you would need to raise the temperature of 200 g of water from 10°C (the temperature of tap water) to 100°C. How much energy would you need?

You know that
- the mass of the water is 0.2 kg (the mass must be in kg to use the formula)
- the temperature rise will be 90°C
- the specific heat capacity of water is 4200 J/kg°C

Put the numbers into the formula:
Energy needed = 4200 × 0.2 × 90
= 75 600 J or 75.6 kJ

Having a bath

How much energy do you use when you have a bath? The answer depends on how hot you like the water, and how deep you fill the bath.

Jane has filled her bath. It holds 200 litres of water, which have a mass of 200 kg. She likes the water very hot, at 45 °C. The water was at 10 °C before it was heated. She has used 4200 × 200 × 35 = 29.4 MJ of energy to heat her bath water.

Jim has a shallow bath; he has used only 100 kg of water. Jim's bath water is at 30 °C. He has used 4200 × 100 × 20 = 8.4 MJ of energy to heat his bath water.

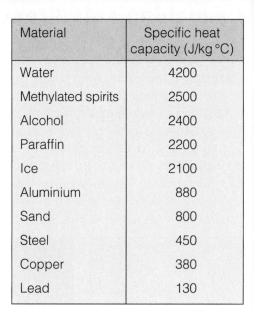

Where does the energy go?

Jane used a lot of energy to make her bath water hot. Eventually the bath water will cool down to the same temperature as the room. The energy will spread out into the room, and make the air in the room (and all the things in the room) a little bit warmer. The energy is still there (remember that energy is conserved) but it is no longer useful. Whenever energy is transferred, some of it is always wasted by being spread out, and usually ends up as heat.

Concentrating energy

Heat pumps are machines that can concentrate spread out energy. The diagram shows how a heat pump works. A refrigerator uses a heat pump, but this time it takes energy from the inside of the fridge and from the food inside (which cools down). This energy is pumped out into the kitchen. You can check this for yourself – at the back of the refrigerator you will find a set of tubes which feel warm because of the energy that has been taken away from the inside of the fridge.

A heat pump also can be used to heat a house by taking energy out of the air or ground and 'pumping' it into the house to warm it. Does this mean that you can get something for nothing? Unfortunately, the pump that drives the fluid around the heat pump uses energy. When all the energy is added up you still get out less energy than you put in, and overall the energy still gets spread out.

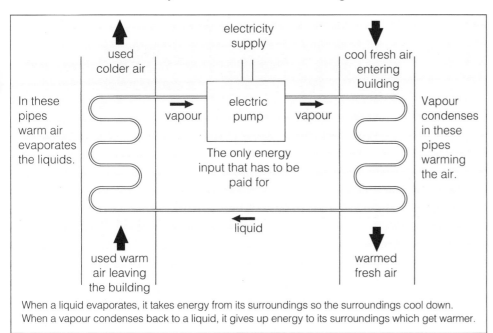

When a liquid evaporates, it takes energy from its surroundings so the surroundings cool down. When a vapour condenses back to a liquid, it gives up energy to its surroundings which get warmer.

How a heat pump works

The tubes on the back of a fridge get warm

Q1 You could save a little money by cooking in copper saucepans instead of aluminium ones. Explain how and why you would save money.

Q2 Ann and Andy are going to buy a new house, and want to keep their fuel bills as low as possible. Make a list of all the different things you would advise them to do to cut down on the amount of energy they will need in their house.

Q3 Calculate the amounts of energy needed to change the temperature of
a 500g of water by 30°C
b 2kg of copper by 10°C
c 900g of ice from –11°C to –1°C
d 1.5kg of sand from 10°C to 30°C.

Q4 An outdoor swimming pool measures 20m by 8m, and is 2m deep.
a When the pool is full, how much water does it hold (in kg)? Remember that 1m³ of water has a mass of 1000kg.
b If the water started at 5°C, how much energy would it take to warm it up to 20°C?

Q5 Sue and Sean are going for a day out in their car. When they get back to their house they find they have used up nearly a whole tank of petrol. What has happened to all the energy that was originally stored in the petrol?

Q6 A 500W heater supplies energy for 100 seconds to a 2kg metal can containing 1kg of water. The temperature rises by 9.8°C. What is the can made from? (*Hint:* first calculate the total energy supplied, then how much of this energy is used to raise the temperature of the water.)

Everyday energy

see science at work

■ **The Earth's energy**
pp 7–14 Energy sources,
pp 19–23 Storing and transferring energy,
pp 30–32 Using energy

Everything we do needs a source of energy.
The pie charts show where Britain gets its energy,
and what the energy is used for.

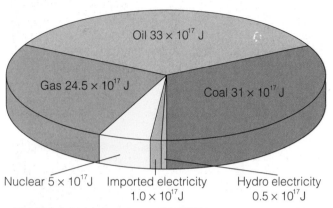

*The Britain's energy sources in 1987.
Britain used a total of 95×10^{17} J*

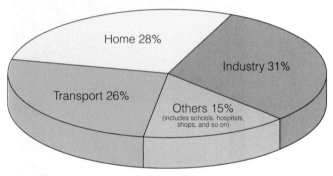

How Britain uses energy

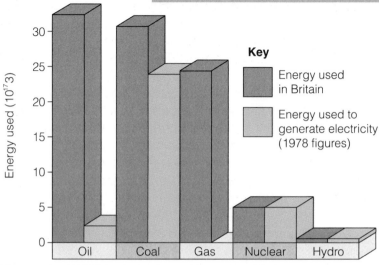

How much of Britain's energy is used to generate electricity

The bar chart shows how much of each source of energy is
used to generate electricity. All of the nuclear energy and hydro
(water) energy is used to generate electricity. Some power
stations are changing from using coal to using gas, so in the
future Britain will use more gas and less coal. The oil that is not
used to generate electricity is used to provide petrol for cars,
diesel for lorries and buses, and fuel for heating houses and
factories. Coal and gas are also used for heating.

   Apart from hydroelectric energy, all of the sources of energy
shown in the first pie chart are non-renewable fuels.

How long will they last?

It is not easy to estimate how long the world's oil or
gas will last, because it depends on too many things.

   Energy experts talk about energy in terrawatt
years (TWyr). One terrawatt is 10^{12} W, so a TWyr
is about 30×10^{18} joules.

   The world reserves of coal are estimated to be
about 8×10^{12} tonnes. This will provide about
7400 TWyr of energy.

   World reserves of oil are estimated at about
400 TWyr. Another 190 TWyr of energy is available
from oil in oil shales and tar sands. This oil will be
more expensive to extract. These estimates include
oil that the oil companies know is there, and oil
which they *think* is available, so even these
estimates could be wrong.

   There is not much natural gas left – only about
400 TWyr.

Q1 Estimate how long the world's reserves of fossil
fuels will last. You can assume that 10 TWyr of oil,
10 TWyr of gas, and 20 TWyr of coal are used each year.
Draw a bar chart to show when each fuel will run out.

Q2 Why are there lots of different estimates of how
long the world's non-renewable fuels will last?

Q3 Some fuels are only suitable for certain uses; for
instance, it is not very easy to use gas to drive
motor vehicles, and you would not use nuclear fuel to heat
your home. Make a list of different uses of non-renewable
fuels, and which fuels are suitable for each use.

Q4 Make a list of all the different uses for energy, and
say what properties the energy must have. For
example, energy used for cooking must be easy to obtain,
fairly cheap, and it must not cause pollution that would make
you or your family ill. You can use your answers to Q3 to help
you answer this question.

How much will we use each year?

This is a difficult question to answer, because the amount of energy needed changes. The amount of fuel used by people all over the world is different; for instance someone living in North America uses about 25 times as much energy in a year as someone living in Asia or Africa.

But countries in Asia and Africa are trying to become more like North America and Europe. They are building more factories, and many of the people would like to own cars and televisions. If these countries become more industrialised they will use more energy.

The amount of energy used also depends on how many people there are. The population of the world is growing all the time, and it is growing much faster in places like Asia and Africa than it is in Europe and North America.

To estimate how much energy will be used each year, scientists have to know how much energy each person will use in different parts of the world, and how much the population is going to grow. Both these things are very difficult to predict. One estimate is that over the next 100 years the *average* demand for energy will be about 40 TW (so 40 TW yr of energy would be needed every year).

The developed world   *The less developed world*

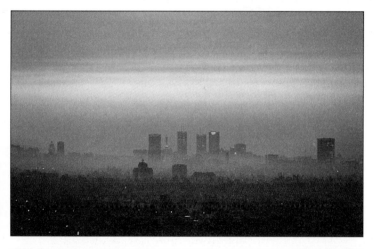

Nuclear Energy

Many people think of nuclear energy as something that will last forever. Unfortunately nuclear power stations need a supply of uranium, and uranium is also a non-renewable fuel. The world's uranium will only last until about 2030.

Here are some things for you to think about:
● How will we make plastics, fertilisers, and some medicines when there is no more oil or gas to use as the raw materials?
● Burning fossil fuels causes air pollution, and contributes to the greenhouse effect.
● Many people in Africa and Asia use wood as fuel. If the wood is cut down faster than it can regrow it is being used as a non-renewable source of energy. Wood is also used to make paper, packing, and in furniture and buildings.
● If forests are cut down many species of insects, plants, birds and animals may become extinct.
● Cutting down forests causes soil erosion, and prevents crops or new forests being grown on the land.
● Forests are the Earth's way of changing carbon dioxide back into oxygen. What will happen if more and more of the forests are cut down?
● Drilling for oil or gas, or mining for coal can be dangerous.

Energy for the future

How can we make our fossil fuels last longer? There are two ways – one is to use them more efficiently, and the other is to find some alternative sources of energy.

Using energy more efficiently

There are lots of different ways of using energy more efficiently, or of using less energy. Some of them can be done easily and cheaply. For instance:

● If you cycle to school instead of going by car then that saves some energy.
● If your family went on holiday by train instead of by car, that would be using energy more efficiently.
● Insulating houses and buildings stops heat escaping to the outside world, and so less energy is needed to keep the house warm.
● Fluorescent lights are much more efficient than ordinary light bulbs, so if everyone uses fluorescent lights they are lighting houses and buildings more efficiently.
● If drivers of cars drive more slowly, they use petrol more efficiently.

Other ways of using energy more efficiently are too expensive for individual people to try. For instance, power stations can be made more efficient by reusing some of the hot water. About 42% of the energy used by a power station is wasted when hot water is cooled before going back to the boilers. If the power station was near a town or near factories, this hot water could be used to heat the buildings. Some power stations do this already – they are called 'combined heat and power schemes'.

When machines are designed, they can be designed to work more efficiently. New engines for cars ad aeroplanes are being developed that use less fuel. New household equipment (like refrigerators) can be designed to use less energy. New washing powders can get clothes clean without needing very hot water, so less energy is used to heat water.

see science at work

■ **The Earth's energy**
pp 18, 20 Storing and transferring energy
pp 30, 32 Using energy
Extension exercises 4 and 7

■ **The Earth's energy**
pp 13, 14, 21, 22
Extension exercises 2, 5, 8

Q1 The amount of petrol a car used to travel a certain distance depends on its speed. The table shows you how far two different cars will travel on one litre of petrol at different speeds.

Speed	Kms travelled/litre of petrol	
	1250 cc car	2200 cc car
60	12.0	8.0
80	10.0	7.5
100	8.0	7.0

a If the journey is 20 km long, how much petrol will each driver save if they travel at 80 km/h instead of 100 km/h?
b How much will they save if they travel at 60 km/h instead of 100 km/h How much longer will the journey take?
c People have to pay for petrol, but most people drive as fast as they can. Why do you think they do not save energy (and money) by driving more slowly?

Q2 The table shows how far different forms of transport will travel for one megajoule of energy, and how many passengers each form of transport will carry.

a Which form of transport is the most efficient if it is carrying only one passenger?
b Which form of transport is the most efficient if it is full? (Hint: multiply the distance travelled by the number of passengers.)
c Draw a bar chart to illustrate your results.
d List the advantages and disadvantages of each form of transport.

Transport	Metres/ MJ	Maximum no. of passengers
Small airliner	3	80
Bus	70	50
Car	300	4
Train	25	500

Alternative sources

Biomass
Biomass means any fuel that comes from living things. Animal dung can be used to make methane which can be burned. Household rubbish can be used to produce fuel, or burned directly to produce heat or to generate electricity.

Hydroelectric
Hydroelectric power stations use falling water to generate electricity. They usually need a dam to trap the water.

Solar
Solar energy can be used to generate electricity, or to heat houses or water. The equipment needed for heating houses or water is relatively simple, but expensive. However the running costs are low once the equipment has been installed. Solar energy can also be used in furnaces, where very high temperatures are needed.

Very high temperatures can be obtained in solar furnaces.

Wind
Wind energy can be used for generating electricity, or for pumping water. Electricity can be generated on a small scale (by individual turbines) or on a large scale ('wind farms'), and is ideal for use in isolated areas.

Geothermal
Geothermal energy (energy from 'hot rocks') can be used to generate electricity if the temperature of the rocks is high enough, or for heating houses or water. Hot springs could also be used for heating.

Tidal
The tides can be used for generating electricity by building dams, or barrages, across river estuaries.

Waves
Waves can be used for generating electricity, either in the open sea or using generators on cliffs. Generators are built at the ends of narrow sea inlets. The motion of the waves forces air up and down the pipe in the centre of the column. The moving air turns the turbine, which generates electricity.

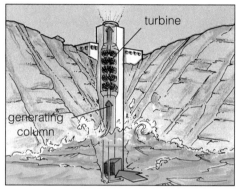

Fusion
There are two kinds of nuclear reactions: fission (where uranium atoms split apart) and fusion (where two hydrogen atoms join together). Fission is used in nuclear power stations, but so far the only way that fusion reactions can be used is in the hydrogen bomb. Scientists have spent a lot of time and money trying to find ways of controlling fusion reactions, but so far they have not succeeded. There is plenty of hydrogen available in water, so fusion would be a good way of generating electricity if the reaction could be controlled.

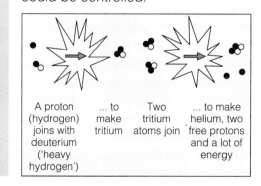

A proton (hydrogen) joins with deuterium ('heavy hydrogen') ... to make tritium. Two tritium atoms join ... to make helium, two free protons and a lot of energy

Q3 Find out more about the renewable sources of energy on this page. For each source you need to answer the following questions.
a Is a constant supply available, or does it depend on the weather?
b Is the energy available everywhere, or only in certain parts of the world? Would it be useful in Britain?
c Would there be any pollution, or an effect on wildlife or the local people?
d Is the technology available, or would the government need to spend money on developing new technology?
e What could this source be used for? (For instance, could it be used to run cars or aeroplanes, or for generating electricity, or could it only be used for heating?)

Revision – a science in itself

Good thorough revision will improve your examination results dramatically. Here are some hints to help you succeed.

● Avoid a last minute panic. Never leave your revision until the night before, or even the week before.
● Avoid revising with the radio or TV on. The excuse that it helps you concentrate is false. Experiments have shown that people lose concentration as soon as there is any unwanted noise. Speech and music are worse in this respect.

| Week 1 revision | | | | | | |
Monday	Tuesday	Wednesday	Thursday	Friday	Saturday	Sunday
4–5pm Science Module 1	4–5 History	4–5 French	4–5 Science 4			
tea	tea	tea				
6–7 Maths Module 2	6–7 Science Module 3	6–7 Science				
7–8 English	7–8 Technology	7–8 Geography				

Making a start

Well before your exam make a revision timetable allocating time between your subjects. Mark on your plan the days when you are going to revise your science, and the time you are going to spend on each module. Try to cover more than one subject a night. If you count up the hours available you will see how little time you have. The essential thing is to start early.

Find a quiet well lit part of your house. Start your revision early in the evening – your brain is fresher, and if you finish early you will have more time to relax afterwards. You must be well rested and maintain your normal sleep pattern. Don't work through the night before your exam.

IM READY FOR THE NEXT FIVE MINUTE WALK.

How to revise efficiently

The technique here is to revise hard for say 25 minutes and then have a complete break for 5 minutes. Repeat this technique throughout the evening's revision period. You would never make your body work non-stop by working or jogging all day without a rest. Revision with timed breaks is more efficient and causes you less strain.

The next stage is to carefully go through all your work, making sure that you understand what you are doing. Mark in your book passages or sections which you do not understand. Use them to remind you to consult your teacher. Once you understand your work, learning the facts becomes much easier. Use a pencil or a coloured outlining pen to mark the important sections of the work.

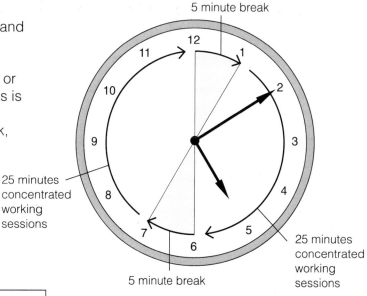

5 minute break

25 minutes concentrated working sessions

25 minutes concentrated working sessions

5 minute break

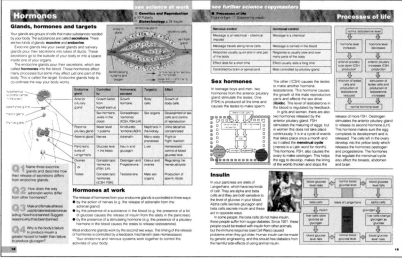

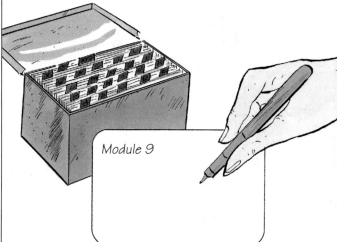

Module 9

How often should you revise?

Experiments have shown that your memory improves if you review your work:
● after ten minutes
● again after one day
● again after one week.

A review of the work is a brief re-read of the important facts, perhaps only the important ones you have marked with your outlining pen. The summary pages which follow this section are designed to help here. Some students summarise their main facts in a card index system.

The ten minute review fits in with your planned short breaks. After a rest period, briefly revise the same work again before you start to learn a new section.

Further brief revisions the next day and the following week (your revision timetable will help) fixes the work in your long term memory.

Some students find that it helps to write brief notes as they revise. They have the satisfaction of seeing the pile of paper grow and they can practise writing quickly (and neatly).

Remember: revision must occur often and you must repeat it at the right intervals.

Practise answering examination questions

This is an important aspect of successful revision. It needs to be started a few weeks before the examination, and after your initial careful revision stage. Ask your teacher for copies of past examination papers. Try to do these papers in the correct time. After doing the questions check them against your notes and this book.

Past papers help you get to know the style and timing of the examination papers. You will begin to understand the way the questions are asked. Learn how to answer the different styles of question and how key words such as 'Describe, Explain, Comment on' and so on are to be interpreted.

Success in examinations

If you have followed the advice on revision you will have all the essential facts in your memory. A final revision of your summary sheets and a good night's sleep are all that's needed.

   Make a careful note of the dates and times of your exams. Be sure to turn up in good time and with the correct equipment:
● two pens and at least one sharpened pencil
● a rubber, a pencil sharpener, and a ruler for the diagrams
● any special equipment for the exam such as a calculator, compass or protractor
● a watch so that you can check your progress through the exam.

In the examination room

Good examination technique can make a lot of difference to your grade. Here is some advice for answering long questions:

1 Carefully read the instructions on the paper, check how many questions must be answered and work out how long you need to spend on each one.
2 Instructions such as 'Careless and untidy work will be penalised' and requirements to spell words correctly mean what they say. If you don't you will lose marks.
3 When you are told to open the paper, read through all the questions carefully. If you have a choice, make it after you have read them all. As a rule, start with your second best question, then answer your best question, and then do the others in order of preference. Do not spend too long on the early questions. Keep to your time allocation. Answer all the questions. It is easier to get the first five marks in a question than the last five. If you can't do part of a question, leave a gap so that you can come back to it later.
4 Do make sure that you answer the question you have been asked.

Here is some advice for multiple choice questions.

1 Read the instructions to check how to mark the answer sheet.
2 Carefully read the coding instructions for each question.
3 Make sure you are putting the mark (A, B, C …) against the correct question number.
4 Read all the alternatives before you decide on your answer.
5 Do not waste time puzzling out a difficult question; leave it out and return to it later.
6 If you have to guess an answer, try to eliminate as many wrong answers as you can
7 Make sure that you answer every question.

Homeostasis helps to keep the environment of your internal body cells steady.

☐ Feedback mechanisms help to keep the conditions in the internal environment steady.

☐ Many body processes are controlled by feedback mechanisms.

Example 1 The rate and depth of breathing is affected by the pH of your blood. This pH changes when the amount of carbon dioxide in your blood increases or decreases.

Example 2 Body temperature is kept at about 37°C by activities of the body controlled by centres in the brain. These centres detect changes in blood temperature as it flows through the brain.

Example 3 The release of hormones such as ADH, FSH, ICSH and insulin.

Kidneys help to maintain the body in water balance.

☐ The kidney filters the blood.

☐ The concentration of urine leaving the kidney is changed by the action of antidiuretic hormone on the collecting duct of the nephron.

Immunity is your body's resistance to disease.

☐ Antibodies made in the plasma help your body fight disease.

☐ Immunity may be innate, natural or acquired.

☐ In passive acquired immunity you receive a dose of antibody.

☐ In active acquired immunity you receive a dose of antigen and your body makes the matching antibody.

☐ The development of immunisation programmes has reduced the number of deaths from infectious diseases.

Hormones are secreted by endocrine glands into the blood.

☐ Hormones affect many body processes and help coordinate the way the body works.

☐ A woman's fertility can be helped by medical treatments, including giving different kinds of hormones. Maintaining the fetal environment is one of the tasks of the placenta.

Coordination within the nervous system is helped by chemical transmitters at the synapses.

☐ The autonomic system controls the activity of many internal organs.

☐ Many drugs act on the nervous system and so change the way the body works.

☐ Chromosomes are thread like structures in the nuclei of cells.

☐ Chromosomes are in pairs.

☐ Each plant and animal species has a specific number of chromosomes.

☐ Genes are carried on chromosomes.

☐ Mutations are spontaneous changes in genes or chromosomes.

Further information about these facts can be found in:
Further Science pages 24 and 25 (chromosomes and genes)
Science at Work: Genetics and Reproduction pages 18-20.

☐ Genes control an individual's physical and chemical characteristics.

☐ Alternative forms of a gene are called alleles.

☐ One allele may be dominant over another. The non-dominant allele is recessive.

☐ Mitosis is the cell division that produces new somatic cells.

☐ Daughter cells produced by mitosis are genetically identical to the parent cell.

☐ Meiosis is the cell division that produces gametes.

☐ Cells produced by meiosis have half the chromosome number of the parent cell.

☐ Gametes have only one chromosome from each homologous chromosome pair.

Further information about these facts can be found in:
Further Science pages 28 and 29 (Cell division)
Activities: Mitosis and Meiosis

☐ It is possible to predict the way in which many characteristics are inherited.

☐ Some medical disorders are inherited.

continues

Further information about these facts can be found in:
Further Science pages 30 and 31 (Monohybrid inheritance – Inherited diseases)
Science at Work: Genetics and Reproduction pages 21 – 28
Extension exercise 4: Deepak's Guinea Pigs
Extension exercise 5: Gregor Mendel's Work.

- [ ] DNA consists of two long strands joined together and twisted into a spring-like shape. The strands are made of units called nucleotides.
- [ ] DNA replication occurs when enzymes unwind and separate the two strands. Each separated strand builds up a new strand joined to itself.
- [ ] The DNA of a gene acts as a code for the exact sequence of amino acids in one protein.
- [ ] The basic molecules in DNA (bases) control the amino acid sequence.

- [ ] Selective breeding involves using individuals with the best characteristics to produce offspring.
- [ ] Cloning is a method of reproducing identical copies of a gene, cell or simple organism. It is done by keeping small pieces of tissue or single cells in ideal sterile conditions so that they divide.
- [ ] Genetic engineering involves creating a new strain of organism by gene transferral.
- [ ] Selective breeding, cloning and genetic engineering have ethical and social implications.

- [ ] Individuals best suited to their environment stand a better chance of survival and mating (natural selection).
- [ ] Genetic variation is caused by reshuffling chromosomes and gene mutation.

- [ ] There is a relationship between variation, natural selection and reproductive success in organisms. They are all significant in terms of evolution.

Ecosystems SUMMARY

The Earth's ecosystems are delicately balanced and are easily damaged.

We need energy to survive.
- [ ] We need food energy, heat energy, and energy to work all the machines and tools of modern life.
- [ ] Nowadays we are using more and more energy.
- [ ] Most of our energy has come from burning fossil fuels.
- [ ] Coal, oil and natural gas are all fossil fuels.
- [ ] Burning fossil fuels releases carbon dioxide and other polluting waste gases into the atmosphere.
- [ ] Cars cause a great deal of air pollution.

It has taken millions of years for the atmosphere to form.
- [ ] The atmosphere is being rapidly changed and damaged by pollution gases.
- [ ] These gases include: carbon dioxide, methane, sulphur dioxide, nitrogen-I-oxide, CFCs and surface ozone.

Global warming is the term used to describe the changing weather patterns of the world.
- [ ] The temperature of the Earth is increasing.
- [ ] There are more floods and more droughts in different parts of the world.

- [ ] The sea levels may rise.
- [ ] Global warming is caused by increasing amounts of carbon dioxide.
- [ ] Other gases such as methane add to the effect.
- [ ] The problems of global warming can only be tackled on an international scale.

Microbes are important in the recycling and decay processes.
- [ ] They are especially important in getting rid of sewage.
- [ ] As the numbers of people have gone up so has the amount of raw sewage.
- [ ] Sewage has to be treated to make it safe and to purify the water released at the end of the process.

Recycling is important in nature.
- [ ] Carbon is recycled in the processes of photosynthesis, respiration and decay.

- [ ] Nitrogen is recycled using microbes.
- [ ] Water is always being recycled by living things.
- [ ] Many other elements are also recycled.
- [ ] If nature did not recycle her resources then they would quickly run out.

Earth structure 1 and 2

- [ ] Most evidence for conditions below the Earth's surface comes from the study of earthquakes and the study of the Earth's magnetic field.
- [ ] A seismometer is used to detect earthquakes.
- [ ] P, S and L waves are the three main types of waves produced by an earthquake.
- [ ] The Earth is divided into four layers which have different densities.
- [ ] These layers are called the crust, mantle, outer core and inner core.
- [ ] The outer core is liquid.
- [ ] The velocities of P and S waves are different in the four layers.
- [ ] The Earth has a magnetic field.
- [ ] A study of the Earth's magnetic field shows that the liquid outer core is made of iron.
- [ ] When some rocks form they become magnetised in the same direction as the Earth's magnetic field.
- [ ] The Earth's magnetic field has reversed its direction several times in the past.
- [ ] Studies of ancient magnetic rocks show that the sea floor is spreading.

The theory of plate tectonics

- [ ] Plate tectonics is the theory of plate movements.
- [ ] Plates move and slide over less rigid material below them.
- [ ] Evidence for the theory of plate tectonics comes from the similar shapes of coastlines and the similar rock records of the continents.
- [ ] Plate tectonics has replaced earlier theories about the formation of the Earth's crust which suggested that the Earth was still cooling and contracting.
- [ ] Plate tectonics theory brings together the ideas of sea floor spreading and continental drift.
- [ ] The edges of plates are marked by narrow zones where active volcanoes, earthquakes and young fold mountain ranges are found.
- [ ] Plate movements have affected the global distribution of the Earth's physical resources.

Plate movements 1 and 2

- [ ] There are three types of plate boundaries: constructive, destructive and conservative.
- [ ] Plates move apart at constructive plate boundaries.
- [ ] Plates move towards one another at destructive plate boundaries.
- [ ] Plates slide past one another at conservative plate boundaries.

- [ ] Plate movements may be caused by convection currents within the mantle.
- [ ] The heat to drive these convection currents is created by the decay of radioactive isotopes in the Earth.
- [ ] Ocean ridges form at constructive plate boundaries.
- [ ] Ocean trenches are formed at destructive plate boundaries.
- [ ] Fold mountain ranges form at destructive plate boundaries where the continental crust is folded into anticlines and synclines.
- [ ] Earthquakes are produced by movement along the three types of plate boundaries.
- [ ] Most volcanoes form at constructive and destructive plate boundaries.
- [ ] Plate tectonic theory helps to explain the rock cycle.

Evolution of the atmosphere

- [ ] The early atmosphere was very different from the Earth's atmosphere today.
- [ ] The early atmosphere was formed by volcanic activity.
- [ ] This atmosphere was a reducing environment.
- [ ] Ancient rocks contain evidence of the composition of the Earth's early atmosphere.
- [ ] It has taken millions of years for the Earth's atmosphere to evolve.
- [ ] The two main gases in the atmosphere today are nitrogen and oxygen.
- [ ] Today's oxidising environment developed as plants evolved.

Balance in the atmosphere 1 and 2

- [ ] Today's atmosphere is in a state of approximate balance.
- [ ] The carbon cycle is the balance between the amount of carbon dioxide leaving and entering the atmosphere.
- [ ] Carbon dioxide is lost from the atmosphere by photosynthesis.
- [ ] Carbon dioxide is added to the atmosphere by the respiration of animals and by the burning of fuels.
- [ ] Carbon dioxide is slowly lost from the atmosphere by being dissolved in the seas.
- [ ] The nitrogen cycle is the balance between the amount of nitrogen and its compounds leaving and entering the atmosphere.
- [ ] Human activities affect the balance by putting more carbon dioxide, nitrogen compounds and sulphur dioxide into the atmosphere.
- [ ] Examples of the problems produced by human activities are acid rain and global warming.

continues

Processes in the atmosphere
☐ Water circulates in the atmosphere by evaporation and precipitation.
☐ Clouds form when the atmosphere can no longer hold the water vapour it contains and the water condenses into visible droplets.
☐ When droplets of water condense the precipitation they produce depends on the values of several variables such as temperature, wind speed and rate of condensation.
☐ Types of precipitation are fog, hail, snow and rain.
☐ Winds are produced by pressure gradients in the atmosphere.

Gravity and satellites
☐ Gravity is a force of attraction between all pieces of matter.
☐ Gravitational force between two objects = $\frac{GMm}{r^2}$

where G = universal constant of gravitation
(6.7×10^{-11} N m²/kg²)
M = mass of one object (kg)
m = mass of the other object (kg)
r = distance between the two objects (m)

☐ The tides are caused by the gravitational force between the Earth and the Moon.
☐ Objects moving fast enough around the Earth do not fall to the ground. They are in orbit.
☐ Satellites that take 24 hours to go around the Earth are in geosynchronous orbits.

Exploring space and The Beginning
☐ A light year is the distance that light travels in one year. One light year = 9.5×10^{15} m.
☐ There are different ideas about the universe. Most scientists believe that the universe started with a huge explosion (the 'Big Bang') and has been expanding ever since. Other scientists believe that new galaxies are being formed all the time, so the universe is in a 'steady state'.
☐ Stars can be studied by examining the light emitted by them. The light from most stars and galaxies shows a red shift, because they are moving away from us.
☐ **Hubble's law**:
The greater the distance galaxies are from us, the greater their speed of recession.

The solar system
☐ There are two theories to account for the formation of the solar system: the nebular theory and the catastrophic event theory.
☐ The inner planets are Mercury, Venus, Earth and Mars. They are small and dense.
☐ The outer planets are Jupiter, Saturn, Uranus and Neptune. They are large, and mainly made of gases.
☐ Pluto may once have been one of Neptune's moons.
☐ The asteroids orbit between Earth and Mars.

Materials · SUMMARY

The changing idea of atoms
☐ *Dalton's theory (1805)*
Atoms of different elements have different masses. Atoms cannot be broken up.
☐ *Thomson's theory (1900)*
Electrons are dotted throughout the atom like plums in a pudding. They carry negative charge. The rest of the atom is positive.
☐ *Rutherford's nuclear atom (1911)*
An atom has a tiny nucleus at its centre. The nucleus has a large mass and is positively charged. Very tiny electrons exist around the nucleus and are negatively charged.

☐ *Modern atomic theory*
Atoms contain three main sub-atomic particles. Protons and neutrons have roughly the same mass and are found in the nucleus. Protons have a positive charge, but neutrons are neutral. Electrons have a much tinier mass, and a negative charge, and exist around the nucleus.
☐ The atomic number (Z) of an element is the number of protons (and also electrons) in the nucleus of each atom.
☐ The nucleon number (A) is the total number of nucleons (protons plus neutrons) in each nucleus.
☐ Isotopes are atoms of the same element which have different numbers of neutrons.

continues

Radioactivity

- [ ] Isotopes of some elements can decay naturally into other elements by releasing radiation which can be of three types: alpha (α), beta (β) and gamma (γ).
- [ ] Alpha radiation consists of helium nuclei : $^4_2He^{2+}$
- [ ] Beta radiation consists of electrons
- [ ] Gamma radiation is short wavelength, high energy electromagnetic radiation
- [ ] The half-life of an isotope is the length of time taken for half the atoms in a sample of radioactive material to decay.
- [ ] Nuclear fission is an artificial nuclear reaction. When a large atom is bombarded with a neutron it can split into smaller atoms and release neutrons. Large amounts of energy are produced. This can lead to a chain reaction.
- [ ] Nuclear fusion is the opposite of fission. Small atoms are fused together to produce larger ones, and energy is also released in large amounts.

Organising the elements

- [ ] Electrons are arranged around the nucleus in energy levels or shells.
- [ ] Atoms in the same group of the Periodic Table have the same number of electrons in their outside shells, and have similar chemical properties.
- [ ] Atoms with full outer shells of electrons are more stable than others.

Chemical bonding 1

- [ ] Reactive elements can combine to become very stable, for example sodium and chlorine.
- [ ] Sodium and chlorine react together by forming ions. An electron is transferred from the outer shell of a sodium atom to the outer shell of a chlorine atom. The resulting positive sodium and negative chloride ions have complete outer energy levels and form a stable ionic compound, sodium chloride.
- [ ] Atoms react to become more like noble gases by getting full outer shells of electrons.

Chemical bonding 2

- [ ] Some atoms share electrons to become more stable: they form strong covalent bonds.
- [ ] Molecules containing covalently bonded atoms are neutral. They are only weakly attracted to each other.
- [ ] Two atoms sharing pairs of electrons have a double covalent bond.

Structures of materials

- [ ] Ionic materials have high melting and boiling points because the electrostatic attraction between ions is strong, so lots of energy is needed to separate them. Ionic materials are good conductors only when melted or dissolved in water, because then the electrically charged ions are free to move.
- [ ] Molecular materials have low melting and boiling points because the attraction between molecules is weak, so very little energy is needed to separate them. Molecular materials are poor conductors under all conditions because molecules are neutral.
- [ ] Metals can conduct electricity because each of their atoms contributes electrons to an electron 'cloud'. These electrons are free to move and form a current.

Properties/uses of materials

- [ ] Materials have quantifiable properties, such as electrical resistivity, density, tensile strength, compressive strength and resistance to corrosion.
- [ ] When choosing a material for a job, a range of properties must be looked at, and the best combination found.

Moles 1
☐ A mole of particles is an extremely large number called Avogadro's constant, $L = 6.02 \times 10^{23}$.
☐ If one mole of a material is measured out in grams, this quantity is called its molar mass.
☐ A molar mass of any element is its relative atomic mass in grams (g).
☐ A molar mass of any compound is its relative molecular mass in grams (g).
☐ One mole of electrons has a charge of 1 Faraday, or 96500 coulombs.
☐ Number of moles of a material = $\dfrac{\text{Mass of material}}{\text{Molar mass}}$

Moles 2
☐ Atoms combine in fixed proportions to form compounds. The formula of a compound tells us how many moles of different types of atom will combine with each other.
☐ The volume of one mole of a gas is called its molar volume. At standard temperature and pressure (0°C and 1 atmosphere) this is 22.4 litres or cubic decimetres, dm^3.
☐ A molar solution contains 1 mole of a material dissolved in 1 dm^3 of solution.

Formulae and equations
☐ The valency of an atom is the number of electrons it gains, loses or shares when it combines with another atom.
☐ Some atoms have more than one valency.
☐ Valency theory can be used to work out the formula of a compound. Use the 'crossover' rule.
☐ A balanced symbol equation for a chemical reaction can be written by remembering that the total number of atoms is the same for reactants and products. They are just combined in different ways.

Electrolysis
☐ In electrolysis, two metal plates are immersed in a molten ionic compound or a solution. Electricity passes through the liquid because ions are free to move.
☐ Positive ions (cations) are attracted to the cathode. Negative ions (anions) are attracted to the anode.
☐ Electrolysis can be used to coat one metal with another, for example silver plating.

Energy in chemistry
☐ Exothermic chemical reactions release energy to the surroundings as heat and light. Less energy is used to break chemical bonds than is released by making new ones, so energy is released.
☐ Endothermic chemical reactions take in energy from the surroundings. More energy is used to break chemical bonds than is released by making new ones, so energy has to be added to the system (heat is absorbed).
☐ The difference in energy between products and reactants in a reaction is the enthalpy change, ΔH.
ΔH = heat content of products – heat content of reactants
This is negative for an exothermic reaction and positive for an endothermic reaction.
☐ Some exothermic reactions require an initial input of energy, the activation energy, to start them.
☐ In electrical cells, energy is released in the form of electricity during an exothermic reaction.

Equilibrium
☐ Some chemical reactions are reversible.
☐ At equilibrium, the rates of forward and backward reactions are equal.
☐ Changing the external conditions (temperature or pressure) of a reaction will affect the equilibrium position.
☐ Le Chatelier's Principle states that an equilibrium position moves to oppose any change in external conditions

Materials from oil
☐ Crude oil can be transformed into a wide range of products by three main techniques: separation, cracking and synthesis.
☐ The technique of fractional distillation can be used to separate crude oil into fractions containing small hydrocarbon molecules such as methane. These make good fuels. Heavier fractions are used for road making or for cracking.
☐ Cracking involves breaking down one type of compound, the alkanes, into another type, the alkenes. Alkenes are more reactive than alkanes, and so can be used to make new materials.
☐ Alkenes can also form large molecules called polymers, by adding on to each other. Polymers are very useful in the plastic industry.

Resistance

- ☐ Resistance, R, is measured in ohms, Ω, and is defined by $R = \dfrac{V}{I}$
- ☐ Resistance is a measure of how difficult it is for electrons to flow through a substance.
- ☐ Good electrical conductors have a low resistance.
- ☐ Insulators have a high resistance.
- ☐ Resistors connected in series have the same current flowing through them. The total resistance $R = R_1 + R_2 + R_3$ and is greater than any of the individual resistances.
- ☐ Resistors connected in parallel have the same voltage across them. The total resistance R can be found using $\dfrac{1}{R} = \dfrac{1}{R_1} + \dfrac{1}{R_2} + \dfrac{1}{R_3}$ and is less than any of the individual resistances.

Ohm's law

- ☐ Voltage, V, is measured in volts, V, and is also called potential difference or pd.
- ☐ Current, I, is a rate of flow of electrical charge and is measured in amperes, or amps, A. Current can be defined as $I = \dfrac{Q}{t}$, where Q is charge (in coulombs) and t is time (in seconds).
- ☐ Kirchoff's law says that at any junction in a circuit, the sum of currents flowing into the junction equals the sum of the currents flowing out.

Electrical energy

- ☐ Electrical energy is measured in joules, J.
- ☐ Electrical energy is charge multiplied by voltage. Useful equations are: $\text{Energy} = QV = VIt = I^2Rt$
- ☐ Electricity meters measure energy in kilowatt hours, kWh. 1 kWh means 1000 watts for a period of one hour. So $1\,\text{kWh} = 1000 \times 60 \times 60 = 3.6 \times 10^6\,\text{J} = 3.6\,\text{MJ}$.

Electrical power and safety

- ☐ Electrical power is measured in watts, W.
- ☐ Electrical power is voltage multiplied by current. $\text{Power} = VI$.
- ☐ Fuses protect electrical wiring and appliances by melting and breaking the circuit if too much current flows.
- ☐ Fuses must be fitted in the live connection of a plug or circuit.
- ☐ Earth wires keep the casing of electrical appliances at 0V. No current can flow between you and the casing, so the appliance is safe.
- ☐ Many modern buildings have Earth leakage circuit breakers instead of fuses.

Electromagnetic induction

- ☐ Electric currents can be made in conducting materials by moving a conductor in a magnetic field or by making the magnetic field around a conductor change.
- ☐ Conductors in a magnetic field obey the two laws of electromagnetic induction. The first law says that the size of the induced voltage between the ends of the conductor is proportional to the rate at which the conductor cuts through the magnetic field.
- ☐ The dynamo rule can be used to find the direction of an induced current in a wire.

Using electromagnetic induction

- ☐ The second law of electromagnetic induction says that the induced current in a conductor always opposes the change in magnetic field which caused it.
- ☐ Currents induced in conductors moving in a magnetic field are called eddy currents. An induction motor works by the use of eddy currents. A transformer uses electromagnetic induction to change a.c. voltages.
- ☐ Transformer formula:

$$\frac{\text{number of turns on the secondary coil}}{\text{number of turns on the primary coil}} = \frac{\text{output voltage}}{\text{input voltage}}$$

Static electricity

- ☐ Static electricity is a build-up of electrons in a material. It happens when one material is rubbed against another.
- ☐ Static electricity can be avoided by connecting materials to Earth.
- ☐ Thermionic emission is the 'boiling off' of electrons from a hot piece of metal.
- ☐ In a thermionic diode, electrons flow from a heated filament across a vacuum. They can flow in one direction only: from the cathode to the anode.

Thermionic tubes

- ☐ X-rays are released when electrons gain a lot of kinetic energy and hit an anode.
- ☐ X-ray tubes produce X-rays by accelerating electrons towards a high voltage anode.
- ☐ A cathode ray oscilloscope is another type of thermionic tube.

Feedback

- ☐ Feedback occurs when information about an end result is 'fed back' to the beginning so that it can effect the later outcome.
- ☐ Negative feedback acts against the initial change, and leads to stability and predictability.
- ☐ Positive feedback exaggerates the initial change, and leads to instability and unpredictability.

Waves 1

- [ ] There are many types of wave. Each comes from some kind of regular to-and-fro change. Each wave transfers energy away from its source by this kind of regular change.
- [ ] In a transverse wave, the regular to-and-fro motion is *across* the direction of energy transfer. In a longitudinal wave, the regular to-and-fro motion is *along* the direction of energy transfer.
- [ ] Examples of transverse waves: radio, microwaves, infra-red, visible light, ultra-violet, X-rays, γ-rays, and some earthquake waves.
- [ ] Examples of longitudinal waves: sound and some earthquake waves.
- [ ] Liquid surface waves are a mixture of transverse and longitudinal

Waves 2

- [ ] The hertz (Hz) is the unit of wave frequency (symbol f): one cycle per second.
- [ ] The metre (m) is the unit of wavelength (symbol λ): this is the distance covered by one wave cycle.
- [ ] The metre per second (m/s) is the unit of wave speed (symbol v): the rate of energy transfer through a distance.
- [ ] For any wave, the wave equation relates speed (v), frequency (f) and wavelength λ: $v = f\lambda$
- [ ] The amplitude of a wave is the greatest variation in a cycle from the centre. Amplitude relates to energy content: to loudness in the case of sound waves, and to brightness in the case of light.
- [ ] When a wave passing through one medium hits the surface of a second, one or more of three things can happen:
  Reflection: the wave bounces off the surface, to stay in the first medium.
  Refraction: the wave passes on through into the second medium, often changing direction at the surface.
  Absorption: the wave disappears; its energy appears in some other from.
- [ ] Diffraction and interference are two more features of any type of wave.
  Diffraction: the wave bends round the edge of a second medium.
  Interference: when two waves of the same type pass through the same space at the same time, they 'interfere' with each other. If they have the same amplitude and the same wavelength, then in some places they reinforce each other and have a strong effect, and in others, they cancel each other and have no effect.
- [ ] **Polarisation** can only happen to transverse waves. This limits the directions in which the vibration takes place.

Sound waves

- [ ] All sound sources produce the sound waves by vibration (regular to-and-fro motion). The waves travel through matter by the vibration of particles in a series of compressions and rarefactions.
- [ ] The loudness of a sound wave is measured in units of the decibel (dB).
- [ ] Sound waves in air diverge (spread out).

Sound and Music

There are many types of wind instrument. Each is a tube of air with an open end for you to blow over or through. The other end may be open or closed. These tubes make waves by the process called resonance, which causes a fundamental note and a number of overtones.

A vibrating stretched string in a stringed instrument also produces fundamental and overtone waves.

Frequency and wavelength

- [ ] White light, like that from the Sun, contains waves of many frequencies. Each frequency affects our sense of vision in its own way: we see colour.

Electromagnetic spectrum

- [ ] Visible light has a range of frequencies (wavelengths), but is just a small part of a very large spectrum of radiations we call electromagnetic. Radio waves, microwaves, infra-red, visible light, ultra-violet, X-rays and γ-rays are all part of the electromagnetic spectrum. This list is in order of increasing frequency and decreasing wavelength.
- [ ] Each type of electromagnetic radiation has its own set of sources (natural and artificial), uses and dangers, but they all have the same basic wave properties.

Electromagnetic radiation

- [ ] Electromagnetic astronomy involves the use of satellites and telescopes to detect and analyse electromagnetic radiation from outside the earth.
- [ ] X-rays are used in medicine to produce 'shadow pictures' of broken bones.

☐ **Forces** are measured in newtons (N).

☐ Forces on structures can be compression (squashing) forces, tension (stretching) forces, or bending forces (a combination of compression and tension forces).

☐ **Hooke's law** states that, for a spring in tension, 'the extension is directly proportional to the load'.

☐ A turning force is called a **moment**.

Moment (N m) = force (N) × perpendicular distance (m)

Forces and movement

☐ **Newton's first law of motion:**
If there is no resultant force on an object, it will either be stationary or travelling in a straight line at constant speed.

☐ **Newton's second law of motion:**
The acceleration of an object is directly proportional to the size of the resultant force acting on it, and the acceleration always takes place in the direction of the resultant force.

Force (N) = mass (kg) × acceleration (m/s^2)

☐ If an object is moving in a circle there is always a centripetal force acting in the direction of the centre of the circle.

☐ Momentum (kg m/s) = mass (kg) × velocity (m/s)
Momentum is a vector quantity.

☐ **Conservation of momentum:**
If there is no external force, then:

Momentum before collision = Momentum after collision

Conservation of momentum can be used to calculate the thrust of a rocket.
Thrust (N) = mass of fuel and oxygen used per second (kg/s) × velocity of exhaust gases (m/s)

☐ **Energy** is measured in joules (J). 1 J = 1 N × 1 m

☐ Energy used (J) = force (N) × distance moved in the direction of the force (m)

☐ Efficiency (%) = $\dfrac{\text{useful energy output}}{\text{energy input}}$ × 100%

☐ Power is the rate of doing work, and is measured in watts (1 watt = 1 joule per second).

$$\text{Power (W)} = \frac{\text{force } (N) \times \text{distance } (m)}{\text{time (s)}}$$

☐ Moving objects possess kinetic energy.

Kinetic energy (J) = $\frac{1}{2}$ × mass (kg) × velocity^2 (m/s)^2

☐ The specific heat capacity of a substance is the amount of energy needed to raise the temperature of 1 kg of the substance by 1°C.

Energy needed to heat an object (J) = specific heat capacity (J/kg°C) × mass (kg) × temperature rise (°C)

☐ Energy is conserved: it is never lost but it gradually spreads out and becomes less useful.

☐ The world's reserves of fossil fuels will run out. Energy for the future will have to be supplied by renewable sources.

ANSWERS

Homeostasis

Q1 Examples could include thermostats (eg. central heating, oven) and water cisterns.

Q2 As carbon dioxide dissolves in water (and plasma) to form carbonic acid, the pH will become acidic. The pH will be lower than 7.

Q3 The chemical reactions within cells are catalysed by enzymes. These are protein and their structure and function are affected by pH. All enzymes have an **optimum pH** for their working.

Q4 If there is a decrease in the level of CO_2 in your blood you would expect the rate of breathing to be reduced and the depth of breathing (or volume of each breath) to become less too.

Body Temperature

Q1 Enzyme controlled chemical reactions (eg. the breakdown of glucose in respiration) work best at 37°C.

Q2 Ectothermic animals
  – any fish; any amphibian
Endothermic animals
  – any mammal (eg. cow, whale);
  – any bird (eg, hen, sparrow).

Q3 As babies have a large surface area to volume ratio they could lose body heat very quickly and so their temperature would drop. They would be unable to metabolise at a rate which would produce enough heat to replace that lost. As a consequence the loss of heat could lead to death.

Q4 Sweating involves the evaporation of water from the body surface. Heat is needed to cause the water to evaporate. Heat is lost from the body, reducing the temperature.

Q5 Small mammals have a large surface area to volume ratio and so lose heat quickly. To replace the heat more heat would have to be generated during respiration. It is thought that the rate of generation could not be enough to replace the heat lost in animals smaller than a shrew.

Q6 The advantages are related to being active whatever the changes in external temperature during the day; animals can search for food during the day and night. The disadvantages include having to have sufficient food available (or stored in the body) to enable them to respire and release energy to maintain the body temperature.

Q7 Shivering is a sudden contraction of the muscles of your body. In the contraction the muscles release heat and so blood is warmed as it flows through. If your body temperature is lowered, then the blood temperature falls and this change would be detected by the 'cold centre' in the brain. The brain would then trigger off the action of the muscles.

The Kidney at Work

Q1 a Bowman's capsule is in the outer part (cortex) of the kidney at the end of a nephron. There are two kidneys one on each side of the aorta and vena cava in the abdomen.
b The loop of Henlé is found between the first and second coiled tube of the nephron. The first part (descending limb) goes from the cortex into the medulla of the kidney.
c The bladder is found at the front of the abdomen and is protected by the bone of the pelvic girdle.

Q2 The cells of the body are surrounded by body fluid and this contains water and solutes. If there are great changes in the water and solute concentration in this fluid, then water may enter or leave cells by osmosis. This will affect the way the cells work.

Q3 a The production of sweat would increase.
b The production of anti-diuretic hormone by the pituitary gland would increase and so reduce the amount of water being lost from the kidney and going to the bladder in urine. This reduction is linked to the increased loss of water in sweat.
c As there is the release of ADH then the permeability of the tubules would increase, thus allowing more water to be taken from the filtrate back into the blood.

Q4 Kidneys produce weak urine when a person has consumed a lot of water and/or reduced the loss of water in sweat. The production of weak urine is diuresis. The consumption of a lot of water will cause the blood plasma to become more dilute. This stimulates the pituitary gland and the release of ADH is reduced. Thus the permeability of the kidney collecting duct is such that water is not taken from the kidney filtrate into the blood and so urine containing a lot of water passes from the kidney to the bladder.

Cell Wars

Q1 The breast milk will contain antibodies which will help to protect the newborn child from infection.

Q2 'Booster' injections are needed so that the body will produce antibodies to a level which will protect the body from an infection caused by the antigen microbe that matches the antibody.

Q3 The answer should highlight the ethical issues associated with the procedure eg. the risk taken with one person's life that have saved the lives of many others; the use of a child for the procedure rather than an adult (or even Jenner himself); the certainty and conviction Jenner must have had in order to risk the life of a child.

Q4 The impact of the removal of the threat of infectious diseases could include:
● young children living longer and thus providing additional demands on the income of a family.
● the need for family planning as large families create maintenance problems for the parents.
● increased requirements for education.
● an increase in the young people available for work.
● changing expectations amongst the population as a whole.

Hormones

Q1 Exocrine glands eg. sweat glands, gastric glands, salivary glands, pancreas. All pass their secretions from the secretory cells along ducts.

Q2 Adrenalin acts very quickly and the effects are evident in many parts of the body. This is because adrenalin works in a way linked to the autonomic nervous system.

Q3 It has been banned because of its effects on the reproductive organs and sex drive. It may cause man to become very aggressive and women to develop masculine features (eg. hair on the face).

Q4 Insulin helps to increase the blood glucose level automatically when it has dropped. The blood glucose will supply cells with glucose needed for respiration. If the body cannot produce or release insulin then the body cannot react to sudden demands for glucose. Glucagon helps to reduce the level. It may be possible to control dietary intake to prevent excess blood glucose.

Nerves at Work

Q1 The differences include:
● position of the cell body
● direction of flow of the nerve impulse to the cell body
● location of the cell body in the nervous system

Q2 The impulse is transmitted by a chemical transmitter which crosses the synapse and attaches to the neuron fibre of the next neuron. This triggers off the impulse.

Q3 The effect of the original stimulus or impulse will be sustained thus blocking further transmissions.

Q4 Yes: they prepare the body for the 'fright' reaction.

Q5 Parts such as the anal and bladder sphincter.

ANSWERS

Fetal Environment

Q1 About day 21.

Q2 The placenta acts as:
- a 'lung'
- a place for the exchange of nutrients and waste
- a barrier to certain drugs and microbes
- hormone producer (HCG)

Q3 The mother's arteries carry oxygenated blood, the veins deoxygenated blood. Those of the baby are the 'reverse'.

Q4 The fetus is an individual whose genotype is a product of that of the mother and father's sex cells. Therefore the fetus could be regarded as a 'foreign body', or foreign antigens and so trigger off the immune response in the mother. This does not happen.

Q5 Mitochondria are the organelles in cells where the chemical processes of respiration take place. This releases energy. Energy is needed for the transport of some materials across the barrier of the placenta.

Q6 This is a search for data but the information should include
a thalidomide – deformation of limbs
b rubella virus – affects the development of the eyes.

Reproduction and inheritance

What is DNA?

Q1 Chromosomes are made of DNA, which contains genetic information for controlling all cell activities.

Q2 Genes control characteristics like hair colour, eye colour and blood group. A gene controls the production of a specific protein.

Q3 A nucleotide consists of three molecules – a sugar, a phosphate and a chemical base.

Q4 When the special enzymes have helped DNA to unwind it separates into two strands. The chemical bonds holding the base partners together are broken. New nucleotides add on to their specific partner. Two stands of DNA, identical to each other and to the original piece of DNA, then result.

DNA is too large to leave the nucleus but a small portion, a gene, can unwind. Then a single strand of RNA can be formed which is thin enough to pass through a pore. RNA takes DNA's coded message to the ribosomes where the amino acids are assembled in the correct sequence to make the required protein.

Q6 Complete the table with the missing numbers:
800 amino acids in a small protein
800 triplets in the code
2400 bases in the code
2400 nucleotides in the DNA

Can we change living things?

Q1 Selective breeding is carried out by using individuals with the best characteristics to produce offspring, then repeating the process with each generation.

Q2 Cloning means reproducing identical copies of a gene, cell or simple organism like a bacterium.

Q3 Genetic engineering means removing a gene (or genes) from one organism and transferring it to another organism of the same (or different) species.

Q4 Labradors used as Guide Dogs for the blind should have the characteristics of intelligence, the ability to be trained and obedient, and to be calm and patient.

Q5 It is difficult to clone mammal cells because they are unstable and die quickly.

Q6 Genetic engineering may help your health if defective and disease causing genes could be replaced with healthy ones.

Has it always been the same?

Q1 The Earth's environment has changed as mountains and continents have appeared, and disappeared, during the climatic changes associated with desert and ice age conditions.

Q2 To survive environmental change organisms have to adapt to the new conditions.

Q3 Reshuffling of genetic material happens when crossing over and gene exchange occurs in meiosis, it is also caused by the random arrangement of chromosome pairs before separation into the gametes.

Q4 The combinations of chromosomes equally likely to occur in the gametes are:
ABC ABc Abc AbC
abc abC aBC aBc

Q5 A mutation is a sudden change in a chromosome or DNA. It is important because it can alter the normal development of an individual. The change is usually harmful and can be inherited.

Q6 Mutations have little effect on the population because:
- a mutant gene is unlikely to be present in every gamete, and so may not be passed on to the next generation.
- many mutant genes are recessive and are suppressed by the dominant genes.
- mutant genes may be selected against by the environment. All these limit the spread of harmful genes through the population.

What is evolution?

Q1 Selection is caused by climate, vegetation, the need for food, the need to reproduce, and the effects of predation and competition.

Q2 Individuals which are best fitted to an environment leave the largest number of offspring so their advantageous genes are passed on to the next generation.

Q3 Individuals which are not adapted to an environment are selected against and become rare, they may die without breeding and so their disadvantageous genes are not passed on to the next generation.

Q4 Mammals have more reproductive success than fish because fewer gametes are needed, internal fertilisation is more successful than external fertilisation. Few young are produced and there is greater parental care so their survival to adulthood is more likely.

Q5 Evolution is caused by the accumulation of small changes in a population of related organisms, selection for or against these changes occurs over many generations/millions of years.

Q6 Human activity could alter the course of evolution by changing habitat. In new environments some variations will be advantageous. Selection may allow the development of new species.

Ecosystems

We are damaging the atmosphere

Q1 More fossil fuels being burnt as there are more people and we are all using more and more energy.

Q2 The population of the world has increased rapidly since that time and the release of extra carbon dioxide has increased in a correlating way.

Q3 Non renewable fuels such as oil, gas and coal all take millions of years to form and we are using them faster than they are forming. Renewable fuels come from sources which do not run out, eg. the sun, or that can be replaced, eg. biofuels.

Q4 This answer should be discussed with the pupils. They should consider voluntary reductions of Carbon dioxide emissions and the possible introduction of laws to limit the emissions of CO_2.

The changing atmosphere

Q1 The atmosphere:
- acts as a blanket, trapping heat energy, which keeps the planet warm enough for life to exist.
- provides carbon dioxide for plant photosynthesis.
- provides oxygen for plant and animal respiration.
- prevents all the harmful ultra violet radiation, that reaches Earth from the sun, from reaching the Earth's surface.
- affect the patterns of weather worldwide.
- provides a reservoir of nitrogen for the nitrogen cycle and the production of proteins.

Q2 Sulphur dioxide and nitrogen-I-oxide.

173

Q3 Acid rain.

Q4 Reduce the amounts used in aerosols and fridges, pass laws to ensure their careful disposal from fridges in future, and pass international laws to prevent their future use. Fund research into possible alternatives.

Q5 The ozone layer traps harmful ultra violet rays from the sun.

Global warming

1 The pupils will need a blank map to answer this question.

2 The pupils will need an atlas to answer this question. The cities which are most likely to flood are those which are below 30–60 cm above sea level.

Microbes and sewage

Q1 Respiring using oxygen.

Q2 Microbes work faster at this temperature and so break down the sewage faster.

Q3 By water rates.

Q4 By collecting methane and using it to warm the tanks and to generate electricity they cut down their electricity bills. They make money from selling the leftover sludge and this is used to keep down the water rates.

Q5 The dumped sludge is very rich in nutrients for plant life. It encourages the rapid growth of algae in the sea. It also harms fish and other marine life.

Natural cycles

Q1 Paper, glass, aluminium, plastic, plastic bags, steel cans.

Q2 Recycling reuses natural resources and also saves energy.

Q4 O= oxygen, C= carbon, H= hydrogen, N= nitrogen, Ca= calcium, K= potassium, Si= silicon, Mg= magnesium, S= sulphur, Al= aluminium, P= phosphorus, Cl= chlorine, Fe= iron, Mn= manganese, Na= sodium.

Q5 There is not an unlimited supply of these materials available.

Q6 Carbon, hydrogen and oxygen.

Q7 Nitrogen.

Q8 Carbon and nitrogen cycles.

Q9 Anaerobically means without oxygen.

Q10 Respiration lives off heat energy.

Q11 They all need water to make the cytoplasm found in their cells. The water acts as the solvent in which all the biochemical reactions of life can take place. In other words life processes take place, in solution, in water.

Earth and space

Earth structure 1

Q1 It tells us that the Earth gets hotter towards the centre.

Q2 L waves – because they have the greatest amplitude near to the surface.

Q3 They are received in the order P, S then L.

Q4 The earthquake station is in the S wave shadow zone, but South of the P wave shadow zone.

Q5 The velocities of the P and S waves change with depth, depending on the properties of the materials through which they pass.

Q6 Because liquids are not rigid.

Earth structure 2

Q1 Like the shape of the magnetic field round a bar magnet.

Q2 Magnetic materials in the rocks line themselves up parallel to the Earth's field when the rock is being formed.

Q3 Because magnetism is destroyed when magnets are heated to the temperature of the centre of the Earth.

Q4 In magnetic rocks you can see that the direction of magnetisation has altered.

Q5 You can see patterns of normal and reversed magnetism arranged symmetrically about the centre of the ocean ridge in the middle of the Atlantic ocean.

Q6 All our compasses would point the opposite way.

The theory of plate tectonics

Q1 The shape of the coastline may have changed (erosion or deposition). Present coastlines do not mark the end of the continental crust (the continental shelf marks its end).

Q2 Age × 20 mm = distance moved apart (providing that it is spreading at a constant rate)

Q3 Because scientists could not provide evidence of any mechanism for it.

Q4 Coal only forms in tropical swamps, and these conditions do not occur at the latitude where Britain is today.

Q5 They only occur in narrow zones.

Q6 Kinds of evidence include: similar shapes of coastlines, similar fossils, rocks of similar age which must have formed in a particular climate.

Plate movements 1

Q1 In the oceans.

Q2 In the Pacific Ocean (East Pacific rise spreads about 50 mm a year on each side).

Q3 Because here plates are colliding and at these destructive plate boundaries magma is generated where ocean plate is destroyed.

Q4 Because it does not lie on a plate boundary today.

Q5 They may have been destroyed by erosion, by the forces folding the rocks or destroyed when the rock is recrystallised by the heat generated during metamorphism.

Q6 Plate tectonics helps by explaining:
- how new igneous rocks form, e.g. where volcanoes erupt at constructive and destructive plate boundaries;
- how sedimentary rocks change to metamorphic rocks, e.g. where fold mountains form at destructive plate boundaries.

Plate movements 2

Q1 Because the ocean floor is constantly being destroyed at destructive plate boundaries.

Q2 Because they form on the land and are able to flow before they cool. Pillow lavas form on the sea bed and they cool very quickly in contact with sea water.

Q3 You might see the flow of water out of springs changing, The chemicals dissolved in the water might change.

Q4 They may be able to sense slight movements in the Earth. They may smell gases being erupted. They may hear things at different frequencies to humans.

Q5 The material dumped into an ocean trench would eventually be recycled into the mantle, but it would take thousands of years, and being on the sea bed for this length of time, some would escape into the water.

Q6 In the past the pattern of plate boundaries was not the same as today's.

Evolution of the atmospheres

Q1 No rocks have been found more than 3800 million years old.

Q2 The processes are: photo-dissociation and photosynthesis.

Q3 At about 3500 million years ago the oxygen levels started to increase very slowly. By 2300 million years ago the oxygen levels were less than one hundredth of the present level. There was a sudden rise so that by 1000 million years ago it had reached levels close to today's.

Q4 Levels of carbon dioxide are increasing. The ozone layer is thinning. Nitrous oxide and sulphur dioxide are increasing due to car exhausts and power station emissions.

Q5 As the oxygen levels increased then aerobic lifeforms increased. The existence of an ozone layer increased the protection to lifeforms from ultraviolet radiation. In an oxidising environment, minerals in the rocks weathered differently.

Balance in the atmosphere 1

Q1 Use less carbon dioxide in power stations, heating homes and in transport. Plant more trees to use up carbon dioxide. Encourage marine plants to grow.

Q2 Either low lying areas would have to be abandoned, or the coastal defences would have to be raised – this would be very expensive.

Q3 Possible strategies include better insulation, more efficient machinery, recycling of components, making goods that last longer. Also, cleaner sources of energy that do not produce carbon dioxide.

Q4 Possible strategies:
- Better insulation
- Use alternative sources of energy (solar power and so on).
- Turn down thermostats on heating systems.
- Use waste heat from power stations to heat homes
- Live underground.

Q5 Possible strategies:
- Help with debts (less pressure to cut down forests)
- Help with food for those who live on margins of rainforest
- Buy rainforest to protect it
- Give technical aid to help with alternative crops and use of non-forested lands.

Q6 Possible strategies:
- Taxes on carbon dioxide-producing fuels
- National network of transport using methods that generate less carbon dioxide
- Banning of inefficient means of transport (e.g. one person per car)

Balance in the atmosphere 2

Q1 Acid rain is rain that contains amounts of nitrous oxide and sulphur dioxide dissolved in it. The chemicals formed are nitric acid and sulphuric acid.

Q2 Nitrates in the soil can overspill into water supplies and poison them. High levels of nitrates do cause illness, including a serious illness in small babies. There are international limits on the amount of nitrate in drinking water.

Q3 Nitrogen, ammonia, nitrous oxide.

Q4 Plants, especially those living on poorly drained soils, are unable to survive in the highly acid conditions. If acid rain reaches open water in lakes and streams it may even kill the plants at the base of long food chains. Thus the effect on the simplest of plants could in turn effect many other plants and animals.

Q5 Sulphur dioxide and nitrous oxide emissions are the sources for the gases that create acid rain when they meet water vapour in the atmosphere.

Q6 The ammonia might be released from rocks and soil near the surface of the Earth but may also be coming from deep inside the Earth, thus completing the cycle where nitrates are washing out of surface rocks and are being buried in deep sediments.

Processes in the atmosphere

Q1 A rain drop is formed by tiny droplets of rain joining together to form a bigger drop which eventually falls to the base of the cloud. They can also be formed from hail or snowflakes that melt as they leave the cloud (if the temperature at the base of the cloud is warm enough).

Q2 A hailstone is formed by droplets building rapidly together and this is often a repeated process. A snowflake forms slowly and its temperature never rises above 0°C (otherwise the fine pattern is destroyed).

Q3 Fog forms when air cools below the dew point. This is likely to happen with damp air that is very cool. Cool air becomes more dense and so tends to fall into low ground and hollows which, incidentally, are the places which also tend to be damp.

Q4 The bottom of the cloud is where the warm air rising reaches the dew point and the visible droplets appear.

Q5 Low pressure zones are where warm air is rising. This rising air is what will produce rain, hail or snow. The energy contained in the rising air tends to create storms and windy weather.

Q6 a As height increases the temperature decreases
b as the air pressure decreases the density decreases.

Materials

The changing idea of atoms

Q6 19 protons, 19 electrons and 20 neutrons

Organising the elements

Q1 a 2,1 **b** 8 in each; period 2, 2nd energy level (L to R) 7,6,5,4,3,2,1,0; period 3, 3rd energy level (L to R) 7,6,5,4,3,2,1,0

Chemical bonding 1

Q1 Full

Q2 For example, potassium and iodine

Q5 For example **a** magnesium **b** oxygen

Chemical changes

Properties/uses of materials

Q1 silver

Q2 tin

Q3 bakelite

Moles 1

Q1 12.04×10^{23}

Q2 a 3 g **b** 28 g **c** 82 g

Moles 2

Q1 Standard temperature (273 K) and pressure (1 atmosphere)

Q3 1000 cm^3

Q5 5 g **b** 0.02 mol dm^{-3}

Formulae and equations

Q1 a 1 **b** 2 **c** 2 **d** 3 **e** 4 **f** 6

Q2 a CF_2 **b** Al_2O **c** $FeCl_3$ **d** Na_2O

Energy in chemistry

Q1 a Ammonia **b** positive

Electricity and magnetism

Resistance

Q1 a copper, metal, because they are good conductors.
b plastic as it is a good insulator.
c brass, because it is a good conductor and it does not easily corrode when out in air.

Q2 The thickest one.

Q3 a Yellow, violet, red. **b** green, blue, brown. **c** red, red, yellow.

Q4 Brown, black, brown.

Q5 18Ω.

Q6 Still about 10 Ω, the voltmeter does not change the resistance of the circuit.

Electromagnetic induction

Q2 Copper, aluminium, steel.

Using electromagnetic induction

Q4 16 V

Light and sound

Waves

Q1 The wave comes from deep sea.

Q2 Boats bobbing up and down show that waves transfer energy.

Q3 The waves get their energy mainly the wind

Q5 As well as the transmitter aerial, the sun gives out radio waves. We know the waves transfer energy as something happens in the detector system (the radio set).

Q6 a something happens in our eyes
b we can hear, sometimes even feel, sound waves
c infra-red waves cause burning
d ultra-violet waves darken fair skin and can damage eyes.

Q7 Only the water surface waves.

Waves

Q1 From a fraction of a wave per second to a couple of waves per second.

Q3 320 m/s

Q4

yellow light	600×10^{-9} m
earthquake "S" waves	0.4 Hz
Radio 1 BBC (MW)	$300\ (.105) \times 10^6$ m/s

Q5 Light and radio waves have the same speed (as they're closely related).

Q8 The amplitude of light relates to brightness.

Q10 For light waves passing from air to glass: the speed falls; as the frequency stays the same, the wavelength falls.

Sound waves

Q1 Sound waves cannot travel through a vacuum because they need matter.

Q2 The air pressure at the time.
See Questions 6 and 7 from page 127.

Q2 a 980 m.s **b** 1500 m/s; **c** 6 km/s

Sound and music

Q2 High frequency (small wavelength) waves have a high pitch

Q6 Length is λ: $\lambda/2$, λ, $3\lambda/2$ ... – ie, $n\lambda/2$, where $n = 1, 2, 3$ ...

Q11 Length is $n\lambda/2$, where $n = 1, 2, 3$ ...

Using sound waves

Q6 They need to measure the total distance travelled by the sound: twice the distance to the wall. Then they use speed = distance/time.

Q8 It depends on interference.

Q14 Cancer hazard

Frequency and wavelength

Q4 A coloured filter passes a small range of frequencies and absorbs the others. If a coloured light includes one of the passed frequencies, it will pass; otherwise nothing will pass: the output is black. A coloured surface reflects only a small range and absorbs the rest.

Q6 Using radiation of wavelength 6×10^{-7} m and frequency 5×10^{14} Hz: 3×10^8 m/s

Q7 4.2 and 7.5×10^{14} Hz

Q8 Blue: ultra-violet ('bluer than blue') is a greater danger than infra-red ('redder than red').

Q9 It contains little blue: it isn't hot enough.

Q10 It contains little blue or yellow: it's even cooler.

Electromagnetic spectrum

Q2 About 300 000 km/s (3×10^9 m/s)

Q4 Nuclear weapons, radio-activity, the (heavily shielded) core of a nuclear power station.

Q6 More energy: greater penetrating power.

Q7 The first three letters of the Greek alphabet.

Q9 A shiny surface is a better reflector; a matt dark surface is a better absorber (as for light).

Q10 a 1.2 W **b** 58.8 W

Q11 Higher temperatures

Q13 170×10^6 m/s

Q14 The spectrum shown assumes the radiation is in vacuum.

Q21 Shorter (more energy).

Electromagnetic radiation

Q3 0.2 s

Converting waves

Q2 A loud note has a greater amplitude.

Q3 A high note has a higher frequency.

Q4 They differ in 'quality' – they sound different.

Forces and Energy

Speeding up and slowing down

Q2 b 1 ms^{-2}, 1 ms^{-2}, –3 ms^{-2}
c 850 N, 850 N, 2550 N

Q3 375 N

Moving in circles

Q3 b 5.33 N

The right material for the job

Q4 a 1.07 m^2 **b** 0.19 m^2

Q5 a 5×10^{-8} m^2 or 5×10^{-2} mm^2, 0.25 mm
b 1.5×10^{-6} m^2 or 1.5 mm^2, 1.4 mm
c 5×10^{-6} m^2 or 5 mm^2, 2.5 mm
d 4.5×10^{-5} m^2 or 45 mm^2, 7.6 mm

Momentum

Q2 2.4 m/s, in the same direction as the original motion.

Q3 a 1.125 m/s, to the left
b 2.625 m/s, to the left.

Q4 Car, 2.77 seconds; Truck, 83.3 seconds.

Q5 a 0.172 m/s **b** 0.35 m/s **c** 0.536 m/s

Propellers, jets and rockets

Q4 a 108 kN **b** 216 kN

Q5 a 4.32 MN **b** 10.8 ms^{-2} **c** 16.9 ms^{-2}
d 0.99 ms^{-2}

Energy and temperature

Q3 a 63 kJ **b** 7,6 kJ **c** 18.9 kJ **d** 24 kJ

Q4 a 320 000 kg **b** 2×10^{10} J

Q6 Energy supplied = 50 kJ, energy used by water = 41160J.
Specific Heat capacity of can = approx 450 J.kg °C, so the can must be made of steel.

Everyday energy

Q1 Coal, 370 years; oil, 59 years; gas, 40 years

Energy for the future

Q1 a 1250 cc car, 0.5 litres; 2200 cc car, 0.19 litres
b 1250 cc car, 0.83 litres; 2200 cc car, 0.36 litres; 8 minutes longer

INDEX

INDEX

000023